GOD AND VIOLENCE

GOD AND VIOLENCE

BIBLICAL RESOURCES FOR LIVING IN A SMALL WORLD

Patricia M. McDonald

Foreword by
Ben C. Ollenburger

**Herald
Press**

Scottdale, Pennsylvania
Waterloo, Ontario

Library of Congress Cataloging-in-Publication Data
McDonald, Patricia M., 1946-
  God and violence : biblical resources for living in a small world /
Patricia M. McDonald.
      p. cm.
Includes bibliographical references (p.   ).
  ISBN 0-8361-9269-9 (paper)
  1. Violence—Biblical teaching. 2. Bible—Criticism, interpretation,
etc. I. Title.
  BS680.V55M33 2004
  261.8'73—dc22
                                          2003022509

Chapter 12, "Lion and Lamb," was published in *Horizons*, (23 [1996] 29-47) as "Lion as Slain Lamb: On Reading Revelation Recursively."

Cover: "Cain Kills His Brother Abel," print by Julius Schnorr von Carolsfeld. Reprinted with permission from *Treasury of Bible Illustrations Old and New Testaments*, Dover Publications, Inc., 1999.

To order or request information, please call
1-800-759-4447 (individuals); 1-800-245-7894 (trade).
Website: www.heraldpress.com

To my parents,
Dorothy and Jack

CONTENTS

FOREWORD

According to the Bible, violence erupted, in the form of murder, as soon as there were two potential rivals: Cain and Abel—brothers. It may be significant that the provocation to this first act of lethal violence was religious. Each brother brought an offering to God, who had regard for Abel and his offering but not for Cain and his. No wonder, then, that some have come to see religion, and "monotheism" in particular, as bearing heavy responsibility for the storm of violence across history's pages. Does the Bible share in that responsibility? Does God? After all, Exodus 15:3 declares bluntly (in Hebrew), "Yhwh is a warrior."

God and Violence names both the title of Patricia M. McDonald's excellent book and the concern that prompted it. The nature of her investigation is not in the least abstract; she examines in fine detail the biblical texts themselves. The story of Cain and Abel occupies the second chapter of McDonald's book, and she devotes extended attention to the exodus (chap. 5), in which God acted as a warrior. Throughout, she never forsakes the particulars of the text. This marks one of the book's strong qualities, for it is Scripture that properly forms our thinking and speaking of God, and it is Scripture that routinely troubles our thought and speech . . . and our action, whether in worship or in other forms and forums of public discipleship. At the same time, McDonald does not lose sight of the pressing questions that contemporary readers may have about, or may pose to, the Bible—especially those readers devoted to peace and peacemaking.

McDonald's approach, as she describes it, features narrative and canon. She explains what she means by these terms in her first, introductory chapter. It will suffice to say here that her approach allows her to show the expansion of violence in the story of Israel's advance from the exodus through the period of the judges and into monarchy—indeed, to the end of monarchy. In addition to this broad sweep, in which she treats Genesis, Exodus, Numbers, Joshua, Judges, and Isaiah, McDonald considers three brief narratives from the Old Testament that display creative efforts at defusing violent situations. The story of Abigail and David in 1 Samuel 25 proves especially provocative and instructive. Her discussion of this story also displays McDonald's own narrative skills, which help to make her book accessible to a broad audience.

The Christian canon, of course, includes the New Testament. While Professor McDonald devotes the greater part of *God and Violence* to the Old Testament, she includes chapters on Mark's gospel and Revelation. This is greatly to be welcomed. In some views, Jesus and the New Testament resolve problems created by the Old. McDonald does not pursue this course. She does not deny—she strongly affirms—the radical difference that Jesus makes. At the same time, though, she shows how Mark and John, the seer of Revelation, follow the Old Testament in offering their communities alternatives to the practices of violence in the midst of its reality. Mark does so in four-part harmony—soprano, alto, tenor, and bass (chap. 10)—while John's apocalyptic imagination re-reads and refigures Old Testament texts under the sign of the Lamb.

Throughout the book, Patricia McDonald admits ambiguity. She acknowledges that the Bible, including by way of Mark and Revelation, can be enlisted to justify violence and can be blamed for promoting it—can be and has been. And she is not loath to criticize parts of the Bible, or its "authors," for contributing to the justification or the blame, and to the ambiguity. This will offend some sensibilities, to be sure, while affirming others. *God and Violence* will reward careful reading, regardless. It argues, finally, that the Bible does not encourage but counters violence, even in and despite its most apparently violent parts. And it offers encouragement and resources to those who would seek to counter violence in this continually violent world. In commenting on Revelation, Professor McDonald remarks that "despite the New Testament's insistence of the centrality of Jesus' crucifixion, popular imagination has assimilated God's power to human power" (p. 226). True words, even and especially now.

At the beginning of this Foreword I quoted the Hebrew version of Exodus 15:3—"Yhwh is a warrior." The Greek version says something quite different: "The Lord completely overcomes [or *crushes*] war." The word I have italicized is the same one that Paul uses in Romans 15:33, which says, "The God of peace will soon *crush* Satan under your feet." May it be so.

Ben C. Ollenburger
Professor of Biblical Theology
Associated Mennonite Biblical Seminary

PREFACE

Why can't people live at peace with each other? Those with siblings have been hearing different versions of that question for as long as they can remember; others may have had to wait a little longer, but probably not much longer than it took to get to know the children down the street or at the playgroup.

Having lived most of our lives during the decades of the Cold War, the Europeans and North Americans of my generation tended to assume that we knew the answer: if it were not for the Soviet Union, there would be peace. Quite wrong, we discovered, as the amazing events of 1989 gave way to ongoing catastrophes involving places we still occasionally think of as "the former Yugoslavia." Peaceful expectations were dashed as hope for a settlement in the north of Ireland first grew bright and then dimmed, as television and news reports reminded us of places in "the Gulf" that few of us had thought much about since studying ancient Sumer and Babylon, as the situation between Israelis and Palestinians became increasingly intractable and dangerous, and as it became evident to all that the United States was no more immune to terrorist violence than the rest of the globe. These were just some of the major conflicts on my own radar screen; someone in a different location (anywhere in the Southern Hemisphere, for example) could have a completely different set.

The heightened technological sophistication of our societies increases the possibilities for violence, even as it also increases our resources for coping with its effects and, sometimes, protecting ourselves from them. Consequently, armaments and defense already use up a disproportionate and ever-increasing amount of the Earth's resources. Meanwhile, vast numbers of people are undernourished, undereducated, and with prospects that seem all the bleaker to the extent that they are contrasted with the way of life portrayed by such universal communications as MTV and the advertising necessary to near-global capitalism. This is not a situation that most of us would choose for ourselves or for anyone else. So maybe we need to choose otherwise, which is what this book is about.

The Road Not Taken

One possible way forward would be to get at the roots of violence so that we could develop an all-inclusive theory that includes an account of its nature, origins, and ways of exerting its effects. If we knew all this, we could surely find ways to reduce the harm that results from violence. It certainly is a fine idea. The appendix of this book gives an account and critique of one such theory that is currently being offered. Like many others, it answers some questions but raises many more. In the meantime, there is respite from the fighting, oppression, victimization, enslavement, and other manifestations of the human propensity for trying to control people against their will. Perhaps there is room for a project that takes a different approach.

Resetting the Default

My intention in the chapters that follow is to use the resources of biblical literature to show how the books of the Bible can be used to transform people's imagination, so that readers see situations in a different way and there-fore understand how they themselves might behave differ-ently. It is rather like resetting the default for a particular operation on a computer, so that a pattern of response that no longer works well is replaced by a new one that fits the prevailing circumstances better. The difference between people and computers is, of course, that once a computer's default has been reset by entering the right commands, the new pathway automatically comes into operation thereafter, whereas people are always liable to slip back into old habits, even after they have seen the need to change and have even tried the new way for a while. Nevertheless, we can and do learn to change familiar patterns of thinking about issues, such as what constitutes justice in the courts or in the allocation of resources, how countries should relate to others, how we should treat the environment, who should be educated and how, and so on. With encouragement and practice, we come to imagine points of view other than the ones we set out with. Then, gradually or sometimes quite abruptly, past patterns of behavior are dropped because they no longer serve well.

The violence-reducing strategy advocated here could be seen as a conversion from self-regarding behavior to being at the service of others. Cold turkey. More helpful, however, is to think of it as the process by which people increasingly recognize that their good is best served when everyone's needs are the object of everyone's concern, at least in principle. That formulation makes it clear that the process is ongoing, as the limits of each person's involvement gradually expand.

Such a way of living contrasts with the existing default condition, which consists of people doing that for which their long-term evolutionary inheritance has best equipped them: promoting vigorously their own immediate concerns and less strongly supporting causes that they perceive to be related to their well-being. This has worked more or less adequately for a long time. Yet it is not good enough. Unless it can be construed very broadly indeed, looking out for oneself eventually sets up friction with whatever is excluded, whether it be neighbors; other ideological, ethnic or national groups; or the environment. It may take a while before the people behaving in this way notice that there is a problem—and often, when they do, they can take action that postpones the day of reckoning—but isolationism is not long sustainable in a world where the flow of information is ever increasing. In the end, the tension becomes too great and some form of violence erupts. Then people suffer and things are damaged or destroyed. To reduce this tendency, we need to develop more inclusive ways of seeing the world, so that we are less inclined to set our own good against that of others.

Such a more general approach is flexible enough to take account of the difficulty (if not the impossibility) of deciding on how violence is to be defined. For although there is little question that violence is "bad," people can honestly disagree about what to include under that heading and therefore about what level of competitive or assertive behavior is acceptable and from whom. Thus, when my friend's three-year-old shoots me with a "gun" that looks to me like a piece of wood, he is just having fun. Or is he? (His parents are pacifists; should I "disarm" him?) And what of the adolescent who must always come first in whatever class or league she is in? (It seems not to be good for her or her relationships, but she will probably get into medical school.) There are legitimate differences in evaluating so many ordinary human activities and the people who engage in them. Those who buy ringside seats for boxing or wrestling? All who are not vegetarians? The ambitious parent whose child *must* be accepted by the best kindergarten? The artist who cannot exercise his talent without engaging in what looks like inconsiderate or antisocial behavior? The "perfect" supervisor or administrator who is unaware of the demoralizing effect she has on subordinates? The priest who owns a gun? Those who give tendentious reports of inflammable situations? Nations that control scarce resources to their own advantage? Those who pollute the environment because they can get away with it? And so on, it seems, endlessly.

In other words, if we were not careful, we could spend all our time and energy arguing about what is or is not to be included in a definition of violence. On the other hand, our normal ways of living are always causing us to see situations in a new light and to change our behavior accordingly. What I am proposing, then, is a deliberate version of that natural process: to transform imaginations in ways that make for more peaceable living.

Contrary to much popular thought, the Bible can be a useful resource for such a transformation. First, because the biblical writers have no illusions about the harm people can do to each other, anybody can enter into the world of their text. It is not necessary even to be "good," let alone holy. Among those portrayed in their writings are characters that are far nobler than we are, but many more are like ourselves and worse, often *much* worse. Second, the Bible portrays the complexity of human life and culture in a way that is familiar in its ambiguity: cultural achievements (cities, in particular) are repeatedly recognized as both valuable and potentially dangerous to the point of lethality. Third, the biblical books present recurring reminders of the wider context in which people live their lives. Even though many of the events described in both testaments take place in an area no bigger than Wales or the state of Vermont, the writers always understand them as components of a created world for which a concerned God has plans that go infinitely beyond any time and space coordinates that we can imagine.

If the Bible is being used to help us reimagine and recontextualize our experience, the fact that it contains some violent imagery may actually make it of more use to us than it would be if it were more sanitized. The question then arises: is it fair to claim that the Bible depicts violence as an attractive option? One purpose of this book is to answer with a resounding no. Chapters 2–8 have this as one of their aims, as has chapter 12 on the book of Revelation. The other purpose of *God and Violence* is to demonstrate from a range of biblical texts the way they can provide many (and sometimes surprising) resources for encouraging and enabling more peaceable ways of living.

Some Presuppositions

Readers might be helped by being aware of several presuppositions that ground what follows.

First, the Bible is essentially a religious work. It emerged from the life and worship of Jewish and Christian communities that experienced themselves as graciously addressed by their self-revealing God. For present-day members of those groups, it is, therefore, the Word of God, a sacred book that continues to be foundational to their lives. As a Roman Catholic, I include myself among such people, who do not regard the Bible as "just another book." Readers of *God and Violence* certainly need not share that conviction, but it seems only fair to inform them of it.

Second, and equally important, is that as the written witness to God's self-disclosure, the Bible is also the result of human literary efforts and bears all the marks of that process. So it is appropriate to interpret it in light of the historical situations in which the different books were produced, to the extent that these can be determined. That procedure is known as the historical-critical method and is foundational to these chapters. In more recent decades the historical-critical method has been increasingly supplemented by other techniques, particularly from literary study and the social sciences. To these, too, I am indebted.

Because the biblical texts originated in specific times and situations, readers should pay attention to the literary genre used by the author of any given part of it. The books of the Bible contain writing of many different types. Some of it could loosely be called history, but there is much else besides. If, for example, the myths in Genesis 1–11 or the sagas in Exodus, Numbers, Joshua, or Judges are read as though they are simply historical reportage, the reader will run up against all manner of impossible "facts" and unanswerable questions, such as "Where did Cain's wife come from?" or "How could the desert have supported such huge numbers of people?" Similarly, Mark must be read as a Gospel written forty or so years after the time of Jesus, and the book of Revelation is an example of apocalyptic literature, a type of writing familiar to John's first-century readers but not to us.

Finally, some notes on terminology. B.C.E. denotes "Before the Common Era" and is the exact equivalent of B.C. The abbreviation C.E. ("Common Era," that is, the era common to Christians and Jews) replaces A.D.

Most of what now constitutes the Christian Old Testament is also sacred to Jews as Tanak, consisting of the Law, the Prophets, and the Writings.[1] Yet although the two communities read the same material and can have fruitful dialogue about it, Tanak and the Old Testament are different from each other because of the contexts in which they are read and understood: in one case as the Word of G*d that is interpreted in the light of the Talmud and ongoing Jewish tradition and, in the other, as the Word of the God whose communication with humanity continued in the person of Jesus of Nazareth. There is, therefore, an irreducible difference between Jewish and Christian readings of these texts, a difference that needs to be respected. Because I write as a Christian, my primary concern in chapters 2–10 is with what I shall normally call the Old Testament. This is not with an intent that is super-cessionist or in any way disrespectful of those who read the same books as Tanak, but because it is the customary designation for the books in my own two-testament tradition.

Organization and Rationale

Following the introductory chapter, chapters 2–9 focus on some of the books at the beginning of the Old Testament. Here the tone is set for the serial reader of the Bible, who may get no further if sufficiently offended. But do these books really glamorize violence or are there elements in them that make for peace, sometimes in surprising ways?

The three chapters about the book of Genesis demonstrate that this opening segment of the Bible clearly depicts a world in which violence damages people, whereas peaceable behavior results in the well-being of all. The situation becomes more complex with Exodus. Here we shall look carefully at how the biblical writers come to call the Lord a warrior, and then at tendencies to which this gives rise later. The book of Numbers is a particularly blatant example of the way that a mistakenly militaristic reading of a text can color one's reading of it to the extent that one may miss altogether some arguably much more significant elements of the work. No more than Exodus does Numbers glorify Israel as a successful military power. The book's point lies elsewhere, as is also the case with the book of Joshua, even though in the course of it Israel is described as coming into possession of the land by mostly military means. On the other hand, the narratives from Exodus onward provide evidence of a slow but inexorable increase in Israelite violence that culminates in almost complete societal breakdown at the end of Judges. That breakdown is chronicled in Judges in a way that leaves readers in no doubt of the author's extreme disapproval of what went on. In this case, therefore, the descriptions of violence (and of other, equally reprehensible activities) are intended as the strongest possible counterexample. The hoped for solution implied by the closing words of Judges is an Israelite king, but that experiment proved largely a failure, as can be seen from the society that Isaiah of Jerusalem addresses in the first thirty-nine chapters of the book that bears his name. Civilization is clearly not enough for dealing with human violence.

Chapter 10 considers three narratives from other parts of the Old Testament. This single chapter takes three "soundings" to indicate some other imaginative possibilities that the Bible offers as resources and motivation for constructing nonviolent responses. There are, of course, many other examples that could have been used.

Chapter 11, the first of the two chapters that comprise the New Testament section, is about the Gospel of Mark, and chapter 12 explores the book of Revelation. The integrating feature of this third and final section is not the canon (as it was in chapters 1–9) but the response of the earliest Christians to the figure of Jesus, a response to which the New Testament is the literary testimony. Again it has been necessary merely to sample from the available books. The Gospel of Mark is first considered, as a narrative example of the claims and attitudes that lie at the heart of Christianity. It presents in a particularly stark form the radically countercultural way of living exemplified by Jesus himself and by the teaching about discipleship that the Gospel contains. Taken seriously, this attitude can enable people to change the way they respond to the violence that Mark recognizes as part of ordinary life.

Finally, we shall consider Revelation. Often regarded as a complete betrayal of what Jesus did and taught, in reality it resembles the rest of this testament in restating and developing Christian insights for people in a particular set of circumstances. John writes for people who must live out their commitment to God in cities of the Roman Empire. Because he is thoroughly biblical in his insistence on the goodness of creation and in his ambivalent (sometimes hostile) attitude toward the complex realities of life in imperial cities, John often uses dualistic language that sounds violent, although only rarely does it *function* in that way. The seer's vivid use of imagery and his broad perspective can engage present-day readers whose lives are similarly complex and whose hope for a peaceable outcome to world events often exceeds their expectations.

The overall movement of this book is from Genesis to Revelation. This is because there is often development from one book to the next, particularly in the earlier part of the Old Testament, and it is sometimes helpful to take advantage of the order in which a reader would encounter the material in a liturgical cycle or when reading the Bible from cover to cover. There is a heavy concentration on the first part of the canon: Genesis, Exodus, Numbers, Joshua, Judges, and Isaiah 1–39. To varying degrees, all these books have been used to provide evidence for the common charge that the Bible is a violent book; so has the book of Revelation, at the other end of the Christian canon. There are, of course, many other such books that are not considered here. They include Deuteronomy, some of the Psalms, much of the prophetic writing, and sections of several New Testament books. That many parts of the Bible contain violence is undisputed, but I am convinced that there is far less of it than is generally supposed, that most of what there is should be read as countering violence rather than encouraging it, and that the remainder is very difficult to square with the best understandings of Tanak/the Old Testament and the New Testament.

1

RESETTING THE DEFAULT:
AN INTRODUCTION

For my thoughts are not your thoughts,
nor are your ways my ways, says the LORD.
—Isaiah 55:8

Whoever wishes to become great among you must be
your servant, and whoever wishes to be first among you
must be slave of all.
—Mark 10:43-44

Several years ago, a college student in the Reserve Officer Training Corps came to tell me he was withdrawing from my Foundations of Theology course. An intelligent young man, he had made a bad start that semester and feared for his grade point average. He did not, however, want me to think badly of him. So, as he left my office for the last time, and knowing that I was also teaching an Old Testament survey course for theology majors, he informed me, smilingly, but I think in all seriousness, that although he liked the New Testament well enough, he *loved* the Old Testament because of the warrior God and all the wars that it portrays. I am sure that he did and probably still does. Shocked and dismayed, I watched him walk away.

At least, I thought, he was not caught in the trap of "Old Testament: bad; New Testament: good." But was that really what he thought about the Bible—the Word of God, the text that has for years fascinated and absorbed me as student, teacher, and committed Christian? This book is, in part, a response to the turmoil in which he, perhaps deliberately, left me.

Violence as Default Condition

Violence is the simplest and most spontaneous response to the frustration of people's desires to achieve their purposes, both immediate and long-term. "Sending in the troops" is the popular remedy for a situation that may possibly get out of control. Everyone sometimes gets road rage, wants to throw things, feels like killing another. Yet satisfying as acting on violent impulses can be, it causes vast amount of wreckage, not only of armies, drivers' lives, and the environment, but also of people's physical and emotional integrity and their ability to sustain relationships. The high cost of such behavior is borne by society as a whole: homes and schools cannot be presumed to be safe places for living and learning; many live in fear of mugging or burglary; incarceration becomes a fact of life for some groups; veterans cannot communicate their experiences to others; entire nations are feared and demonized. As Simone Weil once said about violence, "Those who use it and those who endure it are turned to stone."[1] The societies we have constructed frequently encourage and reward violent behavior, even while ostensibly condemning it. Since, for example, our economic structures are based on ever-increasing consumption, we live surrounded by advertisements that tell us we deserve only the best and can have it immediately. Given the unlimited desires and limited means that most of us have, repeated exposure to such claims leads either to a deadening cynicism or to envy and the craving to do whatever it takes to rectify the situation. Similar results come from having life goals that are unrealistically ambitious for oneself or others. Using talents to the fullest and being competitive are, of course, important, yet overemphasizing the need always to outdo everyone else generates intolerable pressures to succeed and a constant fear of failure. So, for example, I observe many of my students striving to maximize the *measures* of their achievement at the expense of the achievement itself. Regarding peers as rivals and their teachers as mere dispensers of grades, they are liable to avoid interesting but potentially difficult courses in the search for that easy A.

Such attitudes produce some academic and economic stars, but they also produce a generally stressful environment in which the potential for violent action is always increasing, because people are encouraged to think that, however much they may have, they deserve even more. They also experience the resentment of those who desire their possessions and status. Consequently, many of the more vulnerable members of society have a pervasive fear of violence, while the more successful live in dread of losing what they have.

When we behave in these ways, we are "doing what got us here," as the athletes say. In a world where resources are limited and entropy rules, there are both long-term and short-term gains from being successful in obtaining for oneself and one's family the best possible circumstances of existence: of food and living conditions, of education and medical care, and the respect of peers. We all want people to pay attention to us here and now, and then to have our achievements and genes make the greatest possible contribution to the next stage of humanity's existence. Inherited from our prehuman ancestors, this tendency to promote one's own cause (if necessary, at the expense of others) underlies many of the factors that have enabled our species to "fill the earth and subdue it" or at least to make significant progress in that direction (Gen. 1:28).

In other words, activity that may harm or disadvantage others is so much bound up with everyday human dynamics that to see violence as a problem that we might one day solve is surely to hope for the impossible. Certain aspects of it may occasionally respond to such treatment: we can treat some diseases that lead people to behave violently, and occasionally reconcile ethnic groups that have traditionally seen one another as a threat to be exterminated. Yet overall the roots prove exceedingly difficult to uncover.

Resetting the Default

There are other ways out of situations that would normally lead to violence and other ways of attaining greatness. These, however, do not happen easily. Engaging in them requires a resetting of the "default" condition and the deliberate choice to use effort, energy, and imagination to employ them. Such courses of action are often much more difficult to undertake and to promote, because they do not produce the instant results that violence seems to promise. To worried spectators on the sidelines, the need to negotiate and build consensus may make those directly involved appear indecisive or to be giving away too much to the opposition. Compared with "surgical strikes," peaceful solutions are cumbersome and slow in their implementation. There is time for things to go wrong and for people to withdraw their support when the going gets difficult. Although risk is certainly involved, such strategies lack the glamour of an all-out fight. Success is never assured until, one day, people wake up and find that their lives are now bound up with the other in a positive way and the wish to harm has evaporated. Such schemes do not make hearts beat faster. They rarely make gripping headlines. Yet ever-growing concern about the extent and escalation of violence suggests that we should find ways to use and augment whatever resources are available for developing and exercising alternative strategies.

Jews and Christians would include in those resources their Scriptures. For Jews, this is the thirty-nine-book Tanak; for Christians, it is the expanded, two-testament Bible. My central claim is that, despite its reputation for being a violent book, Tanak/Bible is a rich and varied place for imagining other and better ways of being that range from mere avoidance of violence against one's neighbor to cultivating an attitude of compassionate service to others. So this project has two aspects. In it, we shall examine various biblical books in the light of that reputation for violence, in order to demonstrate that they do not promote it as an option that is intended to appeal to readers. At the same time, we shall consider, in more or less canonical order[2] a range of biblical texts from both testaments that provides resources and motivation for constructing nonviolent responses.

Recovering Biblical Resources

On the face of it, using the Bible as a resource for peace would appear to be a problematic undertaking. Why would anyone wishing to promote peace want to read a book that is "filled with stories of wars and conflicts"?[3] Why expose oneself to "cheerfully reported genocidal wars"[4] or to "the cruel and vengeful imagination of the Apocalypse"?[5] It is tempting to side with Voltaire when, with heavy irony, he voices his doubt that the contents of the books of Kings and Chronicles (in distinction from their style) are "so divine." He backs his position with a representative list of assassinations described therein and concludes, "It must be admitted that if the Holy Spirit wrote this history, he didn't choose a very edifying subject."[6] Indeed Raymund Schwager has counted about six hundred passages in the Bible as a whole where violence is condemned, but at least a thousand that focus on *the Lord's* violence.[7] Many of these instances read like a projection onto God of the violence that members of Israel or the early church would like to visit on those who reject the community's claim that its members are the particular object of God's care. Even more disconcertingly, there are those for whom all this is not a problem but, rather, part of the appeal of the Bible.

In the Bible and elsewhere, images of violence readily impose themselves on the imagination. My ROTC student needed no convincing of this. He already knew that war, as socially sanctioned violence, is second only to sex in eliciting attention. "In the beginning there was sex, violence, murder, jealousy, rage, seduction, greed, power trips, and snakes," proclaims an announcement for *Genesis: A Living Conversation with Bill Moyers.* Judiciously timed, wars can be the most powerful aid to unifying a country behind an otherwise insecure president or prime minister. They can also boost economies as peace-focused activities never do: what peacetime manufacturing process can command resources comparable with those that a country at war will gladly devote to the production of armaments and defense systems? In wartime, people are mobilized, in both senses of the term: individually energized and, socially, drafted into the military. The armed forces have uniforms, discipline, and bands: all means of unifying otherwise disparate people. In history as it is popularly remembered (if not taught), wars are events and peace is their absence. For public support, even highly regarded peace organizations find it all but impossible to compete with armies, which are the *sine qua non* of almost every country in the world and can step forward to embody the national identity with minimal further effort.[8] Thus, just as (rightly or wrongly) the medieval Crusades stand out in people's minds more than do the much more remarkable (and probably more

numerous) Franciscan, Dominican, and other peace movements of the same era,[9] so biblical texts about violence are
liable to attract an unwarranted amount of attention. One
purpose of this book is to examine some of these stories
from the Bible, to demonstrate that they contain far less
violence than is often assumed and to discover what that
wrong assumption might have been preventing readers
from learning.

There are, of course, biblical passages that encourage
nonviolent attitudes and actions. In the prophetic books,
Isaiah's famous vision of a just and peaceful earth is among
the most powerful (11:1-9). What would we not give for a
world without injustice; one in which predator and prey
live contentedly as neighbors, all children are safe, and
there is "no harm or ruin" (v. 9)? Yet would a lion that ate
hay like an ox really be a lion (v. 7)? As Chesterton noted
in *Orthodoxy*, if the terms of the peace are that the lion is
required to become lamblike, "that is brutal annexation
and imperialism on the part of the lamb."[10]

Again, those who work for peace frequently quote
Isaiah 2:2-5 or Micah 4:1-3 to the effect that in "the days to
come" people

> shall beat their swords into plowshares,
> and their spears into pruning hooks;
> nation shall not lift up sword against nation,
> neither shall they learn war any more (Isa. 2:4).

What, though, are they to do with the clearly related
Joel 3:9-10 (4:9-10 in the NAB)? Here the Lord commands:

> Prepare war, stir up the warriors.
> Let all the soldiers draw near, let them come up.
> Beat your plowshares into swords, and your pruning
> hooks into spears;
> let the weakling say, "I am a warrior."

The ambiguity is no different for Christians when they turn to the New Testament. Some of those who refuse to regard violence as a permissible option (either completely or in part) have explained their position by means of a general reference to Jesus' own example in accepting calmly his unjust execution. Others turn to specific texts, especially to the Sermon on the Mount (Matt. 5–7). Thus, "Blessed are the peacemakers, for they will be called children of God" (Matt. 5:9); "But I say to you, Do not resist an evildoer. But if anyone strikes you on the right cheek, turn the other also" (5:39); or "But I say to you, Love your enemies and pray for those who persecute you" (5:44). Another oft-quoted verse is Matthew 26:52. Here, as Jesus is being arrested in Gethsemane to be taken to his eventual death, he tells a follower who would defend him (Peter, in John's Gospel) to put away his sword, "for all who take the sword will perish by the sword."[11]

The fact is, however, that many wars and acts of violence in the last two millennia have been waged by those who regarded themselves as Christians. To the extent that they used biblical texts to support their position, they tended to refer to Old Testament stories of wars that the Lord instigated, the heroes who led them, and the conduct there deemed appropriate.[12] For example, Christian soldiers in every age have admired figures such as Joshua, Jonathan, and Judas Maccabaeus, and occasional popes and other religious leaders have commanded or fought with armies. Seventeenth-century Puritans fighting in the English Civil War spoke of themselves as God's servants, which arguably encouraged them to ignore aspects of the situation that might otherwise have troubled their Christian consciences.[13] Cotton Mather thought it appropriate to regard Native Americans as Amalekites who could be legitimately wiped out (see Exod. 17:13-16 and 1 Sam. 15:3),[14] and a sermon preached by Samuel Woodward after the conquest of Montreal by the British General Wolfe in 1760 presents the victory in terms of Israel's triumph at the sea in Exodus 14–15. References to "the God of battles" are not uncommon in sermons preached in the northern states during the American Civil War,[15] and soldiers preparing to leave for the war were encouraged to take comfort from Psalm 46 where it says that God is with us and on our side when nations are in "uproar" and "the kingdoms totter."[16]

The New Testament has proved less useful for stiffening military resolve but is occasionally used in that way. There were unionists who interpreted their part in the American Civil War as Christlike inasmuch as it involved liberating slaves. A line from "The Battle Hymn of the Republic" sums up this attitude: "As he died to make men holy, let us die to make men free."[17] Less directly, soldiers who are Christian can point to the fact that in the New Testament neither John the Baptist and Jesus in the gospels nor Peter in Acts ever required a soldier to give up his profession as a condition of being acceptable to God. Furthermore, military metaphors are used even of the Christian life in the New Testament: there is talk of armor in Ephesians 6:13 and 1 Thessalonians 5:8, while the writer of 2 Timothy 2:3 exhorts the reader to bear hardship "like a good soldier of Christ Jesus."[18]

So biblical support can be invoked for very different positions, and mere text trading is generally futile. People do not change their views simply by hearing a reading chosen by their opponents. Yet the very vigor and persistence with which Christians, in particular, have used biblical texts to back up their positions indicates the important role the Bible plays in their identity. The Bible's reputation for violence needs to be addressed yet again, if only because it can so easily be used as a simple and effective way of discrediting the text and those who regard it as sacred.

On Using Narratives and Canon

A more holistic approach is called for. Because Jews and Christians who accept a biblical canon use Scripture as a major resource for forming their vision of the world, it would be worth trying to take into account the whole Bible, at least in principle. This cannot be done directly within the compass of a single volume. So the compromise adopted here is to take samples of books from the two testaments.

Using narratives requires much sustained effort on the part of the reader, who is encouraged to read attentively the biblical text and become more familiar with the stories included there. The benefits are commensurate, however.

First, because it considers entire biblical books and canonical sequences, this narrative approach provides an alternative to using the Bible as a source of isolated ideas and "proof texts" in the manner indicated above. Sound bites, although convenient for some purposes, are of very limited use for discussing complex issues. Narratives are much more satisfactory. Not only do they allow for more nuance, but a story develops as it goes along and can also interact with other stories. Centuries of experience have shown that those who expend effort on world classics such as the Bible (or the works of Homer, Confucius, the Hindu sages, Shakespeare, and so on) can frequently recognize in them significant aspects of their own situations, preoccupations, and ongoing struggles. The Bible is a sacred book for Jews and Christians, which means that they have traditionally constructed much of their worldview in dialogue with its contents. For them, Scripture thus functions as a kind of "big story" that they recognize as vitally related to the life stories that they are in the process of constructing within their communities.

Those who regard the Bible as Scripture do not, of course, pay equal attention to every part of it. That is to say, any religious group or individual uses some sections more than others, and the details may vary over time. People tend to keep returning to the texts with which they are comfortable and which they have found helpful in the past. This happens less in churches that use a lectionary for public worship, for then congregations hear the texts prescribed for that particular day. Occasionally, however, it is salutary to read even more widely in Scripture. Sometimes this results in having unexpected light shone on one's own situations. At other times, the strangeness of the text raises new questions about humanity's propensity for violence and what can be done about it. Either way, horizons are enlarged.

Second, inasmuch as *God and Violence* offers a serious consideration of texts regarded as sacred by Jews and Christians, it contributes to healing the facile and unhelpful split that some Christians make between the Old and New Testament in which Israel's alleged "warrior God" of the Hexateuch,[19] associated with the "law" that is also found there, is contrasted with the Christian God of love, associated with Jesus and "gospel."

Third, and more broadly, studying biblical texts in this way may contribute to expanding people's notions of the human good through the greatly enriched imaginative possibilities that access to these books makes available. The hope is that readers would thereby come to understand their lives better in an increasingly interconnected world.

2

VIOLENCE AND THE INVISIBLE OTHER:
THE FIGURE OF CAIN

Despite the amount of violence that it contains, the Christian biblical canon is bounded by surprisingly peaceful scenes: two accounts of origins (Gen. 1–2) and the presentation of the New Jerusalem (Rev. 21–22). Violence does not begin until Cain murders his brother, Abel (Gen. 4).[1] Then, in Genesis 6–11, one story after another proposes violent behavior as the cause of much of humanity's suffering. Clearly, such conduct is to be avoided, a point made all the more strongly by the sheer volume of this type of material so near to the beginning of the Bible.

Cain's fratricide results from his defective response to what is sometimes seen as an arbitrary act of God, the acceptance of Abel's offering and the rejection of his own (Gen. 4:4-5). If God's action is indeed arbitrary, the root of the violence lies not in Cain but in God, and many readers have taken it that way. What, though, if we can find in the story a good reason for the divine action? What if the text is instead drawing attention to a fundamental dynamic of human society that is derived from the fact that individuals are differently endowed right from birth? In this line of thinking, God's dealings with the firstborn of Adam and Eve are an attempt at shaking Cain out of his unthinking obliviousness to the many advantages he has over his younger brother. The attempt fails, and Cain opts for removing the source of his problem rather than taking up the challenge of living with Abel. The difficulty of accepting and accommodating "the other" is evidenced by the existence in every age of parallels, both individual and social. The story continues: Cain receives protection, founds the first city, and sires those who will produce important elements of culture (4:13-24).

The Setting: A Peaceable Creation

For both Jews and Christians, the biblical canon opens with the first of two stories of creation, a tightly structured account that depicts Israel's lone God creating a good and ordered world for the sheer joy of it. No violence here. This does not normally cause surprise: why should such things be part of a creation story? Nevertheless, the non-violent presentation of reality's dawn is one of the respects in which the Genesis story differs from some of the other accounts of how things came into being and therefore of how the authors viewed the world in which they lived. An example of the latter is *Enuma elish*,[2] the Babylonian creation myth that perhaps underlies this part of Genesis.[3]

In *Enuma elish*, the world and its inhabitants come into existence as a direct result of conflicts between primordial beings. Those conflicts constitute the original chaos out of which the cosmos arises. For the inhabitants of Babylon, "In the beginning" there was, not God creating the heavens and the earth but Apsu's fury at the rowdiness of his offspring. So he planned to kill them all. They, however, got wind of this and killed him first. Consequently, Apsu's widow, Tiamat, provided herself with a small army of monsters and declared war on her descendants. One of them, Marduk, defeated her and then made the earth out of her body. Another god, Ea, formed the human race from the blood of Tiamat's god-monster consort, Kingu.

The six-day creation account in Genesis 1:1–2:4 contains no suggestion of anything like this.[4] Instead, "God said, 'Let there be light'; and there was light. And God saw that the light was good" (Gen. 1:3-4). Recognizable here is the deep satisfaction of artistic creativity. In the middle of the first "day" and at the end of each subsequent day of creation, God views what has been made and notes its goodness. A translation that captures this well is that of André Chouraqui, who has God exclaim each time, "Quel bien!"— perhaps, "How wonderful!"—an appropriate response to people's experience of the world's intricate beauty.[5]

The main difference between the biblical and the Babylonian stories lies in the relative power of the creator in each case. It is, after all, much more impressive to be a highly successful artist who uses minimal (and merely verbal) effort than to struggle to victory in a long-running family feud and then create the world by reworking already existing material of dubious quality: the corpse of a mother who had warred against her offspring. Israel's God is obviously understood as being in a different class from that of Marduk and his ilk. Furthermore, Genesis 1 also suggests that, because humans are made in the image and likeness of this God and given dominion over the created world (1:26-28), violence, strife, and war are not part of God's original intention for humanity. "Having dominion over" others is, therefore, to be understood as having responsibility for their well-being. There is nothing inherently violent about it, however great may be the possibilities for its misuse.

Although the details are quite different, the second story of origins, in Genesis 2:4-25, is similarly peaceful. Here God the potter first makes a human creature ("Adam") from soil (ᵃ*dāmāh*) and then (like any good parent) sets about providing for it the conditions in which it can flourish and, indeed, delight. This chapter is heavily weighted with imagery that would convey paradise to those eking out an existence in a low-rainfall area: the garden itself (2:8), the beautiful and productive fruit trees, the abundant water and mineral wealth, a vegetarian diet (as in 1:29-30), the necessary companion with, as a by-product, the zoological world (2:9-20). Access to the tree of life is implied (2:9 and 3:22), so that humans can expect to live indefinitely in this paradise where an attentive God is on the lookout to notice and fulfill their every need (2:18-23). In the midst of such plenitude, the prohibition of eating from "the tree of the knowledge of good and evil" (2:17) is all but negligible. The snake has to bring it to the woman's attention in 3:1-2. So the tradition in Genesis 2:4-25, like that in 1:1–2:4, portrays the world as essentially nonviolent. The presence of the snake, however, alerts readers to the possibility of developments along other lines.

After Eden

Violence occurs only after things have gone wrong—or, at least, have gone beyond the state of primal paradise. First, in Genesis 3, Adam and Eve disobey God by eating the fruit. Because the snake manipulates the woman into acting on a partial view of the tree, she forgets that it gives knowledge of evil and not only of good (3:5-6). So the primordial pair is expelled from Eden. Almost immediately afterward, in Genesis 4, comes the terse account of how their elder son, Cain, kills his brother, Abel.[6] That text is the focus of the remainder of this chapter.

The Problem of God's Fairness

On the face of it, God's dealings with Cain are simply inexplicable: later generations of commentators would try hard to find some reason for God's refusal of Cain's offering and acceptance of his brother's,[7] because the biblical text does not offer one:

> In the course of time Cain brought to the LORD[8] an
> offering of the fruit of the ground, and Abel brought
> of the firstlings of his flock and of their fat portions.
> And the LORD had regard for Abel and his offering,
> but for Cain and his offering he had no regard
> (Gen. 4:3-5a).

Cain's unprompted offering is described first, as befits his status as the elder brother. In fact, because Genesis 1–3 said nothing about Adam and Eve making such offerings, Genesis 4 posits Cain as the first one ever to make an offering to God—and God refuses it or, on the most benign interpretation of the Hebrew, regards it as inferior to the offering of his younger brother. Although Abel's action here is described at slightly greater length and the author specifies that Abel offered "firstlings" and "fat portions," there is no suggestion that either of them is presenting anything but what Israel would come to regard as appropriate sacrificial offerings, despite the fact that Israel (like most ancient peoples) tended to value animal sacrifice more highly than grain offerings.[9]

The tension is now increased. Having preferred one brother's offering to the other's, God counters Cain's reaction by asking him why he is angry, thereby drawing the reader's attention to Cain's state. God then suggests two possible strategies for him. First, he can choose to try again: "If you do well, will you not be accepted?" (4:7). If that does not appeal to him, there is another way. It involves more risk, because in that case "sin is lurking at the door," desiring him. But Cain is told that he can indeed master sin if he wishes to.[10] In other words, God offers Cain the opportunity to reflect on his situation and make a rational choice about where to go next.

However, Cain ignores God's invitation to make a reasoned decision about his next move. He refuses to trust that the Lord is indeed offering him vitally important (divine) insight into living in the world along with other people. Instead he speaks to Abel[11] and then, in the field, "Cain rose up against his brother Abel, and killed him," as the author says with brutal economy (4:8).

What drives Cain to murder his brother? It would seem that God acted arbitrarily in accepting Abel's offering and refusing Cain's own. Cain experiences utter surprise and confusion at discovering that he has misjudged his position vis-à-vis God, and he interprets what has happened as a divine violation of his very being. For, as the text states, it is "*Cain and* his offering" (Gen. 4:5, emphasis added) for which the Lord had no regard, and in rejecting Cain's offering, God has rejected Cain. Now from a position of hurt pride, Cain cannot (or at least does not) use reason to extricate himself from his anger, despite the help of God's questions and the encouragement either to try again or to master sin. In fact, as subsequent events show, sin almost immediately masters him, and Cain is never again portrayed as making an offering to God.

Indeed one can sympathize deeply with Cain here. Although no society could tolerate a law that allowed someone who resents the success of others to kill them, in circumstances like this, people are not surprised to find themselves in the grip of angry resentment even before they have had time to figure out exactly what has happened. It is not only children who experience the world as, at times, outrageously unfair. And, at such times, who has not received from a loving parent or friend counsel that is obviously wise but on which one is powerless to act? Then those whom we have tried to dispose of by our brutality refuse to remain mute: their cries constitute an unavoidable part of our new circumstances, and the possibilities of further violence increase.

Cain as Oblivious Golden Boy

Why is Cain so surprised by God's preference for Abel's offering? The key is given in the way in which the two characters are set up at the beginning of Genesis 4.

From the outset, Cain has substance, importance, whereas Abel has very little. There are many indications of this. First, although Cain is never referred to as "first-born," his conception and birth represent a completely new beginning. He is from birth termed a man (that is, a male, *'îš*, first used of his own father in 2:23). His mother, Eve, responds to Cain's presence by saying, "I have produced a man with the help of the LORD" (4:1). By contrast, the act of intercourse that led to Abel's conception is not referred to. At his birth Abel is designated merely "his [Cain's] brother," and Eve makes no comment this time around (4:2). Indeed the Hebrew version of Abel's name *(hebel)* sounds the same as a word denoting "a breath," or "vanity"—something so slight that it should not even be attended to.[12]

Abel's positioning in the text reinforces the idea that Cain, and not he himself, is the one who is heading for success. For when the two are introduced in Genesis 4:1-2, the pattern of their names is a chiasm of the form: Cain—Abel—Abel—Cain, a pattern repeated immediately afterward in verses 3-5a. In these verses, then, Abel's name is twice enclosed by that of Cain: Abel is hemmed in by his brother. Even if this arrangement is interpreted positively, to suggest that Cain is supposed to be protecting Abel, it still implies the younger one's inferior position and, of course, will turn out to be heavily ironical. Overall the reader learns nothing of Abel apart from his name, his shepherding activity (Cain gets the family "business" of tilling the soil), and the fact that his offering of one of "the firstlings of his flock" pleased God (4:4).[13] In fact, except where the text refers to Abel's occupation and offering in verses 2 and 4, Abel is never referred to without being called Cain's brother (vv. 2, 8-11). He will have neither wife nor progeny, and his early death ensures that his character develops no further. From his birth he nowhere relates to a human being, except by being the brother of his murderer and, in the Greek but not the Hebrew Bible (see n. 11), by his wordless assent to Cain's suggestion that the two of them go out into the field (4:8).

That Abel is completely overshadowed by his older brother is not stated: it did not need to be in a society where primogeniture counted for so much. Nor is it necessary that Cain be shown taking any advantage of his superior status. He outstrips Abel not by anything that he does but because of what he is, and neither he nor any other human person can alter *that*. Someone who happens to have most of the features that his or her society regards as particularly desirable may occasionally give thanks for them but is more likely to take them for granted most of the time. (The same applies to groups and even nations.) But what about those who lack such unspoken social advantages? They risk thinking of themselves disparagingly in terms of the gifts that others possess but they themselves lack and will never have. Cain is the advantaged one in Genesis 4. As Adam and Eve's first son, he has all the status of that position, whereas Abel has none of it. It is irrelevant that neither of them gets to reflect on the situation or that the text lacks any hint of resentment on Abel's part. We do not need to be told that Abel will never quite measure up to his older brother; that is just a given—but the point is that it *is* given in the text of Genesis 4, at least for the first-time reader of the Bible. In terms of human status, Cain is superior to Abel, right from Abel's conception.

Choosing the Disadvantaged

So the fact that Cain has always had everything in his

favor may explain why he is brought up short by God's unexplained preference for Abel and his gift. Far from acting in an arbitrary manner, God is in fact manifesting for the first time in the canonical texts the most characteristic feature of *this* God: a strong propensity for favoring the weak over the strong. This is the God who, according to the New Testament, "chose what is low and despised in the world, things that are not, to reduce to nothing things that are" (1 Cor. 1:28). God's strong predilection for people who have an initial disadvantage is a basic claim of the entire Bible. In the Hebrew scriptures it frequently takes the form of favoring younger brothers over older ones: obvious examples are God's choice of Jacob and David, rather than of Esau and Jesse's seven older sons. So if Cain is tacitly assuming (as anyone would in his position) that he will succeed when he makes an offering to God simply because he has had all the advantages so far, he is in for a shock. Abel and his gift communicate effectively with God, whereas Cain and his gift do not. As if to reinforce the point, the author tells how the cry of Abel's blood elicits a divine response (4:10): in the biblical world, victims of injustice have automatic access to God's hot-line. Such stories serve to bring to people's attention those whom they would not otherwise notice.

Life in the Human Family

As many commentators have pointed out, this story of the two brothers is about living as a member of humanity, where all are siblings. Perhaps Cain would have been less hurt by God's refusal of his offering if he had been an only child, but there are no only children in this sense. Cain, like all of us, finds that his destiny is to a large degree dependent on the actions of some perceived nonentity, in this case his younger brother. The key point is that, so long as they stick to shepherding or tilling the soil, Cain is unlikely to be aware of any sense of inferiority that his brother may have.[14]

Cain's unexamined presumption of his social superiority to Abel, the basis of all his everyday actions, is not at all malicious. It does, though, turn out to have consequences, as the brothers' attempts to communicate with God reveal. In a very costly learning experience, Cain suddenly comes to realize that what counts as status among humans does not necessarily impress God: as Samuel is told when choosing a king to replace Saul, "mortals . . . look on the outward appearance, but the LORD looks at the heart" (1 Sam. 16:7).

God's act of putting Cain on notice is much like that of a parent dealing with a pair of children (Gen. 4:6-7). Adult intervention is often required if a stronger child is to become aware of the weaker one and his needs. This dynamic is not limited to children, though. It operates in adults, and at the levels of classes, nations, and civilizations too. In other words, the Cain syndrome—that which made him so surprised that God refused his offering and accepted his brother's—is inherent in human beings and the societies constructed by them. For example, most of us in the west regularly and without serious thought use articles made by slave labor, enjoy fruit picked by nonunionized workers, take much more than our share of the world's raw materials, and so on. We need the voices of prophets, quasi-parental figures, to provide reminders that this is unsustainable human behavior because, however unintentional, it is violence done to the weak.

God's further response in encouraging Cain to deal positively with the "correction" is also typically parental. For what conscientious parent does not at some time risk alienating a child by a tough challenge to go beyond the stage he or she has already reached? Here, too, is a service that people made in God's image and likeness sometimes have to perform for one another at personal and societal levels. The biblical text offers warrant for this necessary but potentially dangerous activity.

Cain is offered two possibilities other than simply giving vent to his anger. He can either find out what the problem with God is ("do well . . . be accepted," 4:7) or be fore-warned about the need to master sin in his next move. However, there is a world of difference between knowing what one should do and being able to act on that knowledge: trusting that one's powers of reason will provide a way forward requires so much more security than does indulging one's anger. In Cain's case, the problem appears to be that he, like many readers of the story down through the centuries, has no idea why God should have rejected him and accepted Abel. So God's advice comes to Cain as from one who has just treated him unfairly in the matter that is of supreme importance to him: his spontaneous desire to communicate with God in a new way, by making an offering of what he had produced. Feeling wounded and resentful, Cain is probably not even listening, as the text suggests when it juxtaposes God's address to him (v. 7: "If you do well . . .") with Cain's proposal to Abel and the act of fratricide (v. 8).

The Roots of Human Violence

Thus right at the outset the Bible locates human violence in a defective response to what Cain mistakenly interpreted as an arbitrary challenge from God, because he was not sufficiently aware of his own advantages as the elder brother. The message is clear: God takes human action very seriously. God cautions Cain at the onset of his anger (4:5), but then gently insists that Cain is henceforth responsible for behaving appropriately. The fact that Cain cannot control significant parts of his world (notably God and his brother) makes no difference in this. So Cain's angry action leads to disaster. Not only is Abel dead, but Cain's own life is at risk from those who now know what humanity is capable of and thus fear for their own lives: they could be Cain's next victims if they do not make a preemptive strike. In answer to Cain's plea, therefore, God gives him the special protection that he needs (Gen. 4:14-15). Yet the lesson is not learned: that people's lack of sensitivity to the weak generates violence and therefore grief for everyone. Thus one of Cain's descendants, several generations down the line, is Lamech, and among his sons is Tubal-cain, "who made all kinds of bronze and iron tools" (4:22); one knows what *they* will mostly be used for.[15] So it is no surprise to find in the next verse a poetic fragment in which Lamech says to his wives,

> "I have killed a man for wounding me, a young man
>   for striking me.
> If Cain is avenged sevenfold,
> truly Lamech seventy-sevenfold"
>   (Gen. 4:23-24).

By this stage, not only has violence become something to boast about, but its cost in terms of human lives has escalated. Cain's descendants have even found a way to corrupt the mechanism that God put in place to protect Cain's life (4:15). The development toward Genesis 6:11, "the earth was filled with violence," is well underway.

Separations, Sexuality, Cities

By putting the Cain and Abel incident immediately after Adam and Eve's expulsion from Eden, the author of Genesis is connecting people's tendency to violence with the condition of humans as those who experience themselves as somehow separated from their origins.

Cain also has to make a number of separations. Thus, as God decrees in 4:11 and Cain bewails in verse 14, he is separated from "the soil," the *'ᵃdāmāh* from which his race was taken (2:7).[16] And, far from fulfilling his original intention of using the product of his daily work as a means of relating to God, Cain's move takes him away from the Lord's presence, out of God's reach (4:14, 16) and into "the land of Nod," that is "the land of Wandering."[17] In this respect, Cain's move is even more radical than his parents' departure from the garden, although the mark that the Lord puts on him ensures that his separation from God is not total (4:15). God's writ runs even in the land of Wandering.

Contrasting with these separations, however, is the note about sexual union. Like his father, Adam,[18] Cain's first act on settling was to cause his wife to conceive his son, Enoch (4:17). Thus, at the biological level at least, Cain's line is assured of continuance (at least until the time of the flood). He will not suffer extinction, as Abel did.

A second consequence is that Cain does not, in fact, remain a fugitive but, even in the land of Wandering, settles down and builds a city that he names after Enoch (4:17). His contribution to culture thus goes far beyond that of his parents. Adam in Eden named the animals as God made and presented them to him and also named the woman (2:19-20; 3:20). By contrast, Cain gets to name that which he has himself "built" (4:17), and by calling his city "Enoch" he is shown to be connecting the work of his hands with the fruit of his procreative activities. Cain gives the world its first trademark, thereby drawing attention to his ability to construct components of culture. There is no mention of his descendants tilling the soil: the separation from the *ʾdāmāh* was complete. Yet, as 4:18-22 attests, Cain's offspring continue to develop civilization, as they variously become nomads with livestock and makers of musical instruments and tools.

Some Conclusions

In the biblical canon, then, violence first erupted because Cain responded inadequately when God challenged him to deal rationally with the results of his first-ever unsuccessful encounter with reality: God's rejection of his offering. The ensuing homicide shows the author's awareness of the power that anger exerts over people. Cain cannot break out of it by making a creative response. The killing has highly ambiguous results: on the one hand, it damages Cain greatly; on the other, civilization begins with Cain's founding of the city that he names after his son (4:17). Therefore Cain's violent behavior cannot be seen in isolation from other human achievements that serve to develop humanity's potential and distinguish people from one another.

The story also testifies to a particular difficulty of living in society. Each person relates to others out of a mixture of weaknesses and strengths. The strengths can turn out to be a problem if they cause us to lose contact with those whom, either consciously or unconsciously, we make feel inferior in those respects.[19] The weaknesses are even more likely to cause us trouble. For everyone sometimes experiences God (or "fate") as arbitrary. At such times, even the most innocuous of individuals can be the focus of the resulting anger that tries unsuccessfully to get rid of this "Abel." Yet, as the text says seven times in Genesis 4:7-11, Abel is Cain's brother, and shedding his blood leads to Cain's banishment from the *ʾădāmāh*, the ground from which they both came. In a way, Cain has killed off a part of his own total being, and this diminishes him. Furthermore, he suffers in being thrust away from the presence of the God with whom he had initially tried to make contact, and out into the wider world. At the same time, however, his exertions there can result in much greater opportunities for human achievement, although at the cost of significant negative developments.

So Genesis 4 presents violence as an almost inevitable (but nonetheless highly regrettable) part of human differentiation, both at the individual and at the societal levels.

It harms the victim and the perpetrator: the murdered Abel and the banished Cain have the same origin and are brothers. Cain's subsequent action in eliciting divine protection for himself makes clear the value of a human life, but even this insight can be put to destructive use: his descendants include Lamech, who boasts that his life is worth seventy-sevenfold vengeance (Gen. 4:23-24). It is surely significant that the genealogical tradition in Genesis 5 does not begin with Cain but with the third son of Adam and Eve, Seth, who is never called Cain's brother.

Therefore Cain is not part of the line from Adam to Abraham that can be traced through Genesis 1–11. The cause of his exclusion is his lack of awareness of his brother, Abel, and Cain's inability to deal with his own anger when God registers protest. Cain's cultural achievements are manifest. His descendants domesticate stock, play musical instruments, and introduce metallurgy (4:20-22). The result of this, however, is to render human culture problematic. So Cain's decision and fate is shown as having wide effects, not only for himself (as a theological dead end who is, nevertheless, protected by God) but also because of the negative cast thrown on human achievements, including cities. It is indeed a cautionary tale.

3

AFTER CAIN:

THE FLOOD, STRONG MEN,
AND MORE CITIES IN GENESIS 6-11

The way forward for Israel, after the impasse of Cain and Abel, is by means of the descendants of Seth, Adam and Eve's third son (Gen. 5:3). In its initial stages, this is no better than the Cain option. For, despite the fresh beginning, the extension of the human line soon leads to the near-total corruption of the violence-filled earth prior to the Flood. In 6:5, the Lord will be concluding that no desire of the human heart is anything other than evil, and the chaos of the Flood ensues.

Impetus to this is given by the strange events described in 6:1-4: the intermarriage of divine beings ("the sons of God/the gods") with the beautiful human women. Unless the mere existence of beautiful women is a problem, there is no human culpability here: the heavenly beings simply "took wives for themselves of all that they chose" (v. 2).[1] These unions are evidently frowned upon by God, whose immediate reaction is to limit the human life span (v. 3). The sons born of the unions become "the heroes that were of old, warriors of renown" (v. 4), that is, successful fighting men. The Hebrew word for them is *gibbôrîm*; its singular is *gibbôr*, of which the basic meaning is "manly," or "vigorous."

Post-biblical Jewish tradition includes clear disapproval of these giants. In 1 Enoch 7:2-5 they are described as first eating all the people's food, then eating the people, and finally each other. Baruch juxtaposes their skill in war and their lack of (God-given) wisdom that caused them to perish (3:26-28).[2] Genesis itself makes no overt criticism of the heroes or their way of life. Yet there is implicit condemnation.[3] For what immediately follows is a note about the Lord's reaction to the evil desires of the human heart:

> The LORD saw that the wickedness of humankind was great in the earth, and that every inclination of the thoughts of their hearts was only evil continually. And the LORD was sorry that he had made humankind on the earth, and it grieved him to his heart (Gen. 6:5-6).

These verses have a doublet in verses 11-12. There the offense is specified as *ḥāmās*, which the New Revised Standard Version translates here as *violence*: "Now the earth was corrupt in God's sight, and the earth was filled with violence" (v. 11).[4] God then sums up the situation: "I have determined to make an end of all flesh, for the earth is filled with violence because of them" (v. 13). That is to say, the exploits of the "heroes of old" are, for God, the last straw in a process in which the accumulation of human violence outweighs any achievements that have accrued. Obviously, the story of Noah shows that the depravity was not total, yet the point is made: beginning with Cain's fratricide, the evil and violence in human society have increased so much that there is no way forward, as the Lord regretfully concludes before deciding to "blot out from the earth" humanity and all the other creatures (6:6-7). So the whole of creation suffers because of human lawlessness. There is wholesale destruction, the effects of creatures' fertility and multiplication (Gen. 1:22, 28) are annulled, and animal life is reduced to one pair of each kind (6:19-20).⁵ God has wasted a lot of effort and has responded to violence with what certainly looks like violence: a reversal of the separation of the waters that, on day three of creation, had brought the Earth into being. Consequently, nearly all the creatures drown.

Chapters 4–6 of Genesis, then, present civilization as including a potential for escalating violence which, when exacerbated by the activities of the warrior-heroes of old (the *gibbôrîm*, 6:4), leads God to send the Flood (chaps. 7–8). Yet even God soon comes to terms with the reality: because Noah was deemed "a righteous man, blameless in his generation" (6:9), he and his family can provide for the continuance of creation (6:14–8:22).

What would happen if people took as their example God's behavior in the story of the Flood? In other words, would it be possible to use this story to justify the destruction of others, provided one were absolutely sure where the blame lay and could avoid doing more than inconveniencing the innocent for a few weeks? Perhaps so, at least in theory, inasmuch as the circumstances appear to conform to later formulations of so-called "just-war theory."⁶ On the other hand, the Flood narrative concludes with God's avowal never to repeat the destruction:

> I will never again curse the ground (*ᵃdāmāh*) because of humankind (*'ādām*), for the inclination of the human heart is evil from youth; nor will I ever again destroy every living creature as I have done. As long as the earth endures, seedtime and harvest, cold and heat, summer and winter, day and night, shall not cease (Gen. 8:21-22).

God even takes practical steps to ensure the permanence of the lesson with the "bow in the clouds" (9:12-17) that will function as a reminder of the divine commitment to Noah and his offspring "and every living creature that is with you, for all future generations" (9:12). The Hebrew word used for the (rain)bow is *qeshet*, the same as that used to denote the human weapon (e.g., Gen. 27:3, where Esau will use it to kill game). God's bow is not, however, a weapon but a thing of great beauty that reminds people of God's commitment. The episode of the Flood ends, therefore, with God establishing a covenant with all that lives: God tried violence once and now knows better.

The opening of Genesis 9 includes two divine adjustments to the original program. They are connected with God's renewed blessing of humanity in the persons of Noah and his children. Blood relates the two ordinances. Thus humans may now kill animals for food, provided that they abstain from "flesh with its lifeblood in it" (9:3-4, NAB; contrast 1:29), and they (and "every animal," v. 5) will face a death sentence if they take human life. In the larger context of Genesis 1–11, the latter regulation should be seen as an attempt at curbing the spirit of vendetta displayed earlier by Lamech in 4:23-24. Thus sevenfold vengeance is replaced by a requirement that only the killer's blood is to be forfeit (Gen. 9:6). That both these permissions are given only after the Flood suggests their concessive nature. In Israel's understanding, God's original design for humanity did not include killing of any sort, even for food.

The disaster wrought by the Flood was evidently insufficient to curb the apparently unacceptable tendency of humans to ground their security in their own capabilities. Now that tendency takes the form of city building, the final event described prior to the genealogy of Abraham that concludes the prepatriarchal narratives of Genesis 1–11 (11:10-32). Until this tower of Babel episode in Genesis 11, with one insignificant exception in 10:12,[7] the word *city* was used solely with reference to the one that the exiled Cain built and named after his son Enoch

(4:17). Then, in Genesis 11:1-9, the writer tells of how people set out to build "a city, and a tower with its top in the heavens," their aim being to "make a name for [them]selves" and to prevent their being "scattered abroad upon the face of the whole earth" (11:4). This, even though "fill[ing] the earth" was what God had told humans to do at their creation in 1:28! Instead, they provoke a divine visitation that results in precisely that scattering (vv. 8-9). In this story, the word *city* is repeated three times (vv. 4-5, 8). Finally, in verse 9, the city is specified as Babel, a name that connects explicitly with the confusion of tongues and implicitly with Babylon, for the Hebrew word for Babylon is *bābel*.

All this confirms a suspicion that the writer views cities negatively. One reason for that may have been Israel's period of exile in Babylon during the sixth century. For the punitive "scattering" of the people because of the "city . . . called Babel" would surely have struck a chord with readers whose recent history included enforced removal from their land and a fifty-year period of exile in Babylon, an experience they interpreted as divine punishment for their infidelity to the Lord. Furthermore, elsewhere in Genesis the word *city* nearly always designates Sodom and Gomorrah or the settlements of Israel's enemies.[8] In particular, it is not used of Salem, King Melchizedek's city (Gen. 14:18) that was traditionally identified with Jerusalem.[9]

That the blame for the confusion of tongues in Genesis 11 is linked with the city of Babylon is significant because, just prior to this episode, Nimrod, the founder of Babylon, is three times designated by the Hebrew word *gibbôr* (10:8-9). This is the only occurrence of the word in Genesis 1–11 except to refer to the "heroes of old" at the opening of chapter 6. The reader is evidently meant to be impressed by Nimrod, who is said to be legendary as "a mighty warrior . . . [and] . . . a mighty hunter before the

LORD" (10:8, 9): this does not sound bad. Yet Nimrod's name can be connected with a verb that means "to revolt" or "to rebel," and the next verse specifies that "the beginning of his kingdom" was Babylon (10:10). This casts a different light on him, especially in view of the story about the tower of Babel in the following chapter.

Conclusion

Within the opening chapters of Genesis, being a mighty man, a despot, a hero (all *gibbôr*) is at best a very doubtful compliment.[10] It designates here only the products of enforced divine-human miscegenation whose birth immediately precedes the Flood (6:1-4) and the founder of Babylon, shortly before the disastrous scattering and confusion of tongues that is linked with that city.[11] This suggests a fundamental ambiguity about heroes and strong men that is shared with cities in general and specifically with Babylon (in Gen. 10–11, the closing chapters of this section), the city to which the Lord's people had been exiled in 587 B.C.E., almost two centuries before the Pentateuch took its final shape. That is to say, the early connection between Cain's violence and his city is explicitly developed (in terms of *gibbôrîm*, not fratricide) in what follows. On the other hand, the association between sexuality and the negative aspects of post-fall life that we noted earlier is not sustained beyond Genesis 4, except perhaps inasmuch as (in a move that blames the victims) women's beauty is alleged to have led directly to the birth of "the heroes that were of old, the warriors of renown" (6:2, 4).

Thus, in Genesis 1–11, violence is not part of the original creation. It comes about only after the expulsion from Eden and Cain's unsuccessful struggle with the lurking demon (4:7) that he conjures up by his inability to rise to his own and God's challenge, a challenge brought on by Cain's failure in the face of his brother's success.

Thereafter the violence escalates and, after the Flood, is recognized and legislated for in kind by divine decree (9:5-6), presumably in an attempt at limiting it. In these chapters, no war has been described, although it is clear that Lamech's spirit of vendetta (4:23-24) could very quickly lead to armed conflict, with weapons supplied by the descendants of Tubal-cain (4:22). Additionally, the renown of the "heroes that were of old" (6:4) was surely understood to include military exploits, as the later Baruch 3:26-28 makes clear. Thus war (i.e., violence in its organized, socially sanctioned form) is probably taken for granted by the authors of this first part of Genesis, but they are not at all concerned about describing it, much less glorifying it. Meanwhile, even the carefully controlled divine reversal of creation that for a while effectively cancels the ill effects of human violence is shown not to be an option for God in the future. Logically, this should deter people from destroying their *own* works: it does not necessarily rule out the destruction of other people and their works. What is needed, therefore, is an increased awareness of one's solidarity with those others. The remainder of the book of Genesis provides some models for this, as we shall see.

4

PATRIARCHAL PEACEMAKING

Genesis 1–11 concludes with a genealogy that links Noah's oldest son, Shem, to Abram and Sarai. This leads into the story of Israel, which begins when God calls Abram and gives him a blessing (12:1-3) that includes a divine promise of progeny and land (Gen. 15). One would expect, therefore, a halt in humanity's downward spiral into conflict that the trajectory of Genesis 1–11 had set up, from Cain to the Flood and the results of human inability to communicate after Babel. This is indeed the case. For the patriarchal narratives in Genesis 12–50 contain relatively little violent behavior from anyone; on the contrary, they depict a significant degree of peacemaking, especially on the part of the patriarchs themselves. Abraham, Isaac, and Jacob are models of those who prosper by the Lord's favor and with scarcely a hint of violence. They are shown as living peaceably with their families and those around them insofar as they can do so. Let us consider these two aspects of each patriarch.

Abraham

Genesis 13 shows Abraham dealing with problems of violence within his clan: here he separates from Lot to prevent further strife "between the herders of Abram's livestock and the herders of Lot's livestock" (v. 7).[1] Later and more ambiguously, he heeds Sarah's request that he produce a child with her slave, Hagar, and deliberately keeps out of the way when this leads to trouble between the two women (16:1-6).

Abraham is similarly unwilling to initiate aggression against outsiders. Thus, in the first story told of him after his call (12:1-9), he is shown trying to gain favor and avoid trouble with the Egyptians among whom he is living because of a famine. Again the circumstances are highly dubious: Abraham practices deceit (the typical ploy of the otherwise powerless) and puts his wife and neighbors at risk for his own advantage (12:10-20). However one evaluates his actions, this is not the behavior of a violent man and, in case the issue were in any doubt, he is described as behaving in the same way with regard to the people of Gerar (20:1-18), as does his son Isaac (26:1-11). On the other hand, even by our standards Abraham does not always lack courage: in 18:16-33 he is prepared to bargain with God in an attempt at averting the destruction of innocent people in Sodom—in particular, no doubt, his nephew Lot.

A different light is cast on Abraham in Genesis 14. This is not surprising, because the chapter tells a story that has no obvious connection with the surrounding material. Nevertheless it contributes significantly to the portrait of Abraham found in Genesis. In chapter 14, he goes to war against four kings to rescue Lot and his family from captivity. Abraham clearly succeeds as a warrior, for he and his 318 retainers achieve alone what the alliance of five local kings could not.[2] The operation sounds most impressive: Abraham runs the defeated enemy out of the area and retrieves all possessions and captives (vv. 15-16). The events of the battle are recounted with great economy (vv. 14-16), reflecting that of Abraham in dispatching his adversaries. The story concludes by describing at greater length the aftermath of the victory. Even here, nonmilitary aspects of the patriarch's character are emphasized. Thus, after having been blessed by Melchizedek the priest, Abraham gives tithes to him and, on grounds of piety and honor, refuses to profit personally from the spoil. At the same time, he ensures that those with him receive their due (vv. 17-24). So the traditions found in Genesis 14 take for granted Abraham's military skill and his willingness to fight when the demands of his family's safety and honor drive him to it. However, in much the same way as the book of Joshua will characterize its eponymous hero, the text of Genesis seeks to emphasize not Abraham's ability to fight but rather the piety, restraint, and magnanimity he shows afterward.

Isaac

Abraham's son Isaac is consistently the recipient of other people's actions, rather than being an actor in his own right. Such actions as he does perform are conciliatory rather than aggressive or even assertive. Within his family, he accepts Rebekah, the wife that his father produces for him (Gen. 24), and does not prevent her from ensuring that her favored son, the younger twin Jacob (25:28), receives the blessing of the firstborn in defiance of birth order and Isaac's own intention (27:1-40). Rebekah then enables Jacob to escape from his older brother's wrath (27:4–28:5), a strategy that, incidentally, leads to Jacob marrying the daughters of her own brother, Laban (27:46; chap. 29).

As far as outsiders are concerned, Isaac emulates Abraham in fearfully risking the honor of his wife and the integrity of those among whom he lives by trying to pass off his wife as his sister so as to avoid trouble for himself while living in the land that God had told him to reside in (26:1-11). Although his scheme does not work as planned, Isaac nevertheless secures protection for himself and Rebekah by these means (v. 11).

Isaac then goes on to prosper to an extent that worries Abimelech, the king of the Philistines of Gerar, among whom he is living at the time. When Abimelech tells the patriarch, "Go away from us; you have become far too numerous for us" (26:16, NAB), Isaac complies without a word (v. 17). He is, in fact, acting from a position of strength. For his becoming "numerous" (or "powerful," as in the NRSV) has an implied God-given inevitability about it. Even though the same Hebrew root (*'sm*) was not used when Isaac himself was designated to inherit God's promise to Abraham, his father (26:2-5), the cognate adjective *numerous* (*mighty*, NRSV) in 18:18 did describe the "nation" that Abraham was to become. The fulfillment of that promise was therefore the cause of Isaac's abundant family and Abimelech's consternation. More immediately, the author of Genesis links this flourishing with the Lord's blessing of Isaac: "The LORD blessed him, and the man became rich; he prospered more and more until he became very wealthy" (26:12-13; see also vv. 3-4). So one is surely to conclude that Isaac's future is assured without his needing to do more than accede to Abimelech's request that he leave the area.

The theme of Isaac's essential security becomes explicit in what follows. First, in Genesis 26:17-22, he is shown quietly abandoning two sets of wells that he has dug, because the herders of Gerar dispute his claim to them. After the digging of the third well (about which there is no dispute), Isaac's conduct is implicitly commended by the Lord, who appears to him in the night. Isaac is told not to fear, because the Lord is with him and promises blessing (26:24; see also vv. 3-4, 12). Then Abimelech, his army general, and another adviser approach Isaac in Beersheba and request a covenant with him (vv. 26-31) because, they say, "We see plainly that the LORD has been with you" (v. 28). So they, too, have somehow come to recognize that of which the reader has just been reminded yet again through the theophany to Isaac in 26:23-25. Abimelech and his entourage are willing to acknowledge Isaac's superiority a second time.[3] Isaac's restrained behavior has thus paid off: it has allowed him to prosper and to live at peace (vv. 29, 31) with those who used to "hate" him (v. 27). He has all that he needs for living, as the finding of water at this point underscores (v. 32). We shall find this lesson repeated in the book of Joshua: that the Lord's presence with the people gives them a security that is sometimes evident to their enemies. In Isaac's case, that presence gives them sufficient protection by means of an unexpected peace treaty, not by force of conquest.[4]

Thus, as Genesis depicts Isaac, his wife Rebekah is subtly in charge of the major events within the family. In his dealings with neighbors, Isaac is nowhere presented as even self-assertive, let alone aggressive, and yet he is favored by God, acknowledged as superior by his enemies, and given whatever he needs to flourish: flocks, herds, work animals, and water. He dies "old and full of days" (35:29).

Jacob

There are resemblances between Isaac and his son Jacob. He is introduced as "a quiet man, living in tents," in contrast to the "skillful hunter" Esau (Gen. 25:27; not *gibbôr*). Although he tricks his brother Esau out of his birthright and blessing (25:29-34; 27:1-40), the first is done by driving a hard bargain when Esau presents himself as desperate for food, and the second occurs only at the instigation of his mother (27:6-13). Jacob further heeds Rebekah in fleeing to Haran to avoid being killed by Esau (27:41-45) and, while there, does all he reasonably can to live at peace with his difficult father-in-law, Laban (29:1–30:43). When this does not work out (largely

because Jacob prospers at Laban's expense), he flees a second time. Whatever one may think of his guile, Jacob is anything but confrontational (see 31:20, 27-28) and uses his
anger only to protest his innocence in all his dealings with
Laban up to that point (31:36-42).[5] On returning to his own
country, he goes to extraordinary lengths to ensure a peaceful meeting with Esau, of whom he is very much afraid, and
with good reason (32:3–33:3).[6] Later, in the cycle of stories
centering on Joseph (chaps. 37–50), Jacob's initiatives with
regard to his family are few, sometimes unwise (e.g., the
favoring of Joseph, son of his preferred wife Rachel, in Gen.
37), and mostly concern the tension he experiences between
his family's need for food and his extreme reluctance to let
Rachel's other son, his beloved Benjamin, travel to Egypt
with his brothers to obtain it.[7]

The only occasion on which Jacob interacts (even indirectly) with outsiders is in Genesis 34. Here two of Jacob's
sons, Simeon and Levi, ostensibly avenge the rape of their
sister, Dinah, by Shechem, son of Hamor. They do this by
deceiving and then killing the men of Shechem. After that,
the other brothers devastate and loot the city. This story
contrasts Simeon and Levi, who at least deceived their
negotiating partners (34:13) with their father, Jacob. The
latter, on first hearing the news of Dinah's situation "held
his peace" until his sons came home (Gen. 34:5),[8] was not
involved in their vengeful scheme (cf. v. 11 with v. 13), and,
at the end, protested (however ineffectually) about the risk
at which their hotheaded actions had put him with respect
to his neighbors (v. 30). It is a complex and subtle text: one
cannot be sure whether, finally, the author is implicitly
criticizing Jacob for his lack of initiative or whether he
regards the actions of Jacob's sons as unreasonable and
shortsighted and therefore a foil for those of their father.[9]
At the end of the book of Genesis, the violence of Simeon
and Levi counts against them (Gen. 49:5-7),[10] and so it is

likely that Jacob's nonaggressive behavior in chapter 34 is to be regarded positively and as part of the book's generally peaceable portrait of the patriarchs.

But was Jacob always such a peaceable character? This cannot be taken for granted. In the real world, dynasties are not usually built up by such people, so it might be worth examining whether the Bible contains any traces of a Jacob who was more prone to violence. In other words, is there any evidence that the present biblical tradition results from a choice to include texts in which Jacob does not fight for the land and the elimination of those in which he does? That suggestion has been made at various times. Thus biblical scholar John Skinner wonders whether Genesis 48:22, perhaps a reference to Jacob as a successful fighter, might not "carry us back to a phase of the national tradition which ignored the sojourn in Egypt, and represented Jacob as a warlike hero who had effected permanent conquests in Palestine, and died there after dividing the land among his children."[11] In the verse, Israel (Jacob) says to his son, Joseph, "I now give to you one portion more than to your brothers, the portion that I took from the hand of the Amorites with my sword and with my bow."

In favor of understanding Genesis 48:22 as a remnant of older traditions that were later superseded, is the fact that this is the only biblical text in which Jacob is portrayed as an aggressor. Such an argument assumes that stories of Jacob's warlike exploits used to be prevalent but were suppressed or forgotten when Israel came to understand its tenure of the land in light of the Exodus experience and its aftermath. The difficulty is, of course, that the absence of such traditions makes the position all but impossible to substantiate from this one verse alone. So let us consider 48:22 alongside other relevant traditions about Jacob, to see whether they might provide support for such an interpretation of the verse.

In Genesis 48, the dying Jacob bequeaths to his son Joseph some land: "one portion more than to your brothers" (v. 22).[12] The word here translated as *portion* is, literally, a *shechem*, one that Jacob had captured from the Amorites with his sword and bow (Gen. 48). *Shechem* in ordinary speech means "shoulders," and thus in this context could denote a mountain slope (as in the RSV) or two of them, such as a portion of land (as in the NRSV). Some reference to the city and region of Shechem must be intended, however, given Jacob's association with the place in Genesis 34.[13] So the New American Bible simply transliterates the Hebrew as *Shechem* and thus has Jacob bequeathing the city of Shechem to Joseph. The New American Bible editor admits in the note to 48:22 the obscurity of "the meaning of the Hebrew and the historical reference in this verse." The main historical problem stems from uncertainty about how, when, and for how long Shechem came to be in Israelite hands (see, e.g., Joshua 24 and Judges 9).

There are other problems too. For, apart from being the only place in the Bible in which any patriarch is said to acquire land by conquest, Genesis 48:22 stands in tension with a tradition found in two other texts—Genesis 33:19 and the related Joshua 24:32—which state that Jacob *bought* a small piece of land in the city of Shechem (or very close to it) from Hamor's descendants for a hundred pieces of money.[14]

It is far easier to make sense of the two texts in which Jacob buys land. Genesis 33:19 specifies that what he bought was "the plot of ground on which he had pitched his tent," an area big enough for one tent—or a grave. In fact, the long-term significance of this piece of land is that it was used as a burial ground for the bones of Joseph, which the Israelites brought up from Egypt with them (Josh. 24:32; Gen. 50:25; Exod. 13:19).

In this account, the parallel between Jacob and Abraham is clear. For even though the function of Jacob's purchase becomes apparent only later in the story,[15] the strand of the tradition according to which this patriarch buys the small plot of land in Shechem (Gen. 33:19) is reminiscent of Abraham's purchase of the burial cave of Machpelah, near Hebron (23:3-18). That cave was the one piece of Canaanite land that was traditionally regarded as belonging to Israel before the Exodus. In Genesis 23 its purchase was described in meticulous detail. Eventually Sarah, Abraham, Isaac, Rebekah, Leah, and Jacob were buried there. However, there was never any question about burying Joseph's bones there, when they were brought up from Egypt at the Exodus (Exod. 13:19; Josh. 24:32). Perhaps this is because Hebron was in the territory that eventually belonged to Judah, not to the two Joseph tribes, Ephraim and Manasseh. So it is quite possible that traditions would arise that have Jacob somehow providing a piece of land suitable for Joseph's burial. Shechem clearly fitted this description. It was located in the territory of Manasseh, named after Joseph's elder son, whose descendants would eventually take second place to those of his younger brother, Ephraim (see Gen. 48:8-10). Moreover, the city is close to the common border of the two Joseph tribes. If Jacob bought this plot of land, he is once more emulating Abraham; one can see how such a tradition as Genesis 33:19 might have come into existence.

What, though, about Genesis 48:22, which presents Jacob as bequeathing to Joseph some land, perhaps Shechem, that he had acquired by military means? The connections with 33:19 are geographical (the area of Shechem) and the figure of Joseph, but 48:22 gives no hint that the patriarch is here providing his most successful son with a place to be buried.

As we saw earlier, there is a biblical association

between the sons of Jacob and an act of violence against Shechem. Thus Genesis 34:25 tells how Simeon and Levi used their swords to kill all the Shechemites before the rest of their brothers sacked and looted the city. However, this is clearly a different occasion from the one referred to in 48:22, for no land is taken in the earlier raid, nobody is said to use his bow, and Jacob himself is not involved at all.

In other words, Genesis 48:22 really does stand alone in its witness to a belligerent Jacob. The suggestion that it might be a remnant from earlier times may have inherent plausibility but is impossible to prove.

It is tempting to argue in the opposite direction and see this verse as a later development rather than as representing an earlier stage. There is ample evidence that, like other biblical figures, Jacob "became" more warlike as time went on. One good example, probably from the mid-second century B.C.E., is found in the Book of Jubilees 34:1-9.[16] Here Jacob, Levi, Judah (not Simeon, as in Gen. 34), and Joseph, along with "six thousand men who carried swords" (34:6), go out against a group of at least seven Amorite (Canaanite) kings who have surrounded Jacob's other sons and plundered their herds (34:1-6). The story continues: "And [Jacob] killed them in the field of Shechem," those who escaped were pursued, and Jacob then made the Amorites pay tribute for as long as he remained in Canaan. This text depicts Jacob as one who will fight to rescue his family and their property. Once more, the parallel with Abraham is apparent. Here the relevant story is in Genesis 14, Abraham's victory over the kings. Thus Abraham in Genesis and Jacob in Jubilees both take the initiative in rescuing family members from a group of enemy kings and gain profit in the process. Indeed Jacob prevails against even more kings than did Abraham.

The book of Jubilees is not the only witness to Jacob

as a successful fighter. From the same century, the Testament of Judah includes an account of Jacob killing a giant "twelve cubits tall" in the course of an attack against Canaanite kings, apparently at Shechem.[17] Yet these later, extrabiblical portrayals of a belligerent Jacob cannot be used to establish the idea that Genesis 48:22 is itself a development of the more peaceable character that elsewhere appears in Genesis. That is to say, this interpretation is no better substantiated than is the reverse one: that 48:22 is a leftover from an earlier age that glorified the patriarchs as warriors. We have to conclude that the Bible's portrayal of Jacob is very much like that of the other patriarchs in being surprisingly peaceable. The one verse that suggests otherwise about Jacob has thematic links with other parts of the tradition and suggests intriguing possibilities. It is not, however, sufficient to undercut the bulk of the biblical tradition about him.

Conclusion

In these first three chapters on Genesis, we have seen that, although fratricide is one of the first events of the post-Eden world and although there is both great potential for violence (Lamech and Tubal-cain) and its actuality (heroes become "warriors of renown" in Gen. 6:4, and Simeon and Levi devastate Shechem), the patriarchal traditions of Israel in Genesis 12–50 do not glorify violence any more than did the stories in chapters 1–11. Except in the case of Genesis 14, where a story about Abraham's military activity allows his piety and generosity to shine forth, those who transmitted the traditions usually went out of their way to portray the patriarchs as avoiding conflict where they could, even when alternative traditions may have existed.

As an historical reality, this attitude is characteristic of the politically weak who cannot assert themselves against their more powerful neighbors and yet (in this case) are presented as recipients of a divine promise that will come to fulfillment in God's own time.[18] The ones whom God has chosen are portrayed as essentially nonviolent, although occasional deception (i.e., living by one's wits) seems not to be problematic and would, no doubt, have delighted readers who experienced themselves as equally powerless recipients of God's assurances.

The patriarchs' near-perfect peaceable behavior is very much at odds with the predominant view during the time of Israel's monarchy, particularly in its early days.[19] One would not expect King David, for example, to have ancestors so unconcerned about fighting for land and honor. Yet, interestingly, these are the traditions the Bible presents. The patriarchs' lack of belligerence is, of course, based on their security in the Lord's promise to them of land and progeny.[20] Genesis depicts them as wanderers in Canaan, apparently content to own nothing but the burial cave of Machpelah that Abraham succeeded in buying from the Hittites (Gen. 23).

For the interpretation of the Bible as a whole, it is surely significant that violence is not a predominant characteristic of Israel's most noted ancestors, and that they enjoy greater prosperity than their counterparts who force their will on others in the public sphere.[21] Thus the mild Isaac prevails over Ishmael, of whom it is said, "He shall be a wild ass of a man, with his hand against everyone, and everyone's hand against him" (Gen. 16:12), a saying fulfilled in 25:18. The tent-loving Jacob takes precedence over Esau the hunter (25:27). He curses his sons Simeon and Levi because of their violence (*ḥāmās*, 49:5-7). As the so-called "Joseph cycle" of chapters 37–50 details, the most successful of Jacob's twelve sons is Joseph. He is the object of his brothers' brutality and yet the one who, by the end of the book, has ensured that Abraham's line will not die out because of starvation. Furthermore, he has finally reconciled to one another the members of this highly dysfunctional family.[22] Joseph is also presented as having a place in the highest echelons of contemporary Egyptian civilization. Pharaoh commands him to bring his father and brothers into that society, so that they, too, can profit from his success (45:18-20; 46:31–47:6). Jacob is more than happy to comply (45:25-28), and the night visions that he has at Beersheba, en route for Egypt, give divine sanction to his relocation there.

Therefore one can conclude that Genesis, which opens the biblical canon, presents violence, not as integral to God or to creation, but as an aspect of post-Eden humanity that, although productive in some respects, does not characterize those particularly entrusted with God's promise of land and progeny. Indeed, with the exception of Abraham in Genesis 14 (where virtues other than peacemaking are being lauded), being overtly violent is a disqualification for receiving the promises. Success comes, not through one's own efforts but by fitting into the larger scheme of things, a move that requires a major adjustment of people's natural inclination to ensure their own success, by force if necessary.

In other words, the patriarchal narratives support the resetting of the default, of which we spoke in the Preface and chapter 1: in Genesis 12–50, as in the story of Cain and Abel, God favors those who are either not in a position to exalt themselves at the expense of others or who forgo that option.[23] There is a paradox here, for as recipients of God's favor or promise, they have power that does not express itself as domination of others. The stories of Abraham, Isaac, and Jacob suggest that such power comes as a gift. Yet that is not the whole story: the concluding section of Genesis, chapters 37–50, shows Jacob's sons engaged in a prolonged and painful struggle to overcome their quite understandable resentment of Joseph, as they learn the hard way that they have no alternative but to relate peaceably to one another. Not until all jealous rivalry has given way to reconciliation (Gen. 50:15-21) do the twelve form a unity with which God can subsequently work. This leads us into the book of Exodus.

5

THE EXODUS AND THE
WARRIOR GOD

I will sing to the LORD *for he has triumphed gloriously;*
Horse and rider he has thrown into the sea . . . .
The LORD *is a warrior;*
The LORD *is his name.*
—Exodus 15:1, 3

Introduction

The exodus experience in the thirteenth century B.C.E. is generally regarded as the foundational event in Israel's self-understanding. There are several versions of how Jacob's descendants left Egypt and experienced in a highly dramatic way the saving action of the Lord on their behalf, as they set off on the first stage of their journey to the Promised Land. Not only Jews but also Christians treasure this story as part of their foundational narrative. Many Christians listen each year to the solemn reading of Exodus chapters 14 and 15 during the Easter vigil service. The high point of the liturgical year, the vigil celebrates the resurrection of Jesus: the divine action that underlies the formation of the Christian community.

For many years I attended the Easter vigil and looked forward to listening to the sonorous phrases depicting God's triumph over Pharaoh and his army. Here is told how God, fighting for the Israelites (14:14, 25), delivered them from their enemies, the Egyptians, by drowning them in the Red Sea, and how Israel went on to celebrate the Lord in song as "a warrior" (15:3). For good measure, some of the same text is repeated in the congregation's sung response to the reading: "The chariots of Pharaoh he hurled into the sea. . . . They went down like lead into the mighty waters. Who is like you among the gods, O Lord?"

Then came one year when I was living in Rome. As the reading began, I realized to my profound discomfort and embarrassment that the story was going to sound quite different this time. The one thing I knew for certain about the person seated to the right of me was her nationality: she was Egyptian. What followed was the most unsettling liturgical experience of my life. Here was a grace received in the midst of turmoil engendered by an account of a warrior God who was honored for drowning people whom my neighbor could have counted as her distant ancestors.

In Exodus 14–15, the warrior God makes a first appearance in the Hebrew Bible; it is by no means the last. Indeed at least some commentators find evidence of this figure throughout the rest of the Bible, as far as the book of Revelation. For many Christians it is a most important image, positively or negatively.[1]

The description of Israel's response to this manifestation of divine power (15:1-21) raises further questions about the view of God assumed in these two chapters of Exodus. Although there is little unusual about the way the people celebrated their divine hero with poetry, song, and dance,[2] the object of this triumphalism is the Lord, whom the wider biblical context understands as Lord of all the nations. Post-biblical Jewish tradition came to understand that the Egyptians also are God's children and that the downfall of the wicked does not cause God to rejoice. The Babylonian Talmud, assembled by the early sixth century

C.E., gives in two places the following tradition in connection with the encounter of the Israelites and the Egyptians at the sea: "The ministering angels wanted to chant their hymns, but the Holy One, blessed be He, said, The work of my hands is being drowned in the sea, and shall you chant hymns?"[3] So the question must arise: what kind of parent could bear to see children rejoicing at the death of siblings, as Israel did on seeing "the Egyptians dead on the seashore" (14:30)? One must consider seriously these stories that appear to present God as a warrior who is assumed to take delight in the destruction of human beings.

Can the book of Exodus teach anything about strategies for constructing nonviolent responses to situations that might otherwise evoke conflict? Minimally, the figure of Pharaoh provides, in the earlier chapters of the book, a powerful example of behavior that is *not* to be emulated.[4] For Pharaoh's sequence of actions against Israel eventually leads to disaster for the Egyptian army, which is not at all what he had intended. The problem remains that presenting the Lord as an active warrior suggests that sometimes violence does pay, because that is how Israel manages to escape from slavery in Egypt. As a key text in various theologies of liberation,[5] the exodus story has been the biblical source of much violence by or on behalf of those who (often with justification) have seen themselves as oppressed.

For present purposes, the main benefit to be derived from a careful reading of Exodus may be the indirect one of demonstrating how portrayals of violence in any text can distort other meanings that it may have. The distortion occurs because violent imagery tends to take over the imagination and to absorb the reader's attention. That is to say, people sometimes "find" more violence in texts than is actually there and attribute to it a significance that its context may not warrant.

An example from Native American culture may illustrate this point. It comes from Michael F. Steltenkamp's study of Black Elk, a shaman of the Lakota Sioux.[6] Steltenkamp has shown convincingly that, although "warrior society" is a fitting label for nineteenth-century Plains Indian life, as "now reduced to a commonly shared vernacular, the designation seems explanatory but is not, in fact, as illuminating as it suggests" because of the associations the phrase may evoke for modern readers. Thus the tribes' bellicosity was not freely chosen but resulted instead from a defensive posture because of "pressure exerted on them by other Native groups."[7] Furthermore, the content of such a "warrior society" is not given with the phrase. Steltenkamp quotes a spokesman for the American Indian Movement who says that the meaning of the phrase is far from the "armed forces . . . [and] hired killers" of popular white perception but comes rather from a context in which there are men and women of the nation who have dedicated themselves to give everything that they have to the people. A warrior should be the first one to go hungry or the last one to eat . . . the first one to give away his moccasins and the last one to get new ones. That type of feeling among Indian people is what a warrior society is all about. He is ready to defend his family in time of war—to hold off any enemy, and is perfectly willing to sacrifice himself to the good of his tribe and his people. That's what a warrior society is to Indian people."[8]

That is to say, the *significance* of a society's violence is a function of its total situation and cannot be assessed in the abstract. Thus violent biblical passages cannot be automatically written off as unworthy of consideration: they may be conveying other issues than mere violence, perhaps issues of great importance.

How is this relevant to a reading of Exodus and, in particular, to its portrait of the Lord as a warrior? First, as we shall see later when looking at chapters 1–14, there is ample evidence that the image for God in those fourteen chapters resulted from pressure exerted by Pharaoh, in this case. Second, and more to the immediate point, it warns against imposing on the Lord the reader's own understanding of *warrior*, without careful reference to the biblical text itself.

Clearly, to call God a warrior is to use language analogously: God can never be a warrior comparable with any human exemplar. This is easy to forget, especially on a superficial reading of the story in Exodus. For believing that God accompanies one's army is always comforting, and a people can perhaps be braver the more inclined they are to view God as able and willing to come out in their defense. So how does the first part of Exodus transfer to the Lord the characteristics of a human warrior, with the result that God can then be described in 15:3 as a man of war (*'îš milḥāmāh*, literally, "a man of battle") who fought successfully for Israel?

One approach is to examine carefully the context in which God is termed "warrior," to see how this terminology grows out of the text itself. We shall be studying two aspects of that context: first, the language of 15:3 in its immediate literary surroundings and, second, the buildup to that verse in the preceding fourteen chapters of Exodus. In each case, the object is not to deny that 15:3 calls God a warrior, but to ascertain the terms of the analogy.

Exodus 15

Exodus 15:1-18 contains a poem celebrating God's triumph and Israel's deliverance at the Red Sea. Its language suggests a military climax to the whole operation.[9] We must consider this first, because both its location and its vividness imply that it is intended to contribute significantly to how the exodus event should be understood.

Exodus 15:1-18 opens thus:

> Then Moses and the Israelites sang this song to the LORD:
>
> "I will sing to the LORD, for he has triumphed gloriously;
>   horse and rider he has thrown into the sea.
> The LORD is my strength and my might,
>   and he has become my salvation;
> this is my God, and I will praise him,
>   my father's God, and I will exalt him.
> The LORD is a warrior;
>   the LORD is his name" (Exod. 15:1-3).

The poem goes on to note the dread in which local non-Israelite chieftains greeted the coming of this people and to praise God for the divine commitment to guiding the redeemed people to "the mountain of [their] own possession" and to God's sanctuary (v. 17). The final version of this may have been written long afterwards,[10] and included a contribution from Canaanite models.[11] In Exodus 15:1 it is put into the mouth of "Moses and the Israelites," a song that the latter can continue to sing as long as they remain the people whose foundation this event celebrates.[12]

Joseph Blenkinsopp has suggested that Exodus 15:1-18 "is not so much a victory song as a thanksgiving hymn, and is in no essential respect different from other examples of the genre in Psalms and elsewhere in the Hebrew Bible."[13] But to what extent does the song give thanks for a warrior God? Certainly, this aspect is not missing, for verse 3 states explicitly that "the LORD is a warrior." The two verses before that, however, are another matter. Admittedly, the song is a gloating over enemies. Yet the Egyptian army ("horse and rider") was overcome by drowning in a sea that it had entered while pursuing the

Israelites. That the Lord "has thrown [them] into the sea" is poetic license and does not, in itself, depict a military action. Furthermore, the phrase here translated "has triumphed gloriously" is a Hebrew idiom comprising the double use of one verb to express emphasis: the Lord "has indeed triumphed."[14] The lexical content of the verb that is here translated "to triumph" is connected with "being high up," "becoming exalted."[15] Two of the three other places where it appears in the Hebrew Bible lack even remotely military connotations. Its subject is the rising waters of a river in Ezekiel 47:5 and the growth of the papyrus reed in Job 8:11. The third occurrence, in Job 10:16, is more ambiguous. Here Job speaks of the Lord's power as used against him when he sins, and the following verse (of which the Hebrew is impossibly corrupt) includes a reference to a "host." So apart from this single, textually difficult example, the verb translated "to triumph" is nowhere clearly used in the later traditions that speak of a warrior God. On the other hand, Exodus 15:3 does clearly posit the Lord as a warrior and therefore shines a military aura back on the "triumph" verb, as does the "horse and rider" that denotes the Egyptian army. Let us now look back at earlier parts of Exodus to see where this militarization may have come from.

Exodus 1–14

In what respects is the story found in the first fourteen chapters of Exodus controlled by military language? What is the nature of this "warrior God" who "triumphs" at the sea?

It is very clear from Exodus 1–3 that Israel understood God's saving initiative to have stemmed from divine compassion for Israel's intolerable situation of enslavement in Egypt. God told Moses:

"I have observed the misery of my people who are in Egypt: I have heard their cry on account of their taskmasters. Indeed, I know their sufferings, and I have come down to deliver them from the Egyptians, and to bring them up out of that land to a good and broad land, a land flowing with milk and honey" (Exod. 3:7-8).

The final editor of Exodus reinforces this by appending to it verses 9-10, from a tradition that may originally have been separate:

"The cry of the Israelites has now come to me; I have also seen how the Egyptians oppress them. So come, I will send you to Pharaoh to lead my people, the Israelites, out of Egypt."

From an earlier chapter of Exodus, it is also evident that God is, in a sense, responsible for that situation. The key verses here are Exodus 1:7-10, which describe Israel's growth and the Egyptian response to it. With the addition of italics, verse 7 reads:

But the descendants of Israel were *fruitful* and *prolific*; they *multiplied* and grew exceedingly *strong*; so that the land *was filled* with them.

As many have noticed, this verse is a conglomeration of terms used at strategic points in Genesis; in the following quotations, the Hebrew roots that appear also in Exodus 1:7 are italicized:[16]

•In Genesis 1:28, humanity is told to "*be fruitful* and *multiply*, and *fill* the earth [land]." Exodus 1:7, therefore, depicts Israel carrying out the divine command, to its own immediate detriment.
    •Later, in Genesis 17:2, God tells Abram, "I . . . will

make you exceedingly *numerous*" (the same Hebrew root as the word translated *multiplied* in Exod. 1:7) and four verses later,

• "I will make you exceedingly *fruitful*" (17:6).

• In the following chapter, God's reasoning in deciding to let Abraham in on the divine plan to destroy Sodom and Gomorrah includes the consideration: "seeing that Abraham shall become a great and *mighty* [*strong*] nation" (Gen. 18:18).

All these passages include terminology that is taken up in the description of Israel's fatal flourishing in Exodus 1:7. The list could be widened to include the promises to Isaac (Gen. 26:4) and to Jacob in such passages as Genesis 28:3; 35:11; and 48:4. It could be further extended to show that the Hebrew term translated as *prolific* is used in texts such as Genesis 1:20-22, where it describes the God-given, sheer zoological vigor of the sea creatures and the birds. In Genesis 8:17, after the flood, when Noah is told to bring all the creatures out of the ark, three of the five terms are used to convey what God intends for them: "that they may *abound* on the earth, and *be fruitful* and *multiply* on the earth." That is to say, the words chosen to describe Israel's population explosion in Exodus 1:7 show that its author implicates God in the clearest possible way. The message is that God is beginning to make good the promise to Abraham that his descendants would be as innumerable as the stars (e.g., Gen. 15:5; 22:17).[17]

The effect of this population increase is to strike fear into the Egyptians or, at least, into the "new king . . . who did not know Joseph" (Exod. 1:8). Whether the author regarded fear as a reasonable response is not obvious from the text. From Israel's point of view, one would assume not. Yet the overloaded description of the Israelite population growth in verse 7 would surely be expected to worry a

king who, if he "did not know Joseph," presumably had
no way of knowing that the Lord was behind the dramatic
increase of the Israelites and therefore how to interpret the
phenomenon. Indeed there could well have been cause for
worry if Israel's prosperity were thought to come about at
the expense of other nations such as Egypt. For the reader
knows (from such texts as Gen. 17:2, 6; 26:4; 28:3) that
the multiplying described in Exodus 1 is not merely biological or even human fecundity, such as would be expected
in the first days of creation, but part of the growth of
Abraham's descendants, according to the promise.

In some respects Pharaoh's response here resembles
that of Cain (see chap. 2, above, and Gen. 4). Each per-
ceives a threat to himself in the success of another whose
life is somehow bound up with his own, and each responds
by deciding to eliminate the cause of the threat. Cain's
fratricide leads to banishment and his exclusion from the
genealogical line leading to Abraham. The fate of the
Egyptian king is equally unenviable and takes much longer
to play out. He gets himself, his successor, and his people
increasingly involved in a situation that is hopeless from
the beginning because, in his ignorance (Exod. 1:8), he
decides to go against the dynamic that God established
both at creation and in the choice of Israel.[18] Even the
Hebrew midwives (who "feared God," 1:17) know better
than that.

It is at this point that the Egyptian king begins to think
in military terms and thus establishes a trajectory that will
lead to the Lord's being termed a warrior in Exodus 15:3.
Far from seeing Israel's increased population as a human
resource from which he and his people might benefit,
Pharaoh fears lest Israel "will increase and, in the event of
war, join our enemies and fight against us and escape from
the land" (1:10). He sees Israel as a potential military
threat in the future. It is, of course, far too late to prevent

the population growth, which is already well underway in verse 7 and gathers momentum even as Pharaoh introduces his measures (vv. 12, 20). Quite apart from that, however, is the irony that accompanies this royal concern for long-term military security: the Egyptian king announces his intention of dealing "shrewdly" (or "wisely") with Israel (v. 10), but this will not prevent the one crucial child from slipping through the net. So, in the time of his successor and under the leadership of Moses, Israel will ultimately "escape from the land" (v. 10), the very thing the Pharaoh wished to avoid.

The Egyptians' response arises from their dread of the Israelites (1:12). The immediate form it takes is enslavement of the Israelites: the Hebrew root expressing slavery (*'bd*) occurs five times in 1:13-14 alone. However, that is only the beginning: in the course of trying to counter the perceived threat posed by Israel, Egypt itself will eventually be forced into military activity. In the process, it will lose its firstborn sons (12:29-30) and its army (chap. 14), two categories that are related both to each other (because ancient armies were made up of males) and to the cause of Egypt's dread, the vast numbers of sons born to the Israelites.

What lies behind the Egyptian king's radical misreading of the situation? It is presented as ignorance of how things really are, for even at his first appearance the king is described in terms of *what he does not know*. His successor boasts arrogantly that he does not know the Lord (5:2) and, furthermore, is unable to recognize the Lord's work, even when it is pointed out to him by his own servants (10:7). This characterization of Pharaoh contrasts him unfavorably with the Lord, who *does* know (e.g., 2:25; 3:7, 19; 4:14). It also puts him at odds with the Lord's intention, that Israel (6:7; 10:2) and even the Egyptians (7:5, 17; 8:10, 22;[19] 9:14, 29; 14:4, 18) shall come to know the Lord, although ultimately with very different consequences.

The Pharaoh's ignorance is the basis of all that ensues, from his first pathetic attempts at wisdom or shrewd dealing (Exod. 1:10) to the destruction of the Egyptian army in the sea. The train of events is characterized by an increasing use of force that the Lord knows about from the beginning and must plan to counter. Thus God tells Moses when enlisting him for the project, "I know . . . that the king of Egypt will not let you go unless compelled by a mighty hand" (3:19). Although the next verse terms the Lord's proposed action a striking or "smiting," that with which the Lord plans to strike Egypt is not weapons or even plague but "all my wonders that I will perform in it" (3:20), which probably include events of the exodus, because the Lord is hymned for doing "wonders" (the same root) in 15:11. There is an appropriateness about all this. For, as the narrative describing Moses' call makes very clear (3:1–4:20), the basis of the divine action is the Lord's compassionate response to "the misery of my people who are in Egypt . . . I have heard their cry . . . I know their sufferings" (3:7; see vv. 7-10).[20]

Therefore what Exodus 3:20 shows is that God's initial intention toward Egypt was not violence but rather to use wonders in an attempt at conveying to the Pharaoh who God is: to dispel the king's ignorance by peaceful means. In the course of it, the Egyptian king might have learned that he was wrong in his initial assumption that Israel's flourishing spelled trouble for Egypt (1:9-10). The nonnegotiable element here is that Egypt must come to recognize the Lord,[21] who is working to bring this about through the agency of Moses.[22] There is nothing even remotely warlike about God at this point. Yet a precedent has, perhaps, been set by Exodus 3:20. For when God predicts the need for a divine smiting of Egypt "by doing all kinds of wondrous deeds there," as the New American Bible puts it, the verb to "smite" or strike has been used with God as subject and Egypt as object, albeit in a metaphorical construction.

Later the same verb will be used to designate God's "smiting the land of Egypt," which translates into the slaying of Egypt's firstborn (12:12, 29). Yet this is still not presented as an act of warfare but as the execution of a judicial sentence pronounced on Egypt for its intransigence (or, more precisely, that of its king). Present-day readers may see this as a distinction without a difference: in the concrete circumstances of most modern societies, it is becoming increasingly difficult (if not impossible) to formulate a convincing justification for capital punishment. This is not the presumption of the biblical author, whose objective is to present not a vengeful God but a Pharaoh who initiated the violence by his actions against Israel and therefore incurred penalties from Israel's covenant partner. So Moses is told to say to Pharaoh:

> Thus says the LORD, Israel is my firstborn son. I said to you, "Let my son go that he may worship me." But you refused to let him go; now I will kill your firstborn son (Exod. 4:22-23). [23]

Pharaoh does not learn about this ultimatum until the first nine plagues have run their course, and the story suggests that he has been given ample opportunity to avoid losing his firstborn. Since, in the end, he refuses to comply, the Lord carries out the sentence. Nevertheless, it is a most difficult text: the Lord responds to Pharaoh's stubbornness by means of a killing, as 12:23, 27, and 13:15 reinforce. Its purpose within the narrative may be to raise the tension by showing the height of the stakes.

Exodus 4:22-23 may also have served to reassure Israelites about the Lord's seriousness in their regard, a message of which the negative side is given in the strange tale told in 4:24-26. As Moses is returning to Egypt with his wife and son, God seeks to kill him and is somehow made to desist when Moses' wife, Zipporah, circumcises "her son" (v. 25)[24] and touches her husband's penis with the foreskin. In light of Exodus 4:22-23, quoted above, the point of 4:24-26 may have to do with the Lord's special relationship with the firstborn of the Israelites, who have just been claimed as God's own (v. 22).[25] The text is obscure, however, mainly because not enough is known about the context in which it is to be understood. If it effectively warns Israel not to trifle with this God, it does so at the high cost of presenting the Lord as capricious and violent, at least to many who come to the text in later centuries.

It is evident, then, that the language of striking/smiting Egypt with wonders (3:20), when combined with the divine ultimatum to Pharaoh (4:22-23), conveys a potential for violent action on the part of the Lord against those who "do not know" how things are (i.e., that Israel's increase and relationship with God are part of a divinely instituted and maintained order). God is seen as willing to use divine power to bring down the opposition. The threat of violence made in 4:22-23 will lead to the death of the firstborn: by any standards, God is depicted as acting very violently in 11:4-6 (the preview of the killings) and 12:29. Yet even this does not in itself contribute to the idea of God as a warrior. So let us now consider the use made of specifically military vocabulary in Exodus 1–14, to see where that idea arose.

Military Vocabulary in Exodus 1–14

As we saw, such language was first used by the Egyptian king in 1:10, when he was worrying that if there were to be a war in the future, the huge population of Israel would join the other side and (an odd sequence) "escape from the land." The military aspect of this is not taken up in what ensues, however. No such war is ever again referred to as the story goes on to tell of how the Israelites *did* come to leave Egypt. The idea of God as warrior does not begin here.

More promising is a group of passages that include the use of ṣᵉbā'ôt ("hosts" or "company," the plural of ṣābā') to designate the group of Israelites (and others; 12:38) that left Egypt at the exodus. The word is found only in what is often recognized as the latest layer (Priestly) of the pentateuchal traditions.[26] The point at issue here is the extent to which ṣᵉbā'ôt has a military sense in Exodus 1–14.

There are five verses in which ṣᵉbā'ôt occurs in these chapters. The first, 6:26, follows the listing of "the heads of their ancestral houses" in 6:14-25. This is obviously related to the similar material in Numbers 1 and 26 concerning censuses that were arranged to organize Israel and, perhaps, to find out how big an army it could field if it had to (Num. 1:3 and *passim*; 26:2; see next chapter). But there is nothing in the context of Exodus 1–15 that suggests a military organization of Israel at the time of their leaving Egypt: armed revolt would have been out of the question.

The second use of *companies* in Exodus comes in 7:4. Here God refers to the Israelites as (literally) "my hosts, my people the sons of Israel." The New Revised Standard Version here has God saying, "I will . . . bring [out] my people the Israelites, company by company." Thus the further specification of the "companies" discourages the idea of a militarized Israel as the primary image that even the later tradition uses of them at this stage of the story. If Israel is God's "army," the expression is metaphorical: for an unarmed group moving *away from* its oppressors, the connotation is of a large and organized group of people on the move. Besides, the Lord's action in bringing out the "companies" is referred to in 7:4 (and in 6:7) as "great acts of judgment," a term that sounds more legal than military and connects thematically with God's legal-sounding threat about Egypt's firstborn in 4:22-23, quoted earlier.[27]

The other three examples of the use of *companies* (or *hosts*) are in Exodus 12. The first of them, in verse 17, is clearly part of a developed liturgical tradition that specifies the means by which the Israelites are to keep alive the memory of what God did for them. The other two, in 12:41 and 51, respectively, provide the information that Israel left Egypt after having lived there for 430 years and was brought out by the Lord. Thus, although the word *ṣᵉbā'ôt* is used a number of times, no attempt is made to draw attention to any military connotations that it might have.

The one verse in the account of leaving Egypt that apparently presents Israel as a military assemblage is 13:18. The verse is significantly placed. It follows 13:17, which notes that God did not lead the people by the obvious route:

> For God thought, "If the people face war, they may change their minds and return to Egypt."

The author then informs the reader that "the people [literally: sons] of Israel went up out of the land of Egypt organized-for-war" (13:18, my provisional translation). The Hebrew of the last element of this ("organized-for-war") means literally, "in companies of fifty" (*ḥᵃmûšîm*, related to the Hebrew root for "five," *ḥmš*) and thus "prepared for battle" (as in the NRSV, although there is no word for "battle" in the Hebrew text). So were they armed, as this translation suggests? Except in a very general sense, that is doubtful both in light of the previous verse, where God is trying to prevent the Israelites from experiencing war, and in view of the Israelites' status as slaves: their access to arms would surely have been very limited.

What they obtained from the Egyptians (by open request) was jewelry of silver and gold and clothing (11:2; 12:35-36): nothing that could serve as arms, and there is no mention of weapons. In the few other passages where *ḥᵃmûšîm* is used,[28] words such as *girded, warriors, battle* are associated with the term and thus make explicit there the military nature of the operation. If there is any such context in the case of Exodus 13:18, it is heavily ironical, for in the previous verse God spoke of Israel's unpreparedness for battle and the following one tells about transporting Joseph's bones!

What is described in Exodus 13:18 is a large group of people on the move, their formation being that which a marching army would assume. Nothing in the text suggests that they are to be regarded as armed, however, and there is good reason for thinking they are not.[29] Besides, weapons play no part in the story of their departure from Egypt (see, e.g., 14:13-15, 24-25) and are therefore irrelevant to its continuation. Finally, the formation designated *ḥᵃmûšîm* in 13:18 is never again mentioned in Exodus.

On the other hand, Exodus 13:18 does push in a military direction the interpretation of some aspects of what follows. For example, without 13:18, the Lord's instructions for Israel's encampment (14:1-2) would be taken as referring to a nomadic bivouac (as in, e.g., Gen. 32:8-9 and 2 Kings 5:15). In the present form of the text, that is not quite so evident, for the reader may have the impression from 13:18 that it is against an *armed* Israel that Pharaoh is proceeding (14:3-4). Yet nothing supports the impression of Israel's camp as military in nature.

This feature sharply distinguishes the Israelite encampment from the Egyptian one referred to in 14:9. For in the preceding verses the author has repeatedly mentioned the military might of the Egyptian party. The latter consists of "Pharaoh and all his army" (*ḥayil*, v. 4). As verses 6-7 further specify, this consists of Pharaoh with his chariot, his "people" ('*ammô*, translated as *soldiers* in the NAB and *army* in the NRSV)[30] and "six hundred picked chariots and all the other chariots of Egypt with officers over all of them." In verse 9 they are summed up as "all Pharaoh's horses and chariots, his chariot drivers, and his army" (*ḥayil*, again). The reader is in no danger of forgetting that Pharaoh has mounted a major military expedition against Israel. The meaning of *ḥayil* (used to designate Pharaoh's army in 14:4, 9) is connected to the idea of strength or power. The noun is used again in 14:17, 28, and 15:4, to denote the Egyptian army in connection with its destruction, but it never refers to Israel during the course of their leaving Egypt.

There is, therefore, a qualitative difference of the highest order between the descriptions of a powerful Egyptian army and of an Israel that, although described in 13:18 as "prepared for battle" (or better, "in companies of fifty"), shows no signs of using or even possessing any weapons and that has, in the previous verse, been effectively declared unfit for war by its own God.[31]

It is in light of all this that one must interpret 14:14 and the related 14:25. In Exodus 14:14 Moses is reassuring the fearful Israelites. He backs up his call, "Do not be afraid" (v. 13), by telling them, "The LORD will fight for you, and you have only to keep still" (v. 14). In what happens next, the Egyptians' experience apparently bears out this version of events: they testify, "The LORD is fighting for [the Israelites] against Egypt" (v. 25). Yet the image that Moses employs here in verse 14 ("the LORD will fight for you") is determined by the nature of the force that has come out against Israel. The meaning of verse 25 in its context is: "You, an unarmed group of people on the move by order of your God, are being threatened by the top military technology of the day. God will provide a means for emerging unscathed from that threat." As the story is told, the threat from those preparing to use chariots and horsemen evinces a response from a God who is likewise presented as military, but only metaphorically so. For the destruction of the technology and of those who wield it is caused not by superior weapons of a similar type but by its own limitations —or rather, its misuse. Verses 24 and 25, read:

> At the morning watch the LORD in the pillar of fire and cloud looked down upon the Egyptian army,[32] and threw the Egyptian army into a panic. He clogged their chariot wheels so that they turned with difficulty. The Egyptians said, "Let us flee from the Israelites, for the LORD is fighting for them against Egypt."

Exactly what happened to the Egyptians is, of course, quite inaccessible to historical investigation. The tradition is clear, though, that Israel emerged victorious from the confrontation (in the sense that the Egyptians were prevented from following them through the sea) and that Israel's success occurred without any recourse to arms or, indeed, without any action of theirs that might have brought them credit in the ordinary way.

The event that took place at the Red Sea is not, therefore, a battle in any conventional sense. The "hosts" or "companies" of Israel referred to earlier in Exodus (6:26; 7:4; 12:17, 41, 51) are not even mentioned in chapter 14. The Israelites are a group of slaves trying to make their escape. Although they were once described as leaving the land in "fifties" under God's leadership (13:18), the word *army* (*hayil*) is never used to designate them. Their leader, Moses, insists that they are simply to allow the Lord to save them, which translates into the "actions" of not being afraid and of standing firm (14:13). In this context, it is obvious that to say that the Lord will "fight for" Israel is to speak metaphorically; and yet, given the condition of the Egyptians at this point, it is the one appropriate metaphor. For people are saved from armies only by those who can overcome the opposing military force—which usually, although not necessarily, means other warriors.

There are two stages to Egypt's downfall. First, they panic, and mud clogs their chariot wheels (14:24-25). Had they not been pursuing Israel with their chariots, this would not have happened to them. Then, in verses 26-28, God undoes the extraordinary configuration of the sea that had allowed Israel to reach the other shore and from which the Egyptians had rashly hoped to benefit. Thus the creator God overcomes the overconfident army of Egypt by using the resources of creation, not military procedures of any type.[33]

Israel itself is totally nonmilitary at this point. Moses, following instructions from the Lord, leads "the Israelites" to safety across the sea (14:22). They take no part in the subsequent action, during which the Egyptians die by drowning in water into which they should never have taken their chariots and horses in the first place. In other words, with the exception of 13:18 (of which the strangeness was noted above), the only unequivocally military elements in these chapters are associated with the Pharaoh. So inasmuch as the Lord is committed to enabling Israel to escape, an intervention *interpreted* in martial imagery is all but inevitable, despite the Bible's omission of any description of the Lord as an actual soldier. The Israelites, knowing that their escape from the Egyptian chariots owes nothing at all to their own prowess, must praise the Lord, who is alone responsible for the removal of the threat. How else could they have acknowledged their situation than to posit the Lord as a warrior who was able to annihilate the whole Egyptian army?

In literary terms, then, it is the Pharaoh's propensity for thinking in military categories that starts off the whole process: in 1:10 he immediately interprets Israel's population growth as a military threat in the making. The story then tells how this move of the Pharaoh's culminates in the pursuit of Israel by the full Egyptian army, and it is this, the Egyptian army's involvement, that impels Israel to think of the Lord as a warrior who fought on their behalf.

Yet the Lord is no ordinary warrior. During this encounter, it seems that the Egyptians finally come to experience something of who the Lord is: the account in 14:24 specifies that the divine gaze came down on the Egyptian host and threw them into a panic.[34] What this means, then, is that at the last moment the Egyptians encounter the Lord as a mysterious force that annihilates their military might as exercised against this band of escaping slaves. Conversely, to judge from the Israelites' response in chapter 15, the aspect of the situation that most impresses *them* is their escape from Pharaoh's chariots and horsemen. So, not unnaturally, they praise the Lord as having won a military victory on their behalf. Although quite understandable, this will prove to be a dangerous perception, as we shall see. A God who uses the "weapons" of the created world, however sparingly, can all too easily legitimate the belligerent instincts of those who feel the need to wage human warfare.

This can be seen happening only two chapters later. In 17:8-16, Amalek's attack on Israel occasions development in the direction of the Lord as a warrior who will doom Israel's enemies. This turns out to be both problematic and programmatic. It is problematic because the merciless slaughter that ensued was taken as a precedent within the biblical canon and also in later centuries.[35] The Amalekite attack is programmatic because the Amalekites will come to function as an enemy that forms part of Israel's self-definition, in something like the same way that the Soviet Union did for the west during the decades of the Cold War or that Unionists and Republicans have done for centuries (with some remarkable exceptions) in Northern Ireland. Thus Amalekites repeatedly surface as Israel's enemy at least until the time of David, and even into post-exilic times. For Haman, the villain in the book of Esther, is an Agagite (Esther 3:1), presumably descended from Agag, the Amalekite king whose death is described in 1 Samuel 15. Such "traditional" animosities are highly destructive, because they are transmitted with the respective cultures and prevent reconciliation even among later generations that were not directly involved.

In Exodus, the battle with Amalek follows a series of incidents in which the Lord works with Moses and Aaron (16:1-36) or Moses alone (17:1-7) in responding to Israelite complaints about a lack of food and water.[36] In the second incident, Moses uses "the staff with which [he] struck the Nile" to provide what is needed (17:5). He uses the same staff (now "the staff of God," v. 9) in responding to the threat posed by Amalek. As long as Moses elevates it, Joshua and the band he has chosen defeat Amalek and his people with the sword (v. 13). Implied here is an equivalence of providing water for Israel's continued survival and prolonging that survival by the extermination of their enemies. That the second case involves human deaths appears not to have troubled the author, but it should give modern readers pause.

Within the wider narrative, the story of Israel's response to the attack by the Amalekites has a threefold intention (17:8-16). Building on the story at the sea, it adds to Moses' stature as one who can continue to ensure the Lord's favor for Israel, without which they will perish (vv. 11-12). Second, it introduces Joshua and establishes him as the military deliverer who acts in obedience to Moses and has particular responsibility for Israel's future (v. 14). Third, its concluding verse conveys that the victory, although decisive, is anything but final: "The LORD will have war with Amalek from generation to generation" (v. 16). This expression of the Lord's commitment to Israel in the face of enemies, the only one of its kind in Exodus 16–40, demonstrates very clearly the ethical problem of a God who has come to be thought of in military terms and who favors one group at the expense of others. For it is one thing to be delivered from slavery by one's covenant Lord, but quite another to build on that experience by demonizing whole groups and take it for granted that one's own enemies are God's and will be severely punished.

Conclusion

The story of the exodus and its aftermath, Israel's engagement with the Amalekites, describes two sets of circumstances in which the Lord is responsible for the death of significant numbers of Israel's enemies. In the first of them is outlined a repetition of the pattern that led to Cain's fratricide. That is to say, in recounting how Israel comes to leave Egypt, the author faces the difficulties associated with affirming Israel's basic experience of the Lord as the giver of immense bounties in a world where those among whom they live perceive Israel's success as a threat to their own security. The drowning of the Egyptian army represents the culmination of a process in which Pharaoh has become increasingly ensnared in the consequences of his own foolish misperceptions about the relationship between the Israelites and his own people. Quite gratuitously, but in a not-uncommon reaction to others' success, he sees their growth in population as a threat to Egypt's well-being. So, beginning with Pharaoh's misjudgment about how to "deal shrewdly" with an expanding Israel (1:9-10), the reader follows the buildup of Egyptian militarization and is led to see the events at the sea as the working out of Pharaoh's foolish and malicious stubborn-ness.[37] Certainly, the biblical writer wishes to affirm that these events are under divine control: the Lord directs the events that lead to the drowning of the Egyptians, including the hardening of Pharaoh's heart (e.g., Exod. 7:3). Yet at the same time, the fate of Pharaoh's army is so obviously his own responsibility that careful readers are aware that celebrating the Lord as a warrior involves using language in a highly metaphorical manner.[38] In other words, even as the overcoming of the Egyptians is described in Exodus, the Lord is not a warrior in the same sense that Pharaoh is: the language used is analogous.[39]

The Lord's overthrow of the Egyptians sets a danger-ous precedent, however. For when, shortly afterward, Joshua leads the retaliation against the Amalekite attack on Israel, the Lord is understood as responsible for the long-term belligerence that is to ensue: "The LORD will have war with Amalek from generation to generation" (17:16). That God's (originally compassionate) concern for Israel's well-being is expressed through warlike behavior is no longer argued for, as it was in the exodus event, but is simply assumed.

The misleading simplicity of this move, coupled with the lively hold that violence has on people's imagination, makes it an uphill task to remember the divine compassion (and less immediately, the "good" creation and the general blessings of fertility) that underlies the exodus experience. Indeed the biblical tradition understands that the Egyptians, like all other human beings, were created in God's image and likeness (Gen. 1:26). Moreover, Deuteronomy 23:7, with a focus on Israel's sojourn in Egypt rather than on the circumstances of their leaving, specifically forbids Israel to "abhor any of the Egyptians." But that is a difficult attitude to sustain, especially in the midst of the fear caused by the threatening presence of the current enemy. The story about the Amalekites and especially the claim that God wars against them (Exod. 17:16), should stand, not as a license to do evil in God's name but as a warning about some of the consequences of demonizing those who oppose us, and in particular, a tendency to use God's name to justify long-term belligerence that damages those who had no part in the original quarrel. It is all too easy to resolve the tensions of history and of the biblical witness by neglecting to take into account the wider context of that history. This is an immensely large project belonging to a compassionate creator God who has long-term, even end-time, plans for a humanity that is still in the making. Within that scenario, systematic killing of Amalekites (or of anyone else) does not belong, however appealing it may appear to be as a way of dealing with those who make us afraid.

6

ORGANIZING AN ITINERANT ISRAEL:

THE BOOK OF NUMBERS

Although the book of Numbers is infrequently read and offers few resources for moving away from violent behavior, it will be considered here because it continues the narrative of Exodus and, more significantly, is one of the books that people tend to assume give biblical warrant for engaging in war. The purpose of this chapter is to demonstrate that this latter assumption is not warranted.

Most English translations suggest that, from the outset, Numbers characterizes Israel as a society set up for military engagement, and later chapters do indeed describe battles involving Israelites. As we shall see, however, the reality revealed by a closer reading is less straightforward. Israel as presented in Numbers is not essentially aggressive. The opening chapters of the book are concerned with organization, not mobilization. The groups so formed are never said to take part in any engagements and Israel fights successfully only when enemies seem to leave no alternative or when it believes there is a threat to its ritual purity.[1] That the book of Numbers is not primarily about war may come as a surprise to many. Therefore this chapter draws attention to the general importance of reading in such a way that any violence described in a text is not given more weight or significance than it warrants. As noted in chapter 1, images of violence do draw attention to themselves; in reading Numbers and many other parts of the Bible, we need to make adjustments for that.

Introduction

As the Old Testament tells the story, the Lord promised the descendants of Jacob a land "flowing with milk and honey," but they had to win it for themselves because it was to a large extent already settled in by Canaanites.[2] As they left Egypt, the Israelites were no more than a crowd of liberated slaves under the charismatic leadership of Moses, so military conquest was not the most obvious way for them to gain possession of the Promised Land. Admittedly, at a crucial moment in their history they had experienced their God, the Lord, as fighting for them against the vastly superior army of Egypt. That engagement had left Egyptians dead on the shore of the Red Sea and Israel with nowhere to go except forward in the direction of the Promised Land. When Amalek waged war against the itinerant Israelites, the Lord enabled Joshua to defeat them by military means (Exod. 17:8-16). Yet the remainder of the book of Exodus does not develop the potential for Israel's militarization that is contained in these events. The theme of conquest is first introduced in the partially parallel set of desert traditions to be found in the book of Numbers,[3] and the beginning of that process is very much slower than is often assumed.

The book of Numbers opens by noting that "in the second year after they had come out of the land of Egypt" the Lord instructed Moses to organize a census (1:1-2). With the exception of the tribe of Levi, those to be enrolled are all the males of twenty years and older "fit [or perhaps, "eligible"] for military service," as the New

American Bible translates it. "Able to go to war" is the New Revised Standard Version equivalent, which is rhetorically more problematic (1:3, 45). This designation of the ones enrolled occurs fourteen times in chapter 1. Its use and repetition probably suggests to modern readers that the militarization of Israel was already well underway, a view that is reinforced by some English translations of chapter 2. There, the New American Bible, for example, uses the word *soldiers* twelve times as it describes the organization of the tribes' encampments.

Such an impression is, however, highly misleading. Despite what one hears when listening to the English translations, the usual Hebrew word for "war" or "battle" is not found in the first chapter of Numbers, and those counted in the census are nowhere called "soldiers."

The Hebrew phrase in chapter 1 translated as "fit for military service" (or the like) is *yōṣê' ṣābā'*.[4] The first word here is a participle that means "going out" or "having the ability to go out [to]." The second, *ṣābā'*, means "hosts," "assemblage," or "company," but the exact connotation must be determined from the context each time, depending on whether it denotes warriors, angels, stars or some other collection of beings. The general *presumption* is in favor of a military sense, because that is true of corresponding words in other Semitic languages and is often so in Hebrew.[5] Furthermore, those designated are able-bodied males, the ones who would be called on to defend against an attack. Yet in Hebrew, *ṣābā'* came to have additional, nonmilitary meanings. Thus, when it was used in five verses in Exodus to refer to Israel as it left Egypt,[6] nothing in the context suggested that the "companies" by which the Lord would bring out the Israelites denoted a military group (Exod. 7:4). Rather it seemed that the term there conveyed the orderly nature of the large collection of people that was about to leave Egypt.

In the phrase used so frequently in Numbers 1, ṣābā' clearly designates a *potential* army. The word is also used a dozen times in chapter 2 to denote the units in which the men were enrolled. There the New Revised Standard Version has "company" instead of the New American Bible's "soldiers."[7] The emphasis, however, must surely be on the word *potential*. We have here, as George E. Mendenhall noted, lists that would "serve as a register of those men subject to military duty (or corvée)."[8] As Israel's military potential is not actualized until much later in the book and, even then, does not involve the units set up in these first chapters, the repetition of the terms of the census serves a purpose other than that of suggesting that Israel left Sinai as an army looking for wars to engage in.

The Priestly Concern for Order[9]

Most of the book of Numbers comes from the Priestly tradition.[10] Here as elsewhere in the Pentateuch, the Priestly authors' determination to present Israel as an orderly society is much in evidence. Numbers lists the twelve tribes eight times in all,[11] indicates their size, names their leaders and clans, and details how they were physically distributed in their encampment around the meeting tent (chaps. 1 and 2). It names the two sons of Aaron who are priests with him, specifies their responsibilities and those of the Levites (chaps. 3 and 4), and gives various rules and the sanctions for breaking them (e.g., chap. 5). Details of what each tribal leader contributed to the meeting tent are included (chap. 7), as are the names and tribal affiliations of the twelve scouts sent to reconnoiter the Promised Land (13:3-16). The book provides instructions for Israel's various feasts and rituals (chaps. 6; 8; 9; 10:1-10; 15; 19) and information about how the people gradually made their way to the boundary of the land. The second census, described in chapter 26, also registers all those "from twenty years old and upward . . . everyone in Israel able to go to war" (26:2). Here the expressed purpose is to ensure that tribes of different sizes eventually get a fair allocation of the land (vv. 52-56). This time, the Levites were registered separately, because "there was no allotment given to them among the Israelites" (26:62). The remainder of the book deals variously with such issues as the allocation of the land, details of cultic procedure, and Israel's progress toward the land.

Thus the overall plan of Numbers suggests strongly that in it the interest in order is paramount.[12] Its post-exilic readers, rebuilding their own society after approximately fifty years of exile in Babylon (c. 586-539) would be left in no doubt at all about exactly which ancestral families were included in Israel as it left Sinai some seven hundred or so years previously, and how the earlier society was thought to have been structured. That the restored community had concerns of this type is clear from such post-exilic texts as Ezra 8–10 and Nehemiah 7–13.

If that is the case, the "hosts" to which the able-bodied men could go (chaps. 1–2) are part of that organization: they are not (or not yet) an army as such. Certainly, they would have been available for providing Israel with defense when it was needed. No arms are mentioned in these first two chapters, however, and all that the various groups do is encamp around the tent of meeting and move away from Sinai in an orderly fashion. (Also noteworthy, of course, is the impressive and quite incredible numbers of men reported as "registered."[13]) The resulting arrangement of the non-Levitical tribes is certainly a potential army, and the Levites are described as organized in companies and performing guard duty for the tent of meeting. Yet only Exodus 17 contains any evidence at all for regarding Israel as a group able to field actual military units: there Moses told Joshua to "choose some men" to take with him to fight Amalek (v. 9). There is no suggestion that Israel as a whole was involved, and the census described in Numbers 1 takes place "in the second year after" that departure (v. 1). Furthermore, not until the beginning of chapter 31, with a completely different population and after a second census (see 26:2, 64), is there any mention of arming tribal members (31:3-5). Moreover, the "ranks" created earlier are not mentioned in these verses.[14] Again, not until 31:14, after a retaliatory raid on the Midianites, are the Israelites referred to as an "army," *ḥayil*, the term used at key points to designate the Egyptians who pursued Israel in Exodus 14.

Therefore, even though the Priestly writers may not have been averse to having readers deduce that from the outset the male Israelites constituted a formidable army, their text does not say that. The point of these early chapters of Numbers seems to be rather that from the time Israel left Sinai it was, at the Lord's behest, highly organized. That meant that each tribe had its leaders with judicial and/or administrative functions (see, e.g., Exod. 18:13-37), and its own place in the encampment around the meeting tent. When it was time to move on, the whole of Israel could proceed in orderly fashion toward the Promised Land. This is no wandering rabble, but a disciplined group. The implication is surely that the post-exilic readers in Jerusalem should take note!

Israel's Military Involvement in the Book of Numbers

One function of Numbers 1:4-46 is that it gives the opportunity to list prominent members of the eleven non-Levitical tribes (1:4-19) and to claim for each tribe an impressive number of men who could fight if necessary (v. 46). The important words here are "if necessary." The first report of anything resembling a military operation does not come until 14:40. Even then, it is not formally presented as such: the "companies" and their leaders, listed at such length earlier, are not so much as mentioned here. Indeed there is no evident organization of this operation at all: it could not be described as a campaign. Nor is it an engagement of which Israel can feel proud. After the death by plague of all but two of the twelve scouts who had reconnoitered Canaan (chaps. 13–14), the people decide they will, after all, "go up" to the land promised to them by God (14:40, 42, 44). As Moses warns them, however, the sortie lacks God's sanction and presence (vv. 41-42). So, inevitably, they are badly defeated, beaten back as far as a place called Hormah, a name that means "the destruction" (v. 45).[15] That no connection is made between this initial foray into the land they have been promised and the tribal "companies" established earlier could result from deliberate irony. If this is the case, the author is presenting tribes that are so incompetent in the military sphere that, when the time for engagement finally comes, they simply forge ahead, forgetting all the arrangements that they made earlier. Not exactly models for emulation!

There follow several chapters that specify ritual requirements and tell of various acts of rebellion, after which Israel needs to pass through Edomite territory. In 20:14-17, Moses initiates diplomatic contact with the Edomite king, presenting Israel as a "brother" from whom Edom has nothing to fear.[16] Moses foregrounds the hardships from which the Lord has delivered Israel. He promises, "We will not pass through field or vineyard, or drink water from any well; we will go along the King's Highway, not turning to the right hand or to the left until we have passed through your territory" (v. 17). The Edomite king will not permit even this, and threatens Israel with the sword (20:18). The Israelites make further promises of good conduct: they will pay for any water they or their livestock drink (v. 19). But this and another appeal to reason evoke only renewed refusal and Edom's advance against them "with a large force, heavily armed" (v. 20). One may be intended to think that Edom's conduct is prompted by the sight of the "companies" of "soldiers" that were (allegedly) set up in Numbers 1 and 2 but, although Edom's reaction is surely prompted by fear, the text of Numbers 20 does not specify its terms. The story there finishes with the laconic note that "since Edom refused to let them pass through their territory, Israel detoured around them" (20:21, NAB). Presumably they can do this because Edom is not part of the land that they are to possess (Deut. 2:2-8); in any case, Israel is not keen to fight and here avoids doing so. The whole episode is reminiscent of incidents involving the patriarchs, who characteristically took pains to avoid confrontation. Indeed Israel's concern not to fight against the Edomites in Numbers 20 parallels Jacob's careful orchestration of his meeting with Esau, the brother he had wronged many years previously (Gen. 32:3–33:3) and who is often regarded as Edom's ancestor (Gen. 36:9-19). In the earlier story, Esau had been the one who showed magnanimity (33:4); here it is the descendants of Jacob.

Apart from the disastrous skirmish of chapter 14, the Edom episode in chapter 20 (more than halfway through the book) represents Israel's first encounter with an alien people in the book of Numbers. As the story is told, Moses first engages in serious diplomacy. There is not the slightest hint that he does so as the leader of an army on the march. Moses' diplomatic efforts fail because of Edom's intransigence. So Israel then accepts losing face and being inconvenienced, rather than force a fight. Not a typical army, whatever the language of chapters 1 and 2.

Also atypical is the fact that those who were originally "enlisted" went nearly forty years with only one military engagement to their credit, and that one a catastrophic defeat in which nothing was said about any "companies." For Israel's detour around Edom is followed by an account of Aaron's death (20:14-21, 22-29). Numbers 33:38-40 puts this event in the fortieth year after the Israelites left Egypt; it also links Aaron's death and an incident at Arad, given at length in 21:1-3 (see below). Again, if the contents of the first two chapters are understood in genuinely military terms, for nearly four decades they exert no effect on what follows, by which time any who had been registered would have been too old to fight if, indeed, they were still alive (26:64).[17]

In the next episode, Israel is finally drawn into battle. This occurs, however, through the belligerence of another person, in this case the Canaanite king of Arad. Having heard of their approach, he "fought against Israel and took some of them captive" (21:1-3). They avenge this defeat with a victory that they associate with a vow to the Lord, that they will, in effect, offer their enemies as a sacrifice to God: the "utter destruction" (*ḥerem*) of which the New Revised Standard Version speaks in verses 2-3 is not wanton but cultic, as Susan Niditch has convincingly established.[18] This kind of a God is, of course, highly problematic, even within the Bible itself, where sacrifice in one form or another is a recognized aspect of relating to God, whatever problems later generations may have with it.[19]

After defeating Arad, Israel avoids further trouble by going around Moabite territory (21:10-15) but then is attacked by Sihon, king of the Amorites, who has obstinately refused its request for safe passage (vv. 21-32). Again Israel is shown as trying to proceed peacefully but unable to do so, because others will not allow it. Sihon is therefore put to the sword, and Israel then goes on to take possession of his land and of a further Ammonite city (21:24, 32). Here there is more than simple self-defense, and no indication of a cultic justification for what was done. This is an example of one of the many ways in which violence escalates. Whereas initiating it needs a good reason, continuing in violent behavior often does not. The threshold for engaging in it has been lowered.

Og of Bashan is the next aggressor, although his response could be regarded as more of a defensive move, because Israel was at that point heading for Bashan (21:33-35) and Og might have thought, with some reason, that he was at risk. (He could have tried offering them safe passage, of course.) By this stage in Numbers, the military component has increased: 21:14-15 even quotes from the "Book of the Wars of the LORD," although what is given here is only a listing of certain boundaries in the Transjordan. That the book did not survive may indicate that this was not an aspect of the Lord that people wanted to emphasize.[20]

Israel's reputation as the Lord's people is responsible for Balak of Moab's attempts at persuading the seer Balaam to curse Israel, and its status as such underlies Balaam's refusal to do so (Num. 22–24). Yet no fighting is described in chapters 22–29. What *is* described there, in chapter 26, is a second census in which able-bodied male Israelites are registered. This is because, with the exception of Caleb, Joshua, and Moses himself, the earlier generation has completely died out (26:64). As in chapter 1, those registered are those "of twenty years old or more who are fit for military service" (*yōṣê' ṣābā'*, again; NAB translation of 26:2). This time, the census is explicitly linked with the fair distribution of land when the time comes (vv. 52-56). So the "ranks" are once more filled but, even more clearly than before, there is no indication that the military possibilities are to be actualized or, indeed, that they are the purpose of the exercise.

Overall, then, in Numbers 1–30 the description of Israel's aggression is minimal. Until 31:3, when the Lord commands that men be selected and armed "to go against Midian, to execute the LORD's vengeance on Midian" (see below), they have not initiated an attack on anyone. Their military engagements, all described in one chapter, consist of fighting back when diplomatic efforts have failed, although it must be admitted that they took full advantage of their victory over Sihon in 21:21-32. The Israelites must have used weapons prior to chapter 31, but Numbers gives only one reference to this: the sword, in 21:24.

Chapter 31 is different. In it, Moses conveys the Lord's command to take vengeance on the Midianites who invited Balaam to curse them (chaps. 22–24) and whose women allegedly lured Israel into the immorality and idolatry that "caused" the plague by which the last of the old generation were killed (25:1-18; 26:64-65). The result is full-scale war, carefully organized: a thousand men from each tribe are selected and armed for war (*ṣābā'*, vv. 3-5) and sent out by Moses on the campaign (also *ṣābā'*, v. 6). The use of that word and the twelve-fold organization of those who are to be armed (31:4-5) may encourage readers to link this campaign with the census in chapter 26 that specified the replacements for those counted in chapter 1, who are now all dead. Yet in what follows, the sacral aspects of the war are much more strongly emphasized than are the activities of the fighters themselves. The war is led not by Joshua but by Phineas, the zealous son of the priest, Eleazar (see 25:6-13). He brought with him "the vessels of the sanctuary and the trumpets for sounding the alarm" (31:6). No weapons are mentioned after 31:5. Furthermore, the two verses in which the war is described (vv. 7-8) are relatively inconspicuous among the mass of detail about the different kinds of booty. Most of the rest of the chapter consists of descriptions of its acquisition and selection (vv. 9-18), purification (vv. 19-24), distribution (vv. 25-47), and use (in part) as atonement for the soldiers (vv. 48-54). Also of interest is the note that none of the Israelite soldiers died in the fighting (v. 49) and that they all had to be purified by staying outside the camp for seven days (v. 19, with special provisions for any who touched a dead body) and atoned for (vv. 48-54).

Yet again, therefore, although conquest in battle is part of Israel's tradition, this chapter is not concerned with glorifying the fighting as such, for so little space is given to describing it. Susan Niditch provides ample evidence to support her contention that behind Numbers 31 is a fierce concern for the purity of Israel, a purity threatened by Balaam (whose stock has declined precipitously between Numbers 22 and 31:8) and the dangerously seductive Midianite women. So he and almost all Midianites are exterminated (25:7-8).[21]

Many modern readers will not understand or accept the need for ritual purity that these stories assume. They might, nevertheless, be able to endorse the idea that, Niditch suggests, underlies Numbers 31: that war itself is defiling, however piously and successfully it may be waged. Especially if people have had contact with war veterans or with those who have suffered injury at others' hands, they may also appreciate the wisdom of the text's insistence that the community be very careful about dealing appropriately with the effects of violence on its members and on the community as a whole.[22] Thus, in the attack on the Midianites, no army commanders are named: only the priest's son, Phineas, with whom are associated the sanctuary vessels (31:6). The danger to ritual purity that is posed by war also accounts for the emphasis on the various purifications, particularly of anyone who has killed or has touched a slain corpse (v. 19; see also Num. 19:11-21). Niditch proposes that concern for purity of lineage underlies Moses' shocking insistence that, of the captured Midianite women and children, only virgin females need not be killed. She suggests the other women and boys are sources of impurity because their identity is already fixed as alien (by their maleness or their sexual congress with Midianite males), whereas the virgin women's identity is not, and their association with their Israelite husbands will enable them to become members of the Israelite community.

What Niditch's study of Numbers 31 does make clear is that the Israelites do not engage in violence for its own sake and are aware of the harm that violent action can do to those who undertake it. Present-day readers will probably want to insist that this needs to be supplemented: first, with a corresponding concern about the effects it has on those who are on the receiving end and, second, with a willingness to examine seriously the values for which one would do violence to others. There are probably other ways of maintaining group identity than those put forward by this text.

After chapter 31, the only remaining military activity described in Numbers is a listing of conquests in the land east of the Jordan by members of the tribe of Manasseh (32:39-42). That these are given "in stereotyped phrases"[23] suggests that Israel's engaging in war is becoming routine: fighting is no longer the problem that it was in chapter 31. Now it is taken as "normal" and acceptable, which is a different and much more serious problem, because it has become an unexamined part of society itself. Moses' question to the Gadites and Reubenites ("Shall your brothers go to war while you sit here?" 32:6; see also vv. 29-32) and his instructions to drive out the land's inhabitants (33:50-51) show that more battles are in the offing as Israel prepares to move across the Jordan and into the Promised Land itself.

Conclusion

We have seen that the book of Numbers opens with descriptions of the tribal affiliation, numerical totals, and encampment arrangement of those who could be called on to fight if necessary, and that there is much repetition of language that could bear a military interpretation, and usually does in modern translations. Nevertheless, Israel as it leaves Sinai is not presented as a military society as such.

The book describes no fighting at all until 14:40-45, when the Israelites make an unauthorized and ruinous excursion into the foothills of the Promised Land. Not until almost forty years have passed do they do more than take evasive action (20:14-21; 21:10-20). Even then, the companies ($ṣ^eḇā'ôt$) previously established play no part in the proceedings: they were obviously not maintained as fighting units, even if they ever were such, which is most doubtful. Furthermore, Israel's first engagement (21:1-3) is presented as being in response to Arad's unprovoked aggression, the second (31:21-32) resulted from Sihon's refusal to give Israel safe passage, and the third (31:33-35) comes from Og's presumably fearful resistance to them as they head for his territory. The remaining chapters of Numbers tell of a war against Midian (but with an emphasis on the community's purity), a handful of conquests, and the additional prospect of more such activity to come in the future.

This survey of Numbers has suggested that the Israel presented there is not characteristically aggressive. It is organized on what appears to be military lines, a feature that is somewhat heightened in some English translations and yet belies the people's practice as they move from Sinai toward the land that God promised them. The presumption is that they will come to possess the land by fighting for it, but there is no suggestion that they are eager to fight: they do so only when their way is (unreasonably?)[24] impeded or in response to a perceived threat to their highly developed sense of their own need for purity. These may be regrettable attitudes but they do not of themselves constitute belligerence.

Therefore there is good reason for not letting the military elements in the book of Numbers loom so large that they distract from the other, more fundamental aspects of Israel's self-understanding depicted there. These include its sense of being a strong and numerous people whose existence and continuance depend on the particular care that they receive from their God, a God who requires their trust (chap. 14). Their organization as twelve tribes (plus the Levites), with their named clans and leaders, provides them with what is necessary for sustaining themselves as a group and for relating to the Lord and to those around them as they journey toward the Promised Land.

7

RECEIVING THE LAND AS GIFT:
THE BOOK OF JOSHUA

Much of what was said about Numbers applies also to the book of Joshua. The latter is frequently written off as portraying a God who, finally fulfilling the promise of giving the Promised Land to Abraham's descendants, exterminates human beings in the process and encourages the Israelites to do likewise on their own behalf. There is some cause for taking up such a position. The book's first eleven chapters include descriptions of Joshua, at God's command and sometimes with divine participation, leading Israel to conquer cities that belong to others, first Jericho, then Ai, and finally two other series of cities. These operations leave in their wake extensive destruction of property and human lives. Following a twelfth chapter in which a wider list of defeated kings is given, the rest of the book gives details of the boundaries of Israel's new territories (chaps. 13–22) and an account of events at the end of Joshua's life (chaps. 22–24). One is tempted to echo the question that the Egyptian theologian and pastor Origen (185-243 C.E.) raised as, appalled, he began to study the story of Joshua's attack on Ai in Joshua 8: "What was the Holy Spirit thinking of?"[1]

By no stretch of the imagination, then, can the book of Joshua be described as a peaceable work. It is permeated by military images. The first time the Israelites are mentioned here (1:14), Joshua makes the distinction between armed warriors belonging to Reuben, Gad, and the half-tribe of Manasseh, and their wives and children. The latter are allowed to remain on their allocated territory in the Transjordan while their husbands, sons, fathers, and brothers cross the river to help the other tribes. Thus, whereas in the book of Numbers we saw a slow buildup from organizational concerns to military operations, the book of Joshua picks up where Numbers left off, assuming right from the beginning that Israel is involved in combat.[2]

Nevertheless, although the text could be read as being primarily about God's allowing Israel to win land for itself at the expense of others, there are indications that a more important concern is that of clarifying the circumstances in which, as they understood it, the various tribes were enabled to inhabit cities west of the Jordan River. Largely through the way Joshua himself is presented, the writer situates the taking of the Promised Land in a cultic context and insists that Israel can take none of the credit. So its tenure of the land is never an entitlement and always God's gift to the people.[3]

Furthermore, although Jericho is doomed from chapter 2 on and a military atmosphere pervades the book, no fighting at all is described until chapter 6 and very little after chapter 11. The opening forays (chaps. 6–8) are depicted in terms of solemn religious actions in which obedience to the Lord is paramount. As was the case in Numbers 14, the only time Israel attempts military action on its own initiative (chap. 7), the result is a complete disaster. Moreover, the Israelites' initial success depends on their reputation as a formidable adversary (2:10-11; 9:1-2), but that reputation is derived from the Lord's past actions on their behalf, not from their own military skills. Prior to chapter 12, any Canaanite cities that they eventually inhabit come to them because of the aggression of others and because of Israel's refusal to break a treaty that the Gibeonites tricked them into making.[4] Finally, there are interesting discrepancies between what sounds like total conquest and extermination of people and notes that indicate a different state of affairs.

Therefore one could reasonably interpret the book of Joshua as a clarification of how Israel understands its relationship to the Lord and to its land. This is the position that will be taken in what follows, because it is a reading that is consistent with Joshua's wider canonical context. It is, of course, possible to imagine that anyone could read attentively the whole biblical book and then presume to emulate Joshua or Israel by engaging in military activity. That, however, would require a very high degree of confidence that one was divinely authorized to do so,[5] and the special circumstances that are described in such detail in Joshua should discourage readers from thinking that their situation is equivalent to that of Israel.

We shall consider in four stages the unfolding of the text of Joshua. The first, chapters 1–5, locates what follows in the context of Joshua's privileged relationship to the Lord and his resulting responsibilities to the people. The second, chapters 6–8, shows the people learning the obedience that Joshua already practices. There follow next, in chapters 9–12, descriptions of Israel's main military conquests and acquisitions under Joshua. Finally, taking up an idea of Norman C. Habel, we shall look at Joshua 13–24, concentrating on people who, in those chapters, obtained land in unusual circumstances.[6]

Joshua 1–5: The Sacral Context for What Follows

Although Joshua will lead Israel in overcoming cities, he is no ordinary military leader in the modern sense. Certainly, God commissions him to take over from the now dead Moses, telling him, "No one shall be able to stand against you all the days of your life" (1:5), and assuring him of the divine presence with him. At the same time, Joshua is told that his success is conditional upon his observance of "the entire law" enjoined on him by God's servant Moses (1:7, NAB). As will be evident throughout the book, God is in charge. At the outset, God "commands" Joshua that he is to be firm, steadfast, and unfearing, aware of God's presence with him wherever he goes (1:9). Immediately afterwards, Joshua himself "commanded the officers of the people" to begin to organize the first maneuver, the crossing of the Jordan (1:10).

No fighting is described in the first five chapters. Indeed, as Israel crosses the Jordan and heads for Jericho, they have no need to be belligerent: the city's inhabitants are already well aware of Israel's privileged situation. As the two spies sent to Jericho discover, Rahab the harlot is prepared to wager her own safety and that of her family on her knowledge that "the LORD [their] God is indeed God in heaven above and on earth below" (2:11). Rahab testifies that the incident at the sea and Israel's victories over Sihon and Og (Num. 21) are sufficient to strike fear into "all the inhabitants of the land" (Josh. 2:9-11). As the earlier chapters on Exodus and Numbers made clear, none of those three incidents was initiated by Israel itself. In the first, God acted to protect them from the might of Egypt (Exod. 14). Later Sihon attacked them, after having refused their apparently reasonable request for safe passage through his territory (Num. 21:21-32). Numbers 21:33-35 tells of how Og likewise assailed Israel without any direct provocation, presumably because he felt threatened by this group that was marching toward his kingdom after having subdued Sihon and his territories. The spies who return from Jericho report back to Joshua, "Truly the LORD has given all the land into our hands; moreover, all the inhabitants of the land melt in fear before us" (Josh. 2:24).

Clearly, there will be fighting—the Jericho prostitute Rahab negotiates in advance for the lives of her family (2:8-14)—but not until the author has fully impressed on readers the very particular nature of what will ensue.

The following three chapters continue to establish for readers the basis on which Israel will come to possess the Promised Land. Thus it becomes very obvious that Israel is still assisted by the power of the God who enabled them to cross the Red Sea. First, they solemnly traverse the Jordan River on dry ground (chaps. 3, 4). The incident serves to establish Joshua as Moses' replacement: "The LORD said to Joshua, 'This day I will begin to exalt you in the sight of all Israel, so that they may know I will be with you as I was with Moses'" (3:7).

There is no risk that Joshua will overshadow Moses, however. He does not control the water's flow, as Moses did by stretching out his hand over the sea (Exod. 14:16, 21, 26-27): the Jordan River stops flowing when the priests carrying the ark enter the river (Josh. 3:11-17). Joshua merely orchestrates the crossing of the river by forty fully armed contingents[7] and, presumably, the rest of the people (4:13). However, that is no mean achievement, given the topography of the Jordan valley at this point[8] and the implication that the river would have been in full spate because of melting snow, if the Passover described in 5:10 were being celebrated at its regular spring season. So it is not surprising that the note about the successful completion of the crossing is followed by one about the status of Joshua: "On that day the LORD exalted Joshua in the sight of all Israel; and they stood in awe of him, as they had stood in awe of Moses, all the days of his life" (4:14).

After the note about the significance of the twelve stones (4:20-22; perhaps they are reminiscent of the twelve pillars in Exod. 24:4), the section concludes with Joshua drawing attention to the direct parallel between this event and the crossing of the Red Sea at the exodus (Josh. 4:23-24). He tells the people that in each case God acted "so that all the peoples of the earth may know that the hand of the LORD is mighty, and so that you may fear the LORD your God forever" (v. 24).

In her encounter with the spies, Rahab had testified to the fear in which Israel was already held by "all the inhabitants of the land" (Josh. 2:9). The opening of chapter 5 registers that this latest event, the crossing of the Jordan, causes further disheartening and loss of courage, this time specifying "all the kings of the Amorites beyond the Jordan to the west, and all the kings of the Canaanites by the sea" (5:1). That Israel is armed (4:12-13) may have something to do with their response, but that is not mentioned in connection with the kings' fear in 5:1. What is unquestionably formidable about Israel is the Lord's actions on its behalf. The reader already knows that the basis of Israel's success is Joshua's observance of the law (1:7-9).[9] This is further emphasized by his next two actions, which are anything but military. The first is to circumcise all the Israelites of this new generation who have replaced the ones who proved unfaithful after leaving Egypt with Moses (5:2-9). The second is to keep the Passover. Just as the original celebration in Exodus 12 marked the end of Israel's time in Egypt, this one indicates the end of their time in the desert. On the next day "they ate the produce of the land, unleavened cakes and parched grain" instead of the manna, which promptly ceased (Josh. 5:11-12). Under Joshua's leadership, then, Israel is keeping in close liturgical contact with the Lord. In turn, the Lord provides protection for Israel (in the form of a terrifying reputation) and food from the land in which they will eventually settle. As yet there has been no fighting.

The next event, described in 5:13-15, is programmatic for what follows: Joshua, near Jericho, is faced with an armed figure that turns out to be "the commander of the army [or "host," ṣābā'] of the LORD" (5:14). The incident emphasizes the Lord's control of subsequent happenings. It seems to occur during the siege of Jericho (6:1) and so may be particularly relevant to the capture of that city. Yet it is an interpretive key to all the events described in the book. As Joshua will remind the tribes of Israel at the end, it was not with their sword or bow that the inhabitants of the land were driven out (24:12). In the most obvious sense, this is inaccurate: Israelite weapons *did* overcome those from whom they took the land. However, the heavenly figure is warning them against taking credit for their own achievements, in this case, successful military activities. Like all else in the biblical tradition, the Promised Land is the Lord's gift to them, a gift they hold in trust. Crediting the Lord with gaining it for them does not cancel out the violence by which this was done; indeed, it merely displaces it onto the Lord. At the same time, though, by promoting an attitude of *noblesse oblige*, the reminder of the Lord's involvement in Israel's cause discourages further violence that would come from overweening pride in their conquests.

Joshua interrogates this figure that, with "a drawn sword in his hand," stands before him (5:13). The answer to his first question conveys that the "commander" is neither "one of us, [n]or one of our adversaries," but a being of a different order entirely, as Joshua tacitly acknowledges by his response of immediate prostration.[10] The reader is thus alerted to the highly analogous nature of the language used to describe the "commander." His "sword," then, is not strictly comparable with that of a human warrior: it is not an earthly weapon at all. Next Joshua asks what he is to learn from this individual. It is noteworthy that the reply (from one alleged "soldier" to another) has nothing at all to do with military strategy. Joshua is simply to follow Moses' earlier example by removing his shoes because he is standing on holy ground (Exod. 3:5). The incident concludes with Joshua's simple compliance: "And Joshua did so" (Josh. 5:15).

There is here an indication that the Lord's power is available for Israel's use as it moves into the Promised Land. That it is presented as *military* power (however analogously) is problematic because of the ease with which such convictions become detached from the cultic context in which the writer of the book of Joshua has placed them. That context does not prevent the violence by means of which Israel will take over the land, but does associate it with a particular event in the people's history: the encounter between the ever-obedient Joshua and his heavenly counterpart. Later readers who wish to have access to the Lord's power could imitate Joshua only if they were similarly obedient and had specific authorization from God's messenger.

On Learning to Obey: Joshua 6–8

As was indicated in Joshua 1, obedience to the Lord is the key to Israel's success in this book. So far, the people have followed Joshua's orders with regard to crossing the Jordan, undergoing circumcision, and keeping Passover. Next, without any prompting, they have carried out standard military procedure for taking a city: they have set up a siege against Jericho. That seems to have been successful: "no one came out and no one went in" (6:1). The siege was ended, though, not by conventional means but as the climax of highly controlled liturgical activity: Israel's daily circling of the city, to the accompaniment of blaring trumpets. The ritual importance of Israel's troops is indicated by their position in front of the seven trumpet-blowing priests and the ark of the covenant, and as a rearguard (6:7-9). The troops are not fighting but are on display as part of the liturgical pageant. The account also emphasizes the discipline of the people. They are not to cry out or shout until Joshua gives the order, which he does not do until they have circled the city seven times on the seventh day. Then, at the crucial moment on day seven, all contribute to the shout that accompanies the falling of Jericho's walls. It is very strange military strategy!

The procedure that ensues, putting to the ban, or completely destroying, the whole city of Jericho, is clearly violent by any standards. With the exception of Rahab and her family, all the people are killed. The city and all its contents are burned, and "the silver and the gold, and the vessels of bronze and iron" are "put into the treasury of the house of the Lord" (presumably at Gilgal; 6:24). Susan Niditch makes a good case for understanding the ban as, in this case, a sacrificial offering to God of everything that is valuable, including human life, the most valuable of all. If that is so, the contextualized meaning of Israel's activity at this point is not a glorying in killing and destruction following a military victory that the people have themselves won.[11] However wrongheaded it may seem to later generations, and however dangerous when misunderstood, the ban is intended to honor the God to whom the Israelites must credit the victory, the one whose "commander" arrived just before the description of the siege.

The symbolism of all this is liable to be quite lost on modern readers. Without question, it is an enormous challenge to the imagination. On the one hand, it is all too easy to imagine the military details of the Lord as "fighting for Israel" and to come away with the idea that conquering a region gives one absolute rights over it. (Yet the account does discourage a view of war as an opportunity for gaining plunder: the people are highly controlled before, during, and after the operation.) On the other hand, it is much more difficult to remember the emphasis on Joshua's piety and obedience, and the fact that the "commander of the LORD's army" (Josh. 5:13-14) belongs neither to Israel nor to its enemies.[12]

In the story of the fall of Jericho, then, the primary value emphasized is obedience to the Lord, who is the source of the victory and of any land that they may eventually obtain. This is evident from the way Joshua and the people behave at the time and is further stressed in the tragic tale that follows in Joshua 7. In verse 1, the reader is told that a Judahite called Achan does not abide by the Lord's prohibition of taking for personal use anything that is under the ban (6:18-19): Achan has not handed over all the booty that he acquired in Jericho. Joshua is not yet aware of this problem, however, so he plans and executes the next foray, against the city of Ai ("The Ruin"). (The story is, therefore, an etiology: an explanation of the origin of a particular phenomenon, a ruin, in this case.)[13] In this battle about thirty-six Israelites are killed, the first to be mentioned as dying in this way,[14] and "the hearts of the people melted and turned to water" (7:5). That and the reaction of Joshua and the elders (7:6-9) indicate strongly that the Israelites have no illusions about being able to rely on their own military skills. They are convinced that this one defeat (which is, after all, minor) will completely cancel out the formidable reputation that has preceded them across the Jordan: "The Canaanites and all the inhabitants of the land will hear of it, and surround us, and cut off our name from the earth" (7:9). Most wisely, they do not even attempt to put on a show of force that might reestablish their prestige. Instead they submit a well-placed appeal to God's concern for the divine reputation: "Then what will you do for your great name?" (v. 9). The radical answer is that the one who is at fault must be sought out and located, apparently by lot, and dedicated to the Lord by being put under the ban.

There is much pathos in the continuation of the story, as Achan confesses what he has done. The reader is induced to identify with him at his moment of temptation. He begins, "Among the spoils, I saw a beautiful Babylonian mantle," which he illicitly kept for himself along with some silver and a bar of gold (7:21, NAB). One is led to wonder whether Achan would have found the inherently more valuable precious metals easier to resist in the absence of the mantle. Now, he says, it is all "hidden in the ground inside my tent, with the silver underneath" (v. 21). The consequence of giving in to his admitted covetousness (v. 21; as in 6:18) is that "Joshua and all Israel with him took Achan son of Zerah, with the silver, the mantle, and the bar of gold, and with his sons and daughters, with his oxen, donkeys, and sheep, and his tent and all that he had; and they brought them up to the Valley of Achor" (7:24). Achor means "devastation." There, according to the Hebrew text, "All Israel stoned him to death; they burned [the possessions, including the mantle] with fire, cast stones on them . . . " (7:25).[15] Achan's eye for beauty had caused his own devastation and that of all he owned.

It is very clear, then, that these opening chapters of Joshua, and especially chapters 6 and 7, about the fall of Jericho and its aftermath, intend to convey the supreme importance of doing what God requires. The stakes are very high because it is *the Lord* who offers Israel the land. The story of Jericho also demonstrates Israel's fidelity to an earlier agreement to spare Rahab and her family (6:22-23, 25). The curse that Joshua pronounces on whoever will rebuild Jericho (his eldest and youngest sons will die: 6:26) can be read as an attempt at ensuring that evidence of the Lord's victory will long be available to people. It may also be an acknowledgment that, although they had conquered it, the Israelites knew that Jericho was for some reason not suitable for living in.[16]

Materially speaking, the Israelites gain nothing from taking Jericho except some silver, gold, and vessels of bronze and iron that were destined for "the treasury of the LORD" (6:19). They also acquired the company of Rahab's family and their descendants "to this day" (6:25, NAB: presumably those who composed these stories knew of some non-Israelites in their midst, in which case this is another etiology). What they also come away with is a concrete experience of the Lord's support for them west of the Jordan. The inhabitants of Jericho lose everything, although the Israelites probably would have had quite a different interpretation; notably, that the city's inhabitants and all their possessions had been brought into the sphere where the Lord is honored, albeit through their destruction.[17]

The Lord next encourages Israel to make another attempt at capturing the city of Ai: "Do not fear or be dismayed. Take all the fighting men with you, and go up now to Ai" (8:1). Israel is evidently not looking for war and needs to be told how to plan the onslaught: "Set an ambush against the city, behind it," says the Lord (v. 2). Responsibility for the violence is thus removed from Israel and attributed to God, who actively promotes the destruction of the inhabitants of Ai at the hands of the people. Joshua himself does not fight, but has an important ritual role to play in this event, comparable with that of Moses in Joshua's defeat of Amalek in Exodus 17:8-13. At the crucial moment, when those waiting in ambush are to rush into the now empty city, God directs him to stretch out toward Ai the javelin in his hand, and he stays in this position until the city has been burned and all its people killed (8:8, 26). The ritual execution of the king of Ai (v. 29) has no parallel in the Jericho narrative; the great heap of stones that was raised over the king's body after his hanging suggests that the story is an etiology. Another difference between Jericho and Ai is that in the latter God permitted that the city's livestock and other booty not come under the ban (v. 27). Perhaps the implication is the impossibility of maintaining the strict discipline that the Israelites showed at first, in face of a very strong desire to profit from their depredations. On the other hand, neither conquest provides Israel with a city in which people can live, as both are ruins.

The pericope that concludes chapter 8 (vv. 30-35) shows Joshua implementing God's command of Joshua 1:7-9. Obedience to the law is foundational to his successful leadership of Israel, and so he takes steps to ensure that the people know the provisions of that law. Having built an altar for the Lord on Mount Ebal, Joshua inscribes the law on its stones and then reads aloud "all the words of the law" (8:32, 34). The account emphasizes that every single word was heard by all, "including the women and children, and the strangers who had accompanied Israel" (v. 35, NAB).[18] Their formal renewal of commitment to it will come only at the end of Joshua's life, as his final act on their behalf (chap. 24).

The stories of the engagements at Jericho and Ai, culminating in the reading of the law, certainly emphasize the importance of obeying the Lord. The various etiological elements (e.g., the ruins of Jericho and Ai, the long-term survival of Rahab's descendants, and the heap of stones outside Ai) draw attention to the abiding significance of the past events by which Israel gradually made its mark on the land, under the Lord's guidance. The law itself is an even more significant element of continuity. However, there are strong negative side effects. For although these stories usefully convey that Israel (in the past or present) has absolutely no cause for feeling proud of its military prowess at Jericho and Ai and thus do not encourage the repetition of such exploits, they attribute to God the responsibility for much of the violence that the people carry out. This is quite different from the situation at the

Red Sea, where the Lord enabled Israel to escape from the Egyptians, but without the use of weapons.

In addition, the stories in Joshua 6–8 show the people behaving in ways that are now difficult to understand and therefore to justify. An obvious example of this is the use of the ban to completely destroy people and goods. By contrast, Israel's taking of booty at Ai would be less strange to modern readers, but in context could be read as a downward move into taking what belonged to the real victor, who is God. Another cause of offense for modern readers is Joshua's execution and burial of the king of Ai. Even if he were carrying out procedure that was acceptable (and even required) at the time,[19] and even though the purpose of the story may be to provide an explanation of a familiar heap of stones, the effect is to depict Joshua as acting with a brutality that is uncharacteristic of him overall.

On Being Deceived and Its Consequences: Joshua 9–12

In the meantime, news of Israel's success reaches "the kings west of the Jordan" (9:1, NAB). They respond, not with the fatalism that Rahab of Jericho had led the spies to expect (2:10-11), but by forming a military alliance against "Joshua and Israel" (9:2). This note, which serves to underscore the magnitude of Israel's success so far, also moves the story forward, although in an unexpected way. For the battles in which Israel will gain territory do not come from mere self-defense against this group. They happen, rather, because the inhabitants of nearby Gibeon also regard the Israelites as unstoppable on account of the Lord's commitment to them (9:9-11, 24). But their response is much more creative than that of the kings: they trick Israel into making peace with them. In an elaborate subterfuge, they pretend to be people from a distant land. The Israelite leaders, taken in by the Gibeonites' worn out clothes and stale rations, "partook of their provisions, and did not seek direction from the LORD" (9:14). By doing this, they commit themselves to an alliance with the Gibeonites. Joshua formally makes the agreement, which the leaders seal with an oath (9:15). Their ill-considered move will have consequences that affect all the subsequent events.

The immediate result is that Israel is made to look foolish. Within days of making the treaty, the Israelites arrive at the Gibeonite cities. They thus discover that they have been deceived. Their treaty partners live close by, not in far off lands at all (9:16-17). Albeit reluctantly, the Israelites honor the pact by simply moving into the cities without attacking them (vv. 18b-21). Although their lives are not forfeit, the Gibeonites are reduced to being "hewers of wood and drawers of water for all the congregation" (9:21) and (as Joshua says), "for the house of my God" (v. 23). This is scarcely an honorable way to treat treaty partners, however much one may sympathize with the Israelites who have been duped. It is also against the law as Israel will later understand it: Deuteronomy 29:9-11 specifies that aliens who undertake such menial tasks are part of the covenant people.[20]

Exactly how the story of the Gibeonites' servitude connects with the surrounding material is not clear, however. Subsequent events show Joshua living at Gilgal and Gibeon as a functioning city (Josh. 9:6). It is yet another etiology, intended to account for a situation known to its original audience: "to this day" Gibeonites perform menial service (v. 27). The Gibeonites' resourcefulness, like that of Rahab in chapter 2, has given them a place in Israelite society, although as slaves, not treaty partners. Presumably this is preferable to death. Much more significant is that, apart from this incident, Israel remains faithful to the treaty with the Gibeonites. This will have radical effects. Because of the opposition it provokes, it is the driving force behind later conquests, a two-stage process involving a southern coalition (chap. 10) and a northern one (chap. 11).

Joshua 10 describes how the Gibeonites' alliance with Israel frightens Adoni-zedek of Jerusalem into assembling four other kings, from territories to his south and west, to attack a Gibeon now perceived as large and strong (10:2). With their city under siege, the Gibeonites appeal for help to Israel, their new ally (10:6). Joshua responds with energy and vigor. His surprise attack after an all-night march is backed up by the Lord, who throws the enemy into a panic and augments the slaughter by sending huge hailstones that kill more than did Israel's swords, and by holding up nature's progress until the victory is complete (10:10, 13). All of Israel's army returns safely to camp, after which Joshua (most unpleasantly) uses as an object lesson for Israel his ritual execution of the five kings (10:21, 22-27). The text goes on to detail how Joshua conquered the cities of Makkedah, where the kings had hidden in a cave, and Libnah for no expressed reason (violence and accounts of it escalate). All this before going on to take the cities belonging to Adoni-zedek's four allies: Lachish (and its ally, Gezer), Eglon, Hebron, and Debir. Joshua was able to capture "all these kings and their land at one time" because, the writer suggests, "the LORD God of Israel fought for Israel" (10:42, as in Exod. 14:25, against Egypt). The cause of all this mayhem is the fear that the local kings have of Israel after the alliance that the Gibeonites deceived Israel into making with them. The Lord is understood as protecting Israel from the consequences of its lack of wisdom in dealing with the Gibeonites. Again the text implies that Israel can claim no credit for the victories, but the cost is that both the Lord and Joshua are presented as violent.

By this stage, Israel appears to have a menacing reputation among the neighboring nations. In reality, its renown as a terrifying military force is entirely a theological conceit of the biblical author: careful readers of the biblical narrative must be aware that, apart from the Lord's help mediated through the obedient Joshua, Israel is anything but an enthusiastic or effective fighting force. God's activities on their behalf, especially at the Red Sea, are responsible for the image of them that others find so fearsome. Nevertheless, their formidable reputation continues to elicit military responses. Joshua 11 describes how Israel is attacked, directly this time, by the combined forces of an even larger group of kings from further north. It seems that these forces arrive "with all their troops" in vast numbers and strength: "a great army, in number like the sand on the seashore, with very many horses and chariots" (11:4).[21] Encouraged by the Lord, Joshua deals expeditiously with them too. In addition to leaving no survivors (11:8, 14; as 10:28, 39, 40), "he hamstrung their horses, and burned their chariots" (11:9). In other words, Joshua put their weapons out of commission. In this case, he does not burn the cities, apart from Hazor, which belongs to the ringleader. The chapter concludes with a summary that stresses the completeness of the conquest (although 11:18 says that "Joshua made war a long time with all these kings"). The section ends by noting that Joshua "took the whole land . . . and . . . gave it for an inheritance to Israel according to their tribal allotments" (11:23). Chapters 10 and 11 thus describe a rapid spread of violence that follows Joshua's response to the Gibeonite plea for help in 10:7.

It is important, however, to recall the context in which these two chapters have been placed. The basis was the Israelites' pact with the Gibeonites (chap. 9). Before being tricked into that alliance, Israel had gained very little from its battles. Cultic matters and other religious concerns were very prominent in the text,[22] and the people had attacked only two cities, both of which were totally dedicated to the

Lord by their destruction and the killing of all their inhabitants (6:21; 8:23). In the first, Jericho, the livestock were also killed, and Israel took no booty at all. The prohibitions were relaxed somewhat at Ai, where the victors did keep animals and spoil.

These restrictions might help later readers remember that this text is accounting for Israel's possession of land west of the Jordan and the terms of its tenure. The setting of the stories about Jericho and Ai, including the all-important chapter 7 about Achan, should remind them that this is not about an ordinary war, such as they might engage in at will.[23] Furthermore, in the wider biblical context it can serve as an illustration that, because humans are part of created reality, albeit a special part, all their "possessing" is relative.

One cannot deny that there are big risks involved in reading this part of Joshua. As is often the case, descriptions of devastation and killing attract more than their fair share of readers' attention. In this case, they may also encourage people to see their private feuds as "holy wars" in which destruction is regarded as pleasing to God. Yet those who wrote the book of Joshua used the first chapters of the book to stress the singularity of the situation and the special position of Joshua himself. This could reasonably have been expected to deter people from trying to emulate Israel's leader, except with regard to his courage and piety.[24]

Between 10:7 and 11:23, however, the text describes a victorious sweep of Joshua in which each city involved in the coalitions against Gibeon (10:1-5) and Israel (11:1-5) is summarily and completely dealt with (see above). It is very easy to read Joshua's exploits in this part of the book as a glorification of the hero or even of war itself, with God muscling in like a big brother whose weapons outclass those of the other participants.

Yet even though some parts of it do present violence in

a way that might make it an appealing option for the strong (e.g., Joshua's treatment of the kings and their cities in 10:16-39), this is not the message of the book as a whole. For the context of chapters 10 and 11 suggests that, although Joshua fights, and fights most effectively, what happens is not Israel's doing, at least as a military operation. The leader's exploits are framed by God's insistence about the need to keep the law (1:7-9) and his own reminders to Israel at the end of his life that "it was not by [their] sword or by [their] bow" that the Promised Land became available to Israel (24:12), but through an action of God (24:18). The message here is not that Israel did not kill, but that killing was not the source of their success. Joshua's victories in chapters 10 and 11 are immediately preceded by a reading of the law and by a story in which Israel is deceived by the Gibeonites but still behaves more or less honorably toward them (8:30-35; 9:3-27, see above). It is that behavior that leads Israel to the necessity of fighting in self-defense. In these chapters, Joshua is warlike only when provoked, as was Abraham in Genesis 14, although Joshua fights much more extensively than the patriarch did.

Joshua 10 and 11 include repeated reminders that the one responsible for Israel's victories is the Lord.[25] Israel's traditions here are not straightforward, for they insist that the people came into possession of the land by conquest but, even though sometimes they fought and sometimes did not (when the Lord took their part by, e.g., sending hailstones), they may not gain any glory by it. This attitude is not always sustained, for Joshua 12 consists entirely of a list of kings who were "conquered." Here the credit goes to the Israelites (in the Transjordan) and to Joshua and the Israelites (west of the Jordan): militaristic attitudes have a way of reasserting themselves, even where the basic understanding is that Israel may conquer only when the Lord allows it. Furthermore, the gratuitous inclusion of the city of

Libnah in the list of Joshua's reprisals described in chapter 10 demonstrates how engaging in warfare makes people much more likely to commit further violence on their own account, for political or personal ends. We shall see more examples of this tendency in the book of Judges.

On Learning to Value the Land: Joshua 13–24

What, though, does it mean to say, as the text of Joshua repeatedly does, that the Lord was fighting for Israel?[26] Or that Joshua encountered the commander of the Lord's army in 5:13-15? At worst, it posits God as a warrior, with all the attending problems that such an image generates. The question then would be whether (and why) one should keep the law of such a God. At best, it perhaps expresses Israel's understanding that they have a God-given claim to the cities west of the Jordan. This has caused endless trouble in the past century and the present one. What might it have meant to the original readers?

First, it should be noted that the people of post-exilic times for whom the final version of this book was produced were already in possession of the land—if they wanted it. The Persians who had taken over the Babylonian empire in 539 B.C.E. permitted the exiles and their descendants to return to Jerusalem.[27] Some Jews took up that option. But many preferred to stay where they were, in Babylon or elsewhere. For this latter group of Jews, a strong case that Israel's original claim to the Promised Land was based on a divine gift might have been attractive enough to make them consider returning.

Would this have encouraged them to go to war? Not likely. With the Persians firmly in charge of Judah, there was scant danger that the Judeans would revolt against their overlords. On the other hand, tales of how the previous inhabitants of the cities and their kings were exterminated (whether by Joshua or by God) might have impressed on them the sacred nature of their ancestral claims to the cities and encouraged them to return. The stories are like those in Exodus 1–14, which show that obstinately withstanding the Lord is foolish and dooms one to failure. That the post-exilic Judeans could realistically have taken Joshua's conquest of the land as programmatic for themselves is, however, all but impossible to imagine. Their situation was too different. Those of them who returned to Jerusalem after 538 were not in a position to conquer anybody.[28] Indeed they could not even deal once and for all with the annoyance and ongoing aggression that they received from the inhabitants of Samaria, whose early request to have a part in rebuilding the holy city the Judeans had rudely denied.[29] The consequent rift with the Samaritans was never healed.

However, there are indications in the second half of the book of Joshua that another form of withstanding the Lord might have been a problem. Norman Habel has observed that the book of Joshua as a whole describes how "the Royal lands of Canaan are transformed into a land of family lots."[30] After the kings have been conquered, mostly in chapters 10 and 11, there is a listing of dispossessed kings in chapter 12 (including some belonging to cities not previously mentioned) and a reminder of the territorial division Moses had established for the tribes beyond the Jordan (chap. 13). Then, as Habel notes, each cluster of tribal families is given its divine entitlement (*naḥ^alāh*), usually by lot.[31] Yet the text implies that Israelites may need encouragement to take possession of the land that God is making available to them. For chapter 13 opens with God pointing out to the now-aged Joshua that "very much of the land still remains to be possessed" (13:1) but telling him that he should divide up what they already have. There follows a reminder of the allocations Moses had made in the Transjordan (13:8-33). Then, among the straightforward distribution to the other tribes (as announced in 14:1-5) are several examples of individuals or groups who successfully make a case for receiving either land to which they are not obviously entitled or a greater portion of land. Most prominent in this category are the Kenizzite Caleb, along with his daughter, Achsah (Josh. 14:6-15; 15:13-19); the five daughters of Zelophehad, a man who has no sons (17:3-6); and the Joseph tribes, who have insufficient land (17:14-18). Other examples include Joshua himself (19:49-50) and the Levites (21:1-42). Let us consider these six cases, because they illustrate the conviction that possession of the land is of vital importance to Israel, not only at the level of tribes but also in particular cases, including those of some women.

Before any of the western tribes has received its allocation, Caleb (who may be non-Israelite) approaches Joshua to make his claim (14:6). He reminds Joshua that Moses promised him land because of his complete loyalty to the Lord (14:9) when he, along with other scouts, had spied out the country and brought back their report (Num. 13). Caleb points to his continuing vigor as evidence that he is still loyal to God. Although eighty-five years old, he has the Lord's promise that he will be able to drive out the Anakim from the territory and indeed he does so (Josh. 14:12; 15:14). Joshua blesses Caleb and gives him Hebron (14:13). Caleb's assertiveness is clearly regarded as admirable. So is that of his daughter. On her wedding day Achsah induces her husband to ask her father for some land and, when the request is granted with desert land in the Negev, she obtains from her father an additional and very valuable gift of some pools of water (15:18-19).

More female assertiveness is evidenced in the distribution of land to the descendants of Manasseh. Zelophehad's five daughters, his only children, request and obtain a share in their father's inheritance (17:3-6). In the same chapter,

Joseph's descendants (the two half-tribes of Ephraim and Manasseh) complain that their portion of land is too small for their large numbers, whereupon Joshua encourages them to clear the forest and drive out the heavily armed Canaanites of the plain (17:14-18). Initiative is being promoted. Perhaps Joshua's rebuke of the seven remaining Israelite tribes in 18:3 is intended as part of the same dynamic. For there he chastises them for their delay in taking possession of the land which the Lord their God has given them and sends out three from each tribe to survey the land so that he can allocate it by lot.

When all the other tribes have received their allocation, Joshua himself requests and receives a city from his fellow Israelites (19:49-50). Finally, "the heads of the families of the Levites came to the priest Eleazar and to Joshua son of Nun and to the heads of the families of the tribes of the Israelites" to remind them that God, through Moses, had promised them land too (21:1). Therefore the other tribes divest themselves of part of their own allocations so that it can be assigned to the Levitical families (21:2-42).

Certainly, there is evidence here of fighting for land. Thus Caleb fights for his territory and offers his daughter to the one who will conquer Kiriath-sepher (15:14-15, 16-17). Joshua encourages the Joseph tribes to extend their territory by "driv[ing] out the Canaanites" (17:18). The repeated noting of those whom the Israelites did not "drive out" (15:63; 16:10; 17:13) or conquer (17:12) cannot fail to remind the reader about those whom they did. The Danites, finding their apportioned territory too small, attack and capture the city of Leshem, which they rename Dan (19:47). Yet it is surely significant that, unlike Judges 1, where some of the same material is presented in blatantly militaristic form, the book of Joshua as a whole does not draw attention to the means by which it assumes that Israel came to inhabit Canaan. As Norman Habel notes, in Joshua the understanding is that all the land belongs to the Lord and will be distributed "to any who press their divinely approved land claims in a spirit of total commitment to Yahweh."[32] Theoretically, those later Israelites considering a return to the Promised Land from exile in Babylon could have taken that as a license to fight. Against their doing so, however, is the fact that the adversaries in the stories were Anakim and Canaanites, or non-Israelites, whereas any post-exilic fighting for Judah would have been against other Israelites and, as we shall see, reading the story in Joshua 22 would have discouraged any such ideas.

At least some of the people whom the returning exiles would have encountered in Jerusalem and its environs would have been fellow Israelites,[33] and Joshua 22:10-34 demonstrates very clearly the benefits of dialogue over civil war. In that story, when the tribes whose territory was east of the Jordan built a very conspicuous altar some-where near the river, those in the west regarded it as an act of secession that they were willing to fight to prevent. So they assembled at Shiloh. Before declaring war, however, they sent a delegation to find out why the Reubenites, Gadites, and the half-tribe of Manasseh had set up the altar. What they learned was that the others had acted out of concern to maintain their connection with the Lord, a connection they thought might be at risk because of their geographical separation from the other tribes. The Transjordan tribes explained that they had erected the altar from fear that in time to come "your children should say to our children: 'What have you to do with the LORD, the God of Israel?'" (22:24). They were thus able to convince the other tribes of their piety and their desire to remain part of the Lord's people.

Given that the people are to accept one another's good will, even at a distance and with the Jordan River between them, Joshua in 23:1-10 once more reminds them that, as the Lord was the one who "fought for" them so that they could have the Promised Land (23:3, 9-10) and will continue to do so (vv. 4-5), so they must carefully obey "all that is written in the book of the law of Moses" (vv. 6-8). The rest of the chapter (vv. 11-16) has as its kernel the reminder, given three times in verses 14-15, that "every promise has been fulfilled for you, with not one single exception" (v. 14, NAB). Although there is mention of those who were displaced or who will be in the future (vv. 3-5), the emphasis is rather on the dangers of falling away from such a God, as verses 11-13 and 15-16 specify in vivid detail. The land is important, not for its own sake but because it is the primary instantiation of and metaphor for the Lord's relationship with Israel.

Except for its last few verses, the final chapter of the book depicts a covenant renewal ceremony at Shechem. Here Joshua reminds "all the tribes of Israel" (Josh. 24:1) about God's actions on their behalf, actions that form the basis on which they are to choose whether or not to serve the Lord. When they accept this account of their history and are adamant that they do indeed wish to serve the Lord, Joshua makes a covenant with them, records its terms, and sets up a large stone as witness (vv. 25-27). That the people can go "to their inheritances" is itself evidence of the Lord's fidelity to Israel (v. 28). Joshua's own fidelity has been proven and is sealed by his death, in the account of which he is for the first time given the title used so often of Moses in this book: "the servant of the LORD" (v. 29).[34] The account of the burial (in his descendants' territory) of Joseph's bones "which the Israelites had brought up from Egypt" pushes back even further the people's memory of the Lord's faithfulness (v. 32). The problem, of course, will be Israel's lack of fidelity after the death of the elders who "had known all the works that the LORD did for Israel" (v. 31). The Hebrew form of the book of Joshua gives only a slight hint of this, in Joshua's setting up a stone to deter the people from dealing falsely with their God (v. 27). The book concludes instead with a third burial, that of Aaron's son Eleazar, buried "in the town of his son Phinehas, which had been given to him in the hill country of Ephraim" (v. 33). The Promised Land remains primary in the Hebrew tradition.

By contrast, the Greek version continues further, referring to the ark of God and its service by Phinehas. The note about his death and burial is followed by the information that the Israelites, going off to their own places, proceeded to worship the goddess Astarte, for which the Lord allowed them to be oppressed by Eglon king of Moab for eighteen years, a detail that anticipates the overall theme of the book of Judges, and Judges 3:14 in particular.

Conclusion

The Book of Joshua leaves readers with the impression that the way in which Israel acquired the land—by military action under Joshua's leadership—is part of the tradition but cannot be a source of self-congratulation for the people. That is surely the point of Joshua's repeated reminders that any and all victories were the Lord's doing and not their own. The accounts of the destruction that the Lord had repeatedly urged them to carry out express the conviction that God would indeed have Israel possess the Promised Land: they are not, however, advocating a way of life. What most certainly *does* pertain to everyday life is the text's concluding reminder of the risk (and in the Greek tradition, the actuality) of the people's being unfaithful to the Lord. As always, the Lord is faithful and Israel, in the tradition of humans generally from Genesis 3 onward, is more than likely not to be. For the original, post-exilic readers, the question of belligerence is nowhere in sight. However, it will return to view, accompanied by the theme of Israel's fidelity, or lack of it, in the opening of the book of Judges.

There can be no question that much violent behavior is described in the book of Joshua. Much of it is explicable in terms of specific objectives. They include etiological concerns: stories that account for realities with which the original readers of the book were assumed to be familiar, such as the piles of stones that were said to mark the graves of enemy kings (8:29, 10:22-27), or the remains of ruined cities (chaps. 6–8). The people who composed and transmitted these traditions would not have been shocked by Joshua's brutality on these occasions, although modern readers often are and indeed should be. Another concern of the text is to demonstrate the Lord's power and the inevitability of divine victory. Thus the Lord is frequently said to have ensured the total destruction of Israel's enemies, once by hardening their hearts (11:20). This repeats the pattern found earlier in the book of Exodus. In both places, attributing Israel's victory to the Lord comes at a very high cost, for it presents God as dealing with Israel's enemies by demonizing them and destroying them and their culture.

Readers who can manage to bracket out such real problems can nevertheless find in the book of Joshua material that might help them construct alternative strategies to violence. First, the book provides support for a view of the world that treats all possessions, and particularly the land on which people live, as held in trust from God. In a God-given world, gift is the primary category and possession is never absolute, whatever price one has paid for the object in question. Second, although the hero of the book of Joshua is a military leader, he is not an ambitious seeker after military glory or revenge.[35] What is most emphasized about Joshua is his complete fidelity to God and God's law, and his insistence that Israel aspire to the same ideal.

This is recognized in the text's note about his death, where he is for the first and only time in this document called "the servant of the LORD" (24:29). There is here a deliberate contrast between Joshua and Moses: fourteen times is the latter termed "the servant of the LORD" between Joshua 1:1 and 22:5. Perhaps the delay in according Joshua this honorific title testifies to the high level of risk involved in his vocation, including greed for booty (Josh. 7) and the temptation to break inconvenient treaties (chap. 9). That Joshua was successful enables him to function as a model for those in any profession that requires high levels of initiative and courage, virtues that are always liable to be corrupted into self-seeking and rashness, as we shall see abundantly illustrated in the book of Judges.

8

LEADERSHIP IN A TIME OF VIOLENCE:

THE BOOK OF JUDGES

There is significant development between the book of Joshua and Judges in the presentation of Israel's violence and two related issues: its practice of idolatry and its pattern of leadership. Consequently, whereas in Joshua Israel relates to the Lord in a relatively straightforward fashion, in Judges there is ironical distance.

The introduction to this chapter contrasts the two books by summarizing how each of them presents the themes of violence, idolatry, and leadership. We shall see that, by comparison with Joshua, the book of Judges portrays Israel (1) as much more violent, (2) as more prone to idolatry (i.e., to the worship of gods other than the Lord), and (3) as having leadership that functions in a much more ambiguous way than did that of Joshua. In this chapter we will trace each of these three themes, and conclusions will then be drawn about what readers of the book of Judges may learn about violence and its consequences.

Introduction: From Joshua to Judges

Although the book of Joshua takes for granted that Israel's acquisition of the land involves violence and occasionally describes Joshua's exploits in ways that seem to make war attractive, this is not the overall thrust of the book.[1] The Israelites do not initiate the fighting, except for the ill-fated attack on Ai in Joshua 7:2-5, and their opportunities for battle are mostly provided by enemies who fear them because of the reputation they have gained at the Lord's hand. Besides, the text repeatedly insists that, because the Lord is giving them the Promised Land, they may claim no credit for any of the conquests. Furthermore, strife between or among Israelites does not feature at all in this book. In fact, Joshua 22 consists largely of a morality tale that tells how civil war between the tribes west and east of the Jordan was averted by very simple diplomatic means. The message is that those who think their fellow Israelites are acting in bad faith should ask them about their intentions, rather than launch an attack.

Nor does the Hebrew text of Joshua dwell on Israel as idolatrous, even though in the final assembly at Shechem, Joshua insists that they put away the strange gods that their ancestors had served beyond the River and in Egypt and that remained among them (24:14, 23). The context makes it clear that those gods do not at present endanger Israel, which is emphatically rejecting them in favor of the Lord (24:16, 22, 24).[2] Joshua's speech here (24:20) and, especially, in the preceding chapter (23:7-8, 16) indicates that idolatry is a very real possibility in the future but not a problem during Joshua's lifetime.[3]

Joshua's leadership of Israel is of crucial significance in the book that bears his name. Successor to Moses (1:1-3; 3:7), he shows a total dedication to the Lord that eventually earns him the title "the servant of the LORD" (24:29), the book of Joshua's preferred title for Moses. The text lacks any suggestion that Joshua ever allowed his own agenda to take precedence over carrying out the Lord's will. His attempts to make the Israelites equally obedient to the covenant appear to have been effective, at least as long as he was alive (e.g., 4:14; 24:31). The Israelite leaders in chapter 22 are ready for war with their Transjordanian brethren but solve the dispute diplomatically. They are acting in the spirit of the one who honored the agreement his spies had made with Rahab (6:25) and (although less perfectly)[4] stood by the commitment to the Gibeonites that his imprudent subordinates had been tricked into making because they "did not ask direction from the LORD" (9:14-15; 10:7-14).

Therefore the book of Joshua gives no reason for suspecting that Israel's relationship to the Lord is other than straightforward or that the solemn assemblies of Israel that Joshua calls in 8:30-35 and chapter 24 are anything but genuine encounters between the people and their God. Israel is learning how to live as the Lord's people. Some Israelites were foolish on occasion (e.g., Achan, who withheld booty in Joshua 7), but nobody tries to manipulate the Lord, and so the text lacks irony in what it says about the relationship between God and the people.

The book of Judges describes a very different situation with regard to Israel's violence, idolatry, and leadership. This has consequences for the way they are depicted as relating to the Lord. Here episodes involving violence pervade the narrative. First, from the announcement of Joshua's death in 1:1 until the carefully orchestrated abduction of some Israelite women in 21:17-23, there is aggression against outsiders, against fellow Israelites, or within families. Second, even as they are violent, the people are recurrently unfaithful to the Lord by being idolatrous. Third, Israel's leadership is very different now. In place of "Joshua son of Nun, the servant of the LORD" (Judg. 2:8), a succession of leaders delivers Israel from the oppression that results from the people's infidelity. Most of those "judges" (2:18-19) whose stories are told fail to keep

within the boundaries of what is good for those they are
leading. Thus, in various ways and to differing degrees,
they use their position to further their own cause. This
way of behaving is subsequently taken up by ordinary
Israelites, with disastrous effects that are shown in the series
of vignettes depicting Israel functioning in the absence of a
leader.

As a result, the people relate to the Lord on a different
basis. For despite all the violence, idolatry, and poor leadership, piety (or, minimally, its appearance) is never lacking in Judges. Thus in 1:1 the Israelites ask the Lord who
shall be first to do battle with the Canaanites. The last
chapters depict the tribes repeatedly assembling before the
Lord, first at Mizpah and then at Bethel (20:1, 18, 23, 26),
deciding, with increasing shows of piety (vv. 2, 18, 23, 26-
29), what they are to do about the outrage committed by
the Benjaminites of Gibeah. The Lord, having finally
"defeated Benjamin before Israel" (20:35), is then blamed
for putting at risk that tribe's survival (21:15). The author
offers no comment!

In such a mixture of violence, infidelity, and self-seeking,
readers need to be alert to the question of whether statements about the Lord's involvement in a particular event
are to be taken at face value, as was the case in the book
of Joshua, or are ironical. The author's relative lack of
guidance in this matter is sometimes a problem, especially
for first-time readers. Yet the concluding section of the
book, especially from chapter 19 on, recounts unmistakable
examples of the people (or sections of them) blatantly
holding the Lord responsible for their own outrageous
behavior. It seems legitimate, therefore, to interpret earlier
silences in light of this, although one cannot always be certain. The stakes are high, though. Irony that is not recognized
as such will mislead readers into supposing that the text
intends to blame God for what is merely human violence.

Judges contains at least two powerful claims about the cause of such violence. The more obvious and less interesting claim is that Israel invites oppression by infidelity to its covenant God (2:1) but is repeatedly rescued, usually after crying out to the Lord.[5] This is an important confession of belief in God's continuing fidelity to a people that is self-described as unfaithful time after time. The book of Judges routinely reports that the Lord delivered the enemy of the moment into Israel's hands through the agency of the current judge. Mostly, as in Joshua, such statements are to be taken as simply the point that the author wishes to make. The Calebite judge Othniel delivers them from the king of Aram (Judg. 3:10); Ehud rescues them from the Moabites (3:28); Barak, at judge Deborah's command, routs the army of Jabin, king of Hazor (4:15-16, 23); and Jephthah defeats the Ammonites (11:32).

All is not straightforward, however. For example, Judges 20:35 recounts that the Israelite tribe of Benjamin is defeated by the Lord at the hands of Israel. This should give one pause: that *the Lord* should use Israel to inflict defeat on some of their own number? Furthermore, although it is under the influence of the spirit of the Lord that Othniel judges Israel and goes out to war (3:10) and that Gideon plans his battle against Midian (6:34), the first thing that Jephthah does after receiving the Lord's spirit is to make a most scandalous vow so that he can conquer the Ammonites (11:29-31). More problematic still, Samson has the Lord's spirit (13:25), which rushes on him as he tears a lion to pieces with his bare hands (14:6), kills thirty Philistines in Ashkelon (14:19), and escapes from his bonds so he can kill a thousand more (15:14-16). Judges thus seems to suggest that the Lord is responsible for all manner of outrages, carried out by people whose behavior is at least questionable. Readers may want to check for irony and to interpret incidents in light of the low point reached by Israel at the end of the book. For it may be that at least some of these narratives are intended to show people's propensity for blaming others (any others, including the Lord, if necessary) and the price that a society such behavior pays for. Elsewhere in Judges, however, and particularly in the earlier chapters, the point is simply this: the Lord can and will rescue a chastised and repentant Israel from the harm that results from their infidelity to God.

Alongside this conviction is a second claim, which is implied rather than stated: that some of the worst violence arises from the tendency of the judges, particularly the later ones such as Gideon, Jephthah, and Samson, to have difficulty in sustaining the political and/or personal integrity required to lead the Lord's people. The book recounts the stories of individuals who start out as energetically committed to the Lord's service but sooner or later find themselves promoting their own private interests. The effects from one leader to the next are cumulative, and the final three chapters of Judges, where there is no leadership at all, illustrate the disastrous consequences that such a trajectory has for the community.

Therefore it is not by chance that Israel's experiences of violence, idolatry, and increasingly imperfect leadership accompany their transition from being a covenant people led by Joshua and completely committed to the Lord (Josh. 24) to being a leaderless group in which "all the people did what was right in their own eyes" (Judg. 21:25). The consequences were disastrous. Judges is a very strong object lesson in the kinds of behavior to avoid at all costs. It is now time to consider that lesson in more detail.

Violence as All-Pervasive in Judges
Wars Against Outsiders

Sometimes Israelite tribes fight to acquire the land. For

example, whereas Joshua 15 merely listed the allocation of territory to the tribe of Judah, Judges 1 opens with the Israelites asking the Lord, "Who shall go up first for us against the Canaanites, to fight against them?" and then describes how Judah and Simeon went out and fought various Canaanites and Perizzites (1:3-20).[6] Similarly, whereas Joshua 16:1–17:10 specified the boundaries of Joseph's tribal territory (which include Bethel, 16:1-2), Judges 1:22 informs readers that "the house of Joseph also went up against Bethel," which they subsequently put to the sword (v. 25). Thus Judges draws more attention to Israel's belligerence than did the book of Joshua.

For the most part, however, the fighting is instigated and/or led by judges, against peoples to whom the Lord has allowed Israel to become subject. The author tends to assume that readers know what this subjection would have involved on a daily basis and therefore what liberation from it would have felt like. There is a graphic reminder of this in Judges 6, which gives details of Israel's seven-year oppression by the Midianites. During this time, the people were reduced to living in "hiding places in the mountains, caves and strongholds" (6:2). Growing food and keeping livestock was all but impossible for them, because Midianite raiders destroyed everything (vv. 4-6). Readers first come upon Israel's rescuer, Gideon, when he is threshing wheat. Instead of doing this out in the open, where the wind would blow away the chaff and, incidentally, allow him to breathe freely, Gideon is working underground. He has taken the wheat into the wine press "to hide it from the Midianites" (v. 11). These wretched circumstances give a concrete indication of the plight of Israel as a subject people, the kind of situation from which the various judges will deliver them.

Thus Othniel wages war to rescue Israel from the power of Aram-naharaim (3:8-11). Ehud, of the tribe of

Benjamin, assassinates king Eglon of Moab when paying tribute (3:5-25) and goes on to lead an army that subdues Moab. Deborah incites Barak to fight against Jabin, the Canaanite king of Hazor, into whose power Israel has fallen (4:2). Jabin's army commander, Sisera, is killed when Jael, a Kenite woman who has offered him hospitality, drives a tent peg through his head while he sleeps (4:17-22). Gideon counters the Midianite threat (7:1–8:28). Jephthah goes to war against the Ammonites when his attempts at diplomacy fail (11:1-40). To the degree that the character Samson functions as a public figure, he is little more than a device for killing Philistines (chaps. 13–16). In these cases, then, the fighting is presented as a way for Israel to gain freedom from the various forms of oppression that they experience from those to whom they are subservient.

Civil Wars

The fighting in Judges does not exclude war against one's own people. Gideon exacts cruel revenge on the people of Succoth and Penuel. This is because they had insultingly refused to give him food for his exhausted and famished followers when he and his men were pursuing two Midianite leaders (8:4-9, 13-17). Only those who had victory in hand would receive support from Succoth and Penuel, the people of those cities told Gideon. In the next generation, Gideon's son Abimelech is a kind of anti-judge who has a three-year spell as military leader in Israel and king of Shechem (9:6, 22). He owes his position to his mother's people in Shechem, a city he eventually captures from a usurper, presumably with the help of Israelite troops (cf. 9:55).[7] He then destroys all its inhabitants, demolishes the city, and sows it with salt (9:45). Obviously, kinship ties mean nothing to Abimelech when they get in the way of his plans. After the destruction of Shechem, he burns to death the thousand or so citizens who have taken refuge in the crypt of the temple of their god,

El-berith (9:46-49).[8] Abimelech himself dies after capturing a city called Thebez, when a woman drops a millstone on him as he is preparing to set fire to a tower in which people have taken refuge (9:50-55).

Other civil wars follow those of Abimelech. Thus, although Gideon had managed to appease the Ephraimites when they objected bitterly to his not having called on them at the beginning of his successful campaign against the Midianites (8:1-3), Jephthah has no such success when they do the same to him after his victory against the Ammonites. When they threaten to burn his house, he musters the Gileadites, whom the Ephraimites had previously insulted, and leads them to defeat the Ephraimites (12:1-4). "Forty-two thousand"[9] of the Ephraimites fell at that time" (12:6). The book of Joshua contains nothing comparable with this slaughter of one Israelite tribe by another or with the war that the other tribes wage against the Benjaminites in Judges 20. This latter war results in huge losses on both sides, including not only the destruction of the city of Gibeah, the city that had caused the initial problem,[10] but also the devastation of the whole Benjaminite territory and people, except for six hundred men who escape (20:47-48). In the sequel, Israel slaughters most of the inhabitants of Jabesh-gilead, who belonged to the half-tribe of Manasseh (see 21:8-9), and arranges for the men of Benjamin to abduct and force into marriage young girls who dance at the Lord's feast in Shiloh (chap. 21).[11]

All these examples show that there is a horrifying increase in violence against fellow Israelites, as one moves forward in the biblical canon from Joshua to Judges.

Violence Within Israelite Families

The violence in Judges is not restricted to military action and its immediate consequences—it is exercised even against family members, although not until after the time of Gideon. His son Abimelech executes seventy of his own half-brothers to ensure his succession (9:1-6), despite the fact that Gideon had piously repudiated the idea of a dynasty (8:23). Jephthah sacrifices his only child, a daughter, in fulfillment of a vow that he made to the Lord. A comparison of this outcome with the case of Abraham, whose sacrifice of his son Isaac God first commanded and then prevented at the last moment (Gen. 22), strongly suggests that Jephthah's action was not in accord with God's intentions. The Levite in Judges 19 protects himself from his Benjaminite brethren in Gibeah by deliberately handing over his concubine to mass rape (19:25). He then callously expects her to be ready to travel when, on the next day, he finds her lying at the entrance of the house (19:28). The prosaic tone of these accounts makes it all the more horrifying to a reader with any imagination at all. The editor seems to be suggesting that, even within families, violent behavior was so prevalent that it had ceased to shock anyone anymore.

Israel's Idolatry

Judges 2:11–16:31 presents idolatry as the cause of the God-permitted oppression from which the deliverers repeatedly rescue Israel. In chapters 17 and 18 the idolatry functions as an indication of the extent to which Israel has become estranged from the Lord. Let us look in more detail at this trajectory.

Time and again Israel is characterized as idolatrous. Thus 2:10-11 includes the general statement that "another generation grew up . . . who did not know the LORD or the work that he had done for Israel . . . and worshiped the Baals," that is, the gods of Canaan. Israel's tendencies to worship the gods of those among whom they live are restated in 2:12-13, 17, 19, and again in 3:6. After that, specific examples are given, each the cause of oppression by a particular enemy (3:7-8, 12-14), which ends with the appointment of a major judge (3:9, 14). So, in 4:1, "the Israelites again did what was evil in the sight of the LORD" and the resulting judge, Deborah, elaborates on this in her song. "New gods were their choice," she sings (5:8, NAB), thereby explaining why she had to rescue Israel from Canaanite bondage. After her time, they relapse again (6:1, 10), and Gideon is, therefore, enlisted to deliver them from the Midianites. Although he succeeds in this, he goes on to become guilty of idolatry on his own account. For, in an unmistakable echo of the golden calf incident, in which Aaron had asked the Israelites for gold rings (Exod. 32:2), Gideon asks the Israelites for gold rings from the Midianite booty (Judg. 8:24). These he uses to make a golden ephod, a priestly garment before which "all Israel paid idolatrous homage" (NAB) and which "became a snare to Gideon and his family" (8:27).[12] After Gideon's death, "the Israelites relapsed and prostituted themselves with the Baals" (8:33). The infidelity is radical. Forty-five years later, the same thing happens again (10:6). This time there is a wider assortment of gods. No judge is involved here: the people repent when the Lord follows the logic of the situation and suggests that they cry to those gods for help (10:14, 16). Finally, when in 13:1 they once more "did what was evil in the sight of the LORD," there ensues the Philistine oppression to which Samson's birth is a response.

The remaining chapters, from 17 to 21, record a general societal breakdown in which there are no longer any judges, even of Samson's low standard. To begin with, the cause is still idolatry (chaps. 17 and 18). It takes a different form here, however. Instead of being the worship of other gods, it is a recognizable corruption of the worship that Israel offered the Lord and of the kind of life that was required of the Lord's people.

The main protagonist is someone called Micah, who lives in Ephraimite territory and was once cursed by his mother because he stole silver from her. In 17:2, 4 (but not thereafter), the Hebrew text writes out Micah's name in full: Micaihu. This means "who is like YHWH?" and is highly ironic, because Micah sets up for himself a sanctuary to house (among other things) the idol that his mother had made for him from some of the silver. (The idol is "like YHWH"?) That she hopes this act of piety will cause the Lord to bless her son indicates how little she knows about the God she apparently wishes to serve (17:4). Micah continues to exceed his authority by consecrating as priest, first, one of his sons and, later, a young, wandering Levite who agrees to be "a father and a priest" to him (vv. 5, 7-12).[13] In between these two acts of consecration the narrator introduces the observation that in those days there was no king in Israel, and the people did what they thought best (v. 6). The irony of this would not be lost on readers who are shocked by Micah's original theft and even more by the family's assumption that it can domesticate the Lord. Readers should also wonder why the Levite left the land he had been allocated, a persistent theme in this latter part of Judges.[14]

Micah's confident hope that "the LORD will prosper me, because the Levite has become my priest" (17:13) raises the level of his ignorant wrongdoing and sets the stage for his loss of the shrine and his young Levite to some Danites in search of land on which to live (18:22-26).[15] Without so much as mentioning the Lord, they cynically reintroduce the idea of the cult as a communal activity by convincing the Levite that he would prefer to be the priest of a tribe rather than of just one family; the sight of six hundred armed men standing around may have helped him to decide in favor of their proposal (18:15-20). So he goes away with them to be their priest. When Micah pursues them to register his protest, the Danites bully him into returning home, perhaps to life as an ordinary Israelite (18:22-26; cf. 9:25). In this, they arguably carry out the Lord's will. It is obviously otherwise with their brutal destruction of Laish, a non-Israelite city of "quiet and unsuspecting" people, and their setting up of Micah's carved idol in a long-persisting sanctuary in the rebuilt city that they call Dan (18:27, 30). Here, late in the tenth century B.C.E., after the northern part of Solomon's kingdom, Israel, had separated itself from Judah, King Jeroboam I tried to keep Israelites from going to the temple in Jerusalem (and thus from restoring their allegiance to David's line) by setting up one of two golden calves, as objects of pilgrimage. (The other was at Bethel; see 1 Kings 12:26-29.) Thus the city of Dan, like Jeroboam's own city, Shechem, would have been traditionally associated with the height of idolatry in the minds of the post-exilic Judean readers of Judges.

Clearly, Judges presents Israel's idolatry (including the corruption of Yahwistic worship) as a major cause and indication of the gradual breakdown of Israelite society. At least in its early stages, the problem is connected with faulty leadership: charismatic figures such as Deborah and Gideon do not stem the tendency, and the tradition is evidently not known by the likes of Micah, so that his carved idol ends up in Dan, a sanctuary that later Israel will associate with rank apostasy.

Leadership in Israel
Reliance on Human Prudence

Along with Israel's continuous and, in chapters 17–18, pathetically ignorant idolatry is a growing tendency for people to go beyond what the biblical writer thinks is necessary to procure or safeguard the Promised Land. Such people often undertake schemes of their own that are at odds with earlier (or presumed) norms of conduct, even though they not infrequently invoke divine sanction for them. There are many examples of this in Judges. They can be recognized by the negative judgment that readers are implicitly (or sometimes directly) invited to make on those involved. The examples culminate in the final chapters of the book in which near total disaster is enclosed in the repeated observation that, in the absence of a king, "all the people did what was right in their own eyes" (17:6; 21:25). It is evident that the author strongly disapproves of the situation.

Early Examples. In the first instance, at the opening of the book, an inappropriately specific question is followed by what seems like a minor infraction of an oracular command. The people ask, "Who shall go up first for us against the Canaanites?" (Judg. 1:1). They do not ask the prior question of whether an attack should be made at all.[16] The Lord does give them an answer, however, in this instance overlooking their lack of propriety. The reply is that Judah should be the first to attack, and they are assured of success. However, Judah immediately enlists Simeon to go with them (1:2-3) and, although "the LORD was with Judah" (1:19), their success is not total, for they did not occupy the cities on the plain, where the people had iron chariots. It is not clear whether Simeon's presence has anything to do with this.[17] Even so, as Lillian Klein rightly observes, "From the outset, Israel exerts self-determination, evidencing automatic trust in *human* perception."[18] The course of events described in Judges suggests that this is a problem when it comes to occupying the land that the Lord is giving them as gift.

Klein notes that the difference between the Lord's point of view and that of humans is a key concept in Judges. The contrast is well brought out in the sequence from 2:20 to 3:4, on the significance of the nations that remained in Israel's designated territory. The start and finish of the section (2:20-23 and 3:4) show that the only issue that matters is Israel's fidelity to the covenant, so far as the Lord is concerned. Judges 2:22-23 reads: "In order to test Israel, whether or not they would take care to walk in the way of the LORD as their ancestors did, the LORD had left those nations [that remained after the time of Joshua], not driving them out at once, and had not handed them over to Joshua." The three verses that follow, however, suggest that Israel has a very different view of the situation: the tribes remain to provide military experience for those Israelites who lacked it (3:1-3). As Klein phrases it, "Yahweh's testing . . . is understood as combat training" for the latest generation, which has had no experience of war.[19] The discrepancies between the two views, Israel's and God's, suggest that Israel is concerned only with gaining possession of the land, not with keeping the covenant,[20] and this will lead to disaster.

So throughout Judges it is necessary to ask whether, in any given instance, the biblical text presents the behavior in question as being as divinely approved or as falling outside the area of the permissible. Some examples are difficult to evaluate in this respect, particularly two assassinations near the beginning of the book, one by a judge named Ehud (chap. 3) and the other by a woman named Jael (chap. 4). Is there any evidence that the author disapproves of the deceit and trickery that they used, even though there is no outright condemnation of them and their deeds redound to Israel's benefit? In the case of Ehud, the evidence is very slight indeed, but it is somewhat stronger for Jael. This would be in keeping with the gradual increase in the implicit condemnation of violence throughout Judges.

Ehud is the second of the deliverers raised up by the Lord (3:15). He is able to gain the access and positioning that he needs to assassinate Eglon of Moab by falsely claiming that he has a private "message from God" for the king (3:20). Klein has suggested that, although Ehud musters the Israelites by claiming that the Lord has given them power over the Moabites (3:28), nothing in the ensuing account suggests that the victory comes from anything other than their own exertions. She notes that the Lord allows Israel to triumph but does not fight the battle and remains silent.[21] If these observations are pertinent, Ehud's behavior increases slightly the distance between Israel and the Lord, although the conclusion of the story, that "the land had rest eighty years" (3:30), could imply approval of Ehud's crafty deception of the gullible Moabite king.

The second example involves "Jael wife of Heber the Kenite," in the time of the judge Deborah. Jael drives a tent peg through the temple of the Canaanite general Sisera as he sleeps in her tent after having fled there for refuge following his defeat by Israel (4:17-22). One would expect that the death by any means of one of Israel's prominent enemies would have been regarded as entirely positive, and Jael's action (like that of Deborah earlier in the chapter) has the added purpose of shaming Israel's general, Barak, for his lack of trust in the Lord.[22] Yet the description of Sisera's death in 4:18-21 is prefaced by the information in verse 17 that he deliberately sought out Jael's tent because "there was peace between King Jabin of Hazor and the clan of Heber the Kenite." This explains why, in the presumed absence of Heber himself, Sisera made for Jael's tent. On the other hand, it draws attention to Jael's action as a flagrant breach of the canons of hospitality, on which Sisera ought to have been able to rely. Yet, as with Ehud's assassination of Eglon, Jael's action has a positive outcome, in this case forty years of rest for the land (5:31). Furthermore, according to the word of Deborah, the Lord was somehow behind Jael's action (4:9), and Jael herself is celebrated at length as a hero in Judges 5:24-27. So perhaps the stories of these two assassinations simply demonstrate that the weak must use cunning to defeat more powerful enemies. Not exactly a peaceable message!

Gideon. It is much easier to see the extent to which the next judge, Gideon, is directed at the outset by the Lord but later on by human concerns that are questionable. Although he is slow and in need of great reassurance when God calls him to lead Israel (6:11-40), Gideon's initial conducting of the campaign against Midian is exemplary. Patiently he goes through all the stages by which the Lord reduces to three hundred men the much larger army that Gideon has just assembled (6:34; 7:1-8).[23] Then, after yet more reassurance that he has asked for, Gideon allows the Lord to deal with the enemy while he and his three companies stand in place and put on a "'sound and light' show" that confuses the enemy so that they first fight among themselves and then flee, without anyone in Gideon's army having to fight at all (7:1-22).[24] The implication is that trusting in God and leaving the belligerent to deal with each other can sometimes be effective, although the cost to one's nerves is presumably high.

The writer of Judges thinks that the campaign should have ended at that point, for Gideon's subsequent conduct goes contrary to the instructions that God had earlier given him: to work with minimal recruits. Abandoning the strategy that had just gained him victory, Gideon again swells his ranks. In the account of the rigorous cleanup operation that follows, the Lord's name appears only twice, each time in Gideon's mouth as he threatens vengeance, first to those in Succoth, who have refused to help his followers in their extreme need, and then to the two Midianite princes whom he has eventually captured (8:4-7, 19). His brutality to Succoth and to Penuel, a second city that would not help (vv. 13-17), shows the coarsening of his character now that he has ceased to follow the Lord's instructions and is engaging in violence for his own ends.

The judge's conduct deteriorates further. In his execution of the two princes of Midian, Gideon is presented as indulging in a personal vendetta: he swears "as the LORD lives" that he would have spared them if they had not admitted to killing his relations at Tabor (8:18-19). The implication is that murdering Gideon's own family is more heinous than killing anyone else. As a final insult and offense he tells his firstborn son, who is "still a boy," to kill them (v. 20). The boy is afraid to do so, and Gideon himself dispatches them. Gideon's vindictiveness is a far cry from his earlier obedient and pious behavior, although he seems to revert to that in his subsequent refusal of the Israelites' request to found a dynasty, on the grounds that "the LORD will rule over you" (8:22-23).[25] Unfortunately, he then goes on to ask them for gold from the booty, with results that we saw earlier. Thus, although the Lord allows Gideon to overcome the Midianites and give Israel the customary forty years of peace (8:28), overall his tenure has increased further the distance between himself and the Lord. His hubris and lack of trust prevented him from recognizing the boundaries of suitable activity before he transgressed them. Because Gideon is presented as Israel's current leader, as was Joshua, the effects of his actions are wider than the merely personal. Gideon's initial obedience and piety are exemplary for Israel; his later conduct is not.

Abimelech. As noted above, Gideon's son Abimelech engages in a completely ruthless following of his own interests, regardless of the effect of that on anyone else (Judg. 9). His appointment as king of Shechem and as military chief of Israel (vv. 1-6, 22) apparently owes nothing to the Lord, who is not even named in this chapter. Whether deliberately or not, the sacred name YHWH (LORD) revealed to Moses in Exodus 3:14 is not used in connection with Abimelech, and although "God" is referred to a handful of times, only once does this occur in a situation that is not entirely negative: the speaker is Jotham, the one son of Gideon who escaped Abimelech's slaughter of his brothers. Jotham warns the Shechemites, who have just anointed Abimelech as their king, to listen to his parable if they wish God to listen to them (Judg. 9:7). Apart from this, and following the note that "Abimelech ruled over Israel three years" (9:22),[26] God's only alleged activity is to "put bad feelings between Abimelech and the citizens of Shechem" (v. 23, NAB). As a result, Abimelech's seventy-fold fratricide is avenged, as is the Shechemites' wickedness for having made such a lawless individual their king (vv. 24, 56, 57).[27] It is the perfect working out of the wry statement of the Canaanite king, Adoni-bezek: "As I have done, so has God paid me back" (1:7). In none of these instances, of course, did God have to "do" anything.[28] Human dynamics were quite sufficient, right down to the woman who crushes Abimelech's skull by dropping a millstone on his head, thereby causing her victim to request his armor bearer to kill him with a sword (9:52-55). His one concern at this point is to avoid being remembered as one who was killed by a woman: his reputation is at stake! That Abimelech's vicious behavior provokes enmity between him and everyone else and produces only destruction, including his own, is surely a strong recommendation not to do likewise, as is the book of Judges as a whole.

Jephthah. Israel's next deliverer is the Gileadite, Jephthah. His appointment as military leader by the elders of his tribe is presented as a purely secular, pragmatic affair, in which the elders, in desperate need, come begging for the help of a half-brother whom they have earlier driven out of the family and disinherited (10:18–11:11). Nobody mentions the Lord until Jephthah himself does so in 11:9;[29] then the elders cite the Lord as witness to their agreement (v. 10). Even so, like Gideon, he begins well, for he acknowledges that any victory he may win over the Ammonites will be the Lord's doing (11:9), goes to Mizpah to inform the Lord about the agreement he has made with the elders (11:11), and attempts to appease the enemy by sustained diplomacy in which he rehearses parts of Israel's history (11:12-28).[30] Yet the vow that leads to the sacrificial death of Jephthah's only child indicates a lack of trust in the Lord and a profound misunderstanding of Israel's God, despite Jephthah's prior reception of the Lord's spirit (11:29) and the stress on the importance of his daughter to him: "She was his only child; he had no son or daughter except her" (11:34).[31] That Jephthah is not in harmony with the Lord is reinforced by his immediate (and, for readers, heavily ironic) reaction when, seeing the child as she dances out to meet him, he realizes the situation: "Alas, my daughter! You have brought me very low; you have become the cause of great trouble to me" (11:35). It was *she* who caused trouble for *him*? Jephthah's skewed perspective on the situation is made even more apparent by the fact that all of her concern is for him: he must keep his vow to the Lord, she says (v. 36).[32] Even if he does not trust God, she evidently does. On this occasion, there is no angelic message to stay the father's hand, no ram that Jephthah can substitute for his daughter—this is not a replay of Abraham and Isaac in Genesis 22. Should Jephthah not have known that killing one's child is not what the Lord requires? Had his grief and sense of guilt for his rash vow made him unheeding, not only of his daughter but of the Lord as well? In any case, he kills her in an act of tragically misconstrued piety.

Jephthah's downward spiral continues in the ensuing episode, the final one of his tenure (12:1-6). He begins by falling short of what Gideon achieved, when he fails to appease the Ephraimites, who are threatening to burn down his house because he excluded them from the previous action. Not only does Jephthah fail (again) as a diplomat, he also suggests that in his pursuit of the Ammonites he may still have been relying on his own resources rather than trusting in the Lord. He tells the Ephraimites: "My people and I were engaged in conflict with the Ammonites who oppressed us severely. But when I called you, you did not deliver me from their hand. When I saw that you would not deliver me, I took my life in my hand" (12:1-3). Admittedly, he does then allow that "the LORD gave them into [his] hand" (v. 3), and it is hard to see what he could have told the Ephraimites, who were obviously spoiling for a fight. They got one, and their lost control of the fords at the Jordan River cost them forty-two companies (v. 6). Even so, rather than presenting Jephthah's successful war against Ephraim as a fair retribution for the latter's unreasonable bellicosity, the Hebrew text of Judges 12:1-4 describes it as Jephthah's taking advantage of the situation to avenge his clan, Gilead, against Ephraimite taunts about Gilead's rights to territory claimed by the Joseph tribes, Ephraim and Manasseh (12:4-6). In other words, this part of Judges makes Jephthah's attack seem like a settling of personal scores rather than a response to a threat on his life (v. 1).[33]

Like Gideon, Jephthah is described as having allowed his own agenda to take precedence over Israel's welfare. Furthermore, although he has decisively defeated the Ammonites (11:33), he has also been responsible for killing forty-two companies of Ephraimites, Israelites like himself, allegedly to avenge clan honor. His overall evaluation is implicitly negative too: he judged Israel for but six years. (Abimelech's tenure was only three, but he did not judge Israel at all.) Further, Jephthah is the first of the major judges who is not said to have given the land "rest." His predecessors Othniel, Deborah, and Gideon each gave forty years of it (3:11; 5:31; 8:28) and Ehud, eighty (3:30).

Thus, despite Jephthah's initial good intentions and military victories, Israel is in worse shape, not better, at the time of his death than it was at his accession. His story demonstrates that being a capable fighter is no substitute for trusting in the Lord and being an effective diplomat.

Samson. The career of Samson, described in Judges 13–16, pushes Israel's decline to the limits compatible with its having any leadership at all. The extent of the disaster to come is not evident to begin with, for the events surrounding Samson's birth are not at all ominous, on the face of it. Samson is the son of an Israelite married couple who were previously barren. Admittedly, his father, Manoah, is ignorant of Israel's traditions and distinctly slow on the uptake: one can see why the Lord chose to deal with his unnamed wife![34] The angel announces that Samson is to be dedicated to God as a nazirite "from birth" (13:5). The child receives the best prenatal care available (13:4, 7, 13-14), is blessed by the Lord after his birth (v. 24), and then stirred by the Lord's spirit (v. 25). No other judge is introduced with such care. Aside from Othniel[35] and perhaps the left-handed Ehud,[36] each of the other judges starts out with a handicap that seems far more pronounced than that of having a father who is not very intelligent. For Deborah is a woman, and the man she enlists to lead her campaign refuses to go unless she accompanies him (4:8); Gideon admits to being the most insignificant Israelite of his day and is timid; Abimelech is the son of a non-Israelite concubine; and Jephthah is a prostitute's son who was driven out by his half-brothers.

Yet Samson's birth represents anything but an upturn in Israel's fortunes. Rather, despite all these initial advantages, he will be worse than any of his predecessors, except for the anti-judge, Abimelech. For even though Samson's activities may sometimes benefit Israel by reducing the pressure from the Philistines, he is completely controlled by his desire for a series of variously unsuitable women who, directly or indirectly through associates, determine the events of his life that are chronicled.[37] Readers find that, before they come to the attempted theological explanation of what happens (that God was "seeking a pretext to act against the Philistines," 14:4), they have already been shocked by the way Samson speaks to his parents in 14:1-3. By this stage, they may well be wondering why the Lord would supply Samson with the strength enough to tear a lion into pieces as though it were a kid (14:6). Samson's subsequent behavior makes the question more pressing. For Samson did not tell Manoah and his wife where he got the honey that he gave them and had eaten himself (14:9). This suggests that he might expect them to regard as ritually unclean that food which he found inside a lion's carcass, even if he himself, the one specially consecrated to the Lord, had no qualms about eating it—or about touching dead bodies (the lion or the fresh jawbone of the donkey, 15:15) or hiring a prostitute (16:1). Considering what Samson does with God's spirit, the Lord's fidelity to him is amazing.

In brief, no feature of Samson suggests anything other than a concern for satisfying his own desires. He is as graceless in his interactions with the Lord as he was with his parents. Thus in 15:18 he acknowledges that the Lord has given him victory over the Philistines, but uses that as a lever to demand that he be given water to slake his thirst (vv. 18-19).[38] God complies, as his parents had done, but the reader is once more made to feel the inappropriateness of Samson's attitude and behavior. Thereafter he mentions God only twice more, once in explaining to Delilah about his dedication to God as a nazirite (16:17) and finally, after "the Lord had left him" (v. 20), in 16:28: "Lord God, remember me and strengthen me only this once, O God, so that with this one act of revenge I may pay back the Philistines for my two eyes." Like Gideon and Jephthah, Samson finally wants personal vengeance. This is understandable: Delilah's betrayal has left him a blind and helpless prisoner of the Philistines. Yet the narrator leaves little doubt of the connection between this fate and Samson's foolish propensity for women who belonged to or were in the pay of the Philistines, Israel's current enemy. The last of the judges has evidently squandered the opportunities that were available to him.

Nevertheless, even this highly imperfect instrument of the Lord was able to "begin the deliverance of Israel from the hand of the Philistines" (13:5), inasmuch as he killed several thousand of them—three thousand or so men and women at his death and some smaller number than that during his lifetime (16:27, 30). Even so, his reported achievements are not very great: at his death, Israel is still under Philistine power, as it had been before his birth. Samson is like Jephthah in not being credited with having given the land "rest." Indeed there were times when Samson's "deliverance" made things worse rather than better for Israel: the Judahites preferred to turn him over to the Philistines rather than get further embroiled in the vendetta resulting from Samson's marriage to a Philistine woman (15:9-13). The twenty years in which Samson "judged" Israel must have seemed like a very long time (15:20; 16:31), and there is no reason for thinking that anyone would regret that he had no immediate successor. The office is in utter disrepute. Increasingly, the leadership of charismatic judges is experienced as ineffectual, and the people suffer sorely from the situation. Yet Israel will fare no better without judges.

Life Without Judges: Judges 17–21

As we saw earlier while discussing Israel's idolatry, the culminating disaster begins in Judges 17–18 with the account of Micah. His presumptuous idolatry, made possible by his equally ignorant and well-meaning mother, ended with his spoliation by Danites who are in search of land (itself a problematic notion, because land was understood as a gift from the Lord) and who then establish a shrine in a city built on the ruins of the one they have destroyed.

The final episode of the book, its climax, begins with a Levite's concubine[39] being angry with her husband and returning to her family home (19:1-2).[40] It continues with all manner of inconsideration, abuse of hospitality, brutality, appearance of piety, and escalating violence, and concludes with the socially sanctioned abduction and rape of the Shilonite virgins by the survivors of the newly reinstated tribe of Benjamin, all of their women having been killed.

There is nothing about idolatry in this section, for by this time Israel's connection to the Lord has become totally perverted, and these final stories convey the consequences of that in Israel's life. In fact, there is no mention of "LORD" or "God" in Judges 19, the story of the nameless Levite and his eventually dismembered concubine. In chapter 20, the assembly at Mizpah has the form of an authentic formal gathering of the tribes before the Lord. What occurs there, however, is no honoring of the Lord but merely a human investigation, in which the Levite gives a somewhat tendentious account of the wrongs he has suffered, and those assembled accept without question his version of the events and immediately opt for war.[41] It later transpires that before concluding the session, they also made two very rash oaths that committed them to denying the tribe of Benjamin any posterity and to killing all fellow Israelites who refused to go along with their plan to avenge the Levite (21:1, 5). Of course, one could argue that this total mobilization is a noble action to register protest at the death of the woman, but that is not how it is presented.

When the other Benjaminites (equally stubbornly) stand by the men of Gibeah, the rest of Israel holds another assembly, this time at Bethel. Here they ask God who should go first in attacking Benjamin (20:18). This is the same question they asked (of "the LORD") in 1:1, except that the adversaries here are fellow Israelites and the issue is no longer Israel's acquisition of land. As in 1:1, the question in 20:18 is premature:[42] it should have been preceded by an inquiry about whether they should attack at all, but the assembly had already made that decision without consulting the Lord. So, given that there is no divine assurance of success (unlike in 1:2) and it is not even clear that they heeded the Lord's answer that Judah should go first (20:18),[43] it is not surprising that they are defeated when they launch the attack (20:18-21). They then "wept before the LORD until the evening" and, showing perhaps a greater awareness of what is at stake, they now enquire about attacking "my brother Benjamin" (20:23, NAB). Yet the reader is surely entitled to ask questions about the tone of the positive reply that they receive from the Lord, since the query in this form is even more tragic and the Israelites are again defeated. Finally they include in their question the possibility that they should not go up against "our kinsfolk the Benjaminites" (20:28), and this time the Lord assures them of victory. Even so, readers should note that the statement that "the LORD defeated Benjamin before Israel" (v. 35), which should have been the end of the affair, is followed by an account of the complete ruination of the city by those who had been in ambush, the pursuit of the fleeing Benjaminites, and the systematic destruction of all that had belonged to the renegades, including every woman (20:36-48; 21:16). Thus the author subtly suggests that the pattern is the same as with Gideon and Jephthah: Israel is used to punish the enemy (in this case, Benjamin, which is clearly at fault) but then goes on to commit outrage on its own initiative. Israel as a whole has become like these later judges, which is hardly a commendation from this biblical author.

The Israelites then seem to realize where their conduct has led them. With tragic irony, they spend a day "before God," lamenting, "O LORD, the God of Israel, why has it come to pass that today there should be one tribe lacking in Israel?" (21:2-3). The answer, given in the previous two verses, is that they had slain all the Benjaminite women and at Mizpah had vowed to refuse their women as wives for the six hundred Benjaminite men who escaped the slaughter (21:1). There is no indication that these actions were divinely sanctioned. So the plight of Benjamin has nothing at all to do with the Lord, except that Israel's oath was "by the LORD" (v. 7), which compounds the offense rather than reducing it.

The next step lacks even any affectation of piety. Following the course that it set for itself at Mizpah, Israel simply takes advantage of another oath sworn at that assembly. This conveniently allows them to send a punitive force to Jabesh-gilead, which, for no specified reason, had not taken part in the campaign against Benjamin.[44] There they massacre all the inhabitants except the virgins, who can be given to four hundred of the Benjaminites as part of a kind of reconciliation process in which Israel offers them "peace" (21:13). However, because even then two hundred of the Benjaminites still lack wives, "the people had compassion on Benjamin because the LORD had made a breach in the tribes of Israel" (21:15; it is unclear whether the blame is put on the Lord by the Israelites or by the narrator). So, in one final act of insensitivity to all concerned (including the Lord, whose feast they will desecrate), they come up with a plan by which each Benjaminite will wait in hiding and carry off as a wife one of the girls who dance at "the yearly festival of the LORD" at Shiloh (21:19). The men of the other tribes are confident that they can placate the women's fathers and brothers, if necessary (21:19-22). No problem at all.

What should they have done? The narrator gives no indication. What is clear, though, is that this sequence of events, from the rape of one woman in Gibeah to that of many in Shiloh, is presented as a steep downward spiral into lawlessness, even though the appearance of societal organization may have been maintained by those who seem convinced that they have solved the problem resulting from the Levite's complaint about the injustice done to him by the Benjaminites.

Conclusion

The book of Judges opens with a reminder that Joshua has died. Readers will presume that, even in his absence, the people have retained the unity that was apparent in the covenant renewal ceremony described in Joshua 24. As one defective judge follows another, however, the situation changes. Although most of the judges provided a period of relief from external enemies, the people's progressive degeneration is the dominant theme of Judges. In the end, there is no king (or any other kind of leader), and "all the people did what was right in their own eyes" (17:6; 21:25). This phrase marks off the events of the book's last five chapters, the contents of which form a commentary on it. In this final state, individual Israelites and groups of them engage in a series of ad hoc measures that parody the earlier functioning of their society. Thus Micah knows something about shrines, ephods, and priests, and the Danites know they need land, but neither party honors Israel's traditional understanding that these are not matters to be decided by private enterprise. More pointedly, the unnamed Levite in Judges 19 knows that the men of Gibeah have committed an outrage that concerns the whole of Israel, but his brutal way of notifying them of the event and the self-serving account of it that he gives to the assembly at Mizpah clearly set the stage for the overreacting that ensues: the defeat of Benjaminites (20:36, 45-46) is followed by the destruction not only of Gibeah but also "the remaining towns" (v. 48). Only six hundred men of Benjamin manage to escape the rout (v. 47).

This story of the Levite and his concubine demonstrates that the now-leaderless Israel is open to being manipulated by an individual with something of a case, an economical use of the truth, and a flair for the theatrical (20:4-7). The Israelites go on to extend the corruption of their societal conventions by means of the oaths they make with regard to Benjamin and Jabesh-gilead and the expedients that they adopt to obviate the consequences of their own rashness. By the end, their assemblies are a mockery. Admittedly, they provide a forum for making decisions that keep Israel's social structures formally intact: Benjamin will not perish as a tribe. But the cost of this is violence that is implicitly given divine sanction. Having lamented their plight before the Lord, the next day the people offer sacrifices prior to making their decision about how to avoid Benjamin's extinction (21:3-4). Here the narrator tells stories in which fellow Israelites are treated as mere instruments, to be disposed of at the will of those with the power to decide for them. Thus the men, married women, and children of Jabesh-gilead can be killed so that the virgins are available to be given as wives to the men of Benjamin, who still show no signs of being disturbed by what was done in Gibeah. The narrator is appalled and presumably expects readers to react similarly.

In these final chapters, Israel is in possession of its land and with unity of a sort: the non-Benjaminite tribes came together to fight and to arrange for Benjamin's reinstatement (20:1; 21:15-23). There is, moreover, no evidence that Israel is being attacked by an external enemy (there were Philistines who survived the death of Samson in 16:30, but the remaining chapters of Judges are silent about them). Nevertheless, life is not good. The habit of slaughter has made things worse rather than solving anything. In other words, even after the Israelites' dispersal to their own allotments of land, they cannot live securely because, as the concluding comment of the book says, "all the people did what was right in their own eyes" (21:25). This is not a positive assessment, as the events of chapters 17–21 have graphically shown. So the violence that characterizes almost the whole of Judges finally settles among the Israelites themselves, where no one can endure it. Whether or not the author's intention is to make a case for the monarchy as a preferable system of rule or merely to demonstrate the endless possibilities of corruption to which leaders are subject, the stories told here add up to a powerful cautionary tale about the dangers to society of allowing violence to escalate.

Clearly, the book of Judges is not a pacifist manifesto: its author takes for granted that the Lord wishes Israel to take possession of the land by displacing others and that these others are best killed, so that they do not lead Israel astray. Israel's possession of the territory then typically incites the enmity of surrounding peoples, with whom Israel has to deal. Thus killing enemies is not a problem for this ancient writer. Any case to be made for that view is not to be found in Judges.

As with the book of Joshua, the ideal in Judges is that the Lord, acting through human agency, does what is necessary for Israel to possess the land and to defend it against enemies. Judges, like Joshua, presents as minimal the violence actually required for gaining and holding territory; the rest of it comes from disordered human conduct. The narrative demonstrates that, although people who can inspire others to fight are relatively abundant,[45] it is extraordinarily difficult to find leaders whose selfless fidelity to the Lord and to Israel's total well-being is so great that they are not eventually deflected by personal considerations that lead to disaster. So Israel experiences unnecessary violence, military defeat, and the brutalizing that leads to a loss of understanding of how to live as the Lord's people. Avoiding such dangers requires a high degree of sensitivity to the Lord on the part of Israel's leaders. Joshua was able to attain the necessary standard. For the most part, his successors did not, for reasons that included a tendency to overreact (Gideon), lack of trust in the Lord (Jephthah), lust (Samson), and opportunism (all three men).

So Judges warns readers about the importance of strong and effective leadership, a position with perennial appeal for those with much invested in the status quo and for those who would overthrow it. Readers are also reminded about the need for vigilance on the part of any who seek to carry out the Lord's will in complex situations. The cost of failure is high.

9

ISAIAH 1–39:
CIVILIZATION IS NOT ENOUGH

Introduction

Although there is, at first sight, quite a leap from the end of Judges to the opening of book of the prophet Isaiah, the canonical connection is quite close. The author of Judges implies that Israel's lack of a king (17:6; 18:1; 21:25) is the cause of its societal breakdown that occurred when "all the people did what was right in their own eyes" (17:6; 21:25). In the Christian canon, which adopts the Greek tradition rather than the Hebrew, Judges is followed by the book of Ruth. Set "in the days when the judges ruled" (Ruth 1:1), near its end,[1] this book tells of a young widow from Moab whose strong commitment to her Israelite mother-in-law, Naomi, brings her to the land of Israel, to Bethlehem, which Naomi's family had earlier left during a famine. Whereas in Moab Naomi's husband and sons had died and their Moabite wives were childless,[2] back in Bethlehem the family thrives once more.[3] Thus Ruth marries an Israelite named Boaz. Their union soon produces a child, Obed, the grandfather of David, whom the tradition presents as one of Israel's greatest kings and as the founder of a dynasty that lasted from the late eleventh century until the sixth.

In perhaps the most astute of his actions, David

conquered Jerusalem, the Jebusite city on the hill of Ophel, and made it the capital of his two-part kingdom, which consisted of Judah in the south and Israel in the north. There his son Solomon built the temple. Even when the northern kingdom seceded shortly after Solomon's death, David's descendants continued to rule Judah from Jerusalem until the Babylonian exile that began in 586 B.C.E. It is in the city founded by David that the eighth-century prophet Isaiah of Jerusalem, about 250 years before the exile, takes a hard look at the current situation of "Judah and Jerusalem" (Isa. 1:1) during a turbulent period of their history, when the rise of Assyria is causing discord in the region.

The book of the prophet Isaiah therefore connects with the book of Judges because, taking up Israel's story in Jerusalem during the time of the Davidic monarchy, it makes very clear that, whatever the final editor of Judges had thought, merely having a king is no solution for Israel's ills. The resulting prosperity enabled some to live in great luxury, but they did so in the presence of and at the expense of many more who had practically nothing. Whereas in Judges the problem was one of *general* lawlessness (and indeed Isaiah's message also was available to all Israelites), the prophet's words were aimed particularly at the affluent, whose complacency he needed to disturb. They were the ones now doing "what was right in their own eyes." For themselves and for the kingdom as a whole, the consequences of such behavior were little better than they had been in the time of the judges, despite the greater complexity of society that the monarchy made possible.

Isaiah 1–39 is significant for our present project because it frequently uses vivid imagery to express people's deepest hopes for peace in complex and fraught situations that appear to offer no prospects for it. The prophet further insists that concern for the weak and powerless is an essential condition for the establishment of that peace, which nevertheless transcends anything that humans could achieve on their own.

Modern readers might be tempted to dismiss these oracles as the wishful thinking of a dreamer quite out of touch with political and economic reality; it is likely that many of Isaiah's own contemporaries thought that way too. Yet not all of them did. Several generations of the prophet's disciples collected, augmented, and transmitted his words. Sometimes a reminder of the wider context of our actions is needed to liberate us from the snares in which we have entangled ourselves. Isaiah provides such a reminder, as he writes of Jerusalem and Judah not merely as the locations in which the Lord's people live, but as components and symbols of a much larger project that will (he is convinced) have a positive outcome. Within that project, human actions are vitally important, for good or ill, but are not the determining factor in the end. This leaves his readers with responsibility for living in fidelity to the Lord and to one another, yet without the need to take extreme measures that they may deem expedient but which are not consistent with their integrity as God's people. In the end, God is in charge.

The four sections of this chapter correspond to major divisions within the text of Isaiah 1–39: chapters 1–12; 13–23; 24–27; and 28–39.

Isaiah Chapters 1–12: Civilization Needs Tradition

For this prophet, the focus of the divine activity is to be "the mountain of the LORD's house," symbolically recognized as "the highest of the mountains" to which "all the nations shall stream" in a future event to which Isaiah looks forward (Isa. 2:2). The inhabitants of "Judah and Jerusalem" (2:1) are, therefore, living in a place that will turn out to be theologically significant: a place to which the nations will be drawn by their thirst for the Lord's instruction that will enable them to live aright: "that he may teach us his ways and that we may walk in his paths" (v. 3). Not all ways of living can lead to such an outcome, however: hence Isaiah's expectation that the Lord "shall judge between the nations, and shall arbitrate for many peoples" (2:4).

In those "days to come" (2:2), the world will be very different. In particular, there will be no need to waste resources on war, so metals can be used to make implements such as plowshares and pruning hooks, for use in promoting human welfare rather than the destruction of enemies. Nations can hope to live peaceably together, and young men can spend their time on something more profitable than training for war. In a later chapter, the prophet specifies that the dominion of the child "born for us . . . shall grow continually, and there shall be endless peace" (9:6-7). Isaiah earnestly hopes that the latest royal child will become a good and effective king, a worthy successor to the long-lived and very successful Uzziah, who had died in the year that Isaiah began his prophetic ministry (6:1).[4] Not only in the city but also in the natural world, and among animals in particular, Isaiah prophesies a kind of harmony that goes against all present experience (11:6-9).[5]

The Judah of Isaiah's day is nothing like this. Not peace, but wickedness, corruption, and apostasy characterize society (1:4). As Isaiah presents it, the underlying problem is that the people's own achievements have led them to reject the Lord's claim over them. The Lord laments, "I reared children and brought them up, but they have rebelled against me" (v. 2).

There are strong suggestions that, despite the long-term centrality of Jerusalem in the prophet's thought, urban civilization is a significant component of the present problem. The tradition that locates the origin of cities and culture in the figure of Cain is consistent with Isaiah's position, although he nowhere refers to it.[6] Jerusalem is a major locus of the prophet's experience. His activity takes place in that city and he has access to the royal house (Isa. 6:1-10).[7] Yet he is not impressed by what he sees. He addresses the inhabitants of Jerusalem ("daughter Zion," 1:8) as "rulers of Sodom . . . people of Gomorrah" (1:10), and announces the Lord's judgment against Jerusalem and Judah (3:1). The highly elaborate worship in the temple does not please God—at least when it is combined with "iniquity" (1:13), specified as the denial of justice to those wronged, particularly the orphans and widows, whose rights are most easily violated (1:17). It seems that life itself is not secure: "murderers" inhabit the city (v. 21). The goods of civilization are not what they ought to be— the silver is dross, for example, and the wine watered down (22). Nor can the community's leaders be trusted to work for the good of the whole. On the contrary, Isaiah charges, they are "companions of thieves" and on the lookout for bribes (23). So those who ought to be able to rely on their protection cannot do so. Having "a king in Israel" was clearly no panacea. According to Isaiah, God's solution to all of this is to be a purification that restores to the city justice and therefore fidelity, "as at the first . . . as at the beginning" (vv. 25-26).

There are other indications that the city's present complexity is problematic and about to be undone. Prosperity can be a snare. Thus Isaiah 2 connects material wealth (silver, gold, horses, chariots, 2:7) with the worship of idols. The people are so dazzled by human accomplishments that they have replaced God with the products of their own skills. In 2:11-17 the prophet inveighs against the hubris that accompanies culture in general, and predicts a return to dwelling in caves and crevices in rocks: the antithesis of civilization. Chapter 3 returns to a consideration of how God will deal with Israel's particular version of this sin of societal corruption. Because the "elders and princes" have been "crushing my people" (3:15) by enriching themselves at the expense of the poor (v. 14), the Lord will make ineffectual all the different kinds of respected citizens (2-7). Nor are men alone at fault here, for in the remainder of the chapter and in 4:1, the prophet graphically castigates the haughty and rich "daughters of Zion," who are about to lose their abundance of feminine finery and their social position. Once more, the purification that will ensue is presented in terms of Israel's origins:

> Then the LORD will create over the whole site of Mount Zion and over its places of assembly a cloud by day and smoke and the shining of a flaming fire by night (Isa. 4:5).

The cloud and fire are allusions to the manner of the Lord's presence to the community in Israel's formative period, beginning with the time that they approached the Red Sea and continuing as they moved through the desert toward the Promised Land (Exod. 13:21; 40:38). Isaiah regards subsequent development as a falling away from this early relationship to the Lord: the present situation must be radically reevaluated in light of the earlier experience.

Recalling Israel to its origins and its essential nature, of which it has lost sight, is also the purpose of the following chapter. Here in Isaiah 5:1-7, the carefully tended vineyard turns out to be God's planting, "the house of Israel, and the people of Judah" (v. 7). This is a startling image, given that the Judah and Jerusalem of Isaiah's day was a highly differentiated complex, with military capabilities (2:7; 3:2-3) and with social stratification that enabled the high-living leaders to get away with oppressing the weak. Yet the prophet's point is that civilization does not change either

Israel's basic reality as God's planting or the resulting requirement to yield suitable fruit. Currently, it yields only "wild grapes" (5:2): not right judgment (*mišpāṭ*) but bloodshed, (*mispāḥ*) and a cry (*ṣᵉdāqāh*) instead of justice (*ṣᵉdāqāh*, v. 7). As Isaiah said earlier, the leaders "have devoured the vineyard" of which they and the others are a part (3:14).

From Isaiah 5:8, the prophet expresses the same ideas in other terms. He condemns those "who join house to house, who add field to field" (v. 8). Also censured are people whose primary occupation is the carousing that is taken for granted by the leisured classes of a developed society (vv. 11-12, 21-22). Such a way of life, he suggests, is associated with a total lack of concern for what is right (20-21, 23); he will further condemn these actions in 10:1-4. The threatened consequences of such behavior are dire, for this is God's world. The land will revert to unproductive wilderness (5:9-10, 17) and people will suffer for having offended the Lord. Several images of this are used: they will face exile "because they do not understand" (5:13, NAB), descend to Sheol in large numbers (v. 14), be destroyed by fire (vv. 24-25), or be invaded by a foreign army that the Lord is pictured as having invited in (vv. 26-30).[8]

Because the people do not heed his message from God (6:8-10), a similar threat of exile and the desolation of cities (vv. 11-12) follows the account of how Isaiah came to be a prophet (1-10). Chapter 7 likewise speaks of disaster at the hands of Judah's enemies (vv. 17-20). Yet there will be an awareness of the Lord's presence with them. For the child who functions as a sign for Ahaz will be called "Immanuel" (v. 14). People will then be aware that "God is with us," even though the "curds and honey" of verse 15 suggest conditions of rustic simplicity. In other words, Isaiah is confident that Judah will have an effective leader in their time of political danger. In a similar vein, even though the land will once more bear thorns and briers, people will still live adequately on it, but in a fashion quite different from the luxury that the leaders enjoy in the city of the prophet's day (7:21-25).

Eventually, there will be a restoration, despite the difficulty of the process (6:13). This is because Assyria, the dominant power of the day, will eventually overreach itself, not realizing that it is merely a tool in God's hand (10:5-19). As we might express it: violence sometimes contains the seeds of its own undoing. Then a chastened Israel, a mere remnant, "will lean on the LORD" and therefore return (or repent,[9] 10:20-21). The Davidic child will be established in power (9:1-6): "A shoot . . . from the stump of Jesse" (11:1-9).[10] This act of God will affect all nations and the whole of creation (2:2-4; 11:1-9). It will be located on Mount Zion, "the mountain of the LORD's house" (2:2) and God's holy mountain (11:9). At that time it will be appropriate for "royal Zion" to rejoice (12:6). One imagines, however, that the prophet envisaged it as a very different city from the Jerusalem that he had been confronting in these oracles. The difference will be in the integration of human achievement with people's proper relationship to God. So it is not exactly a matter of returning to the idealized beginning, but of expressing the developed reality in its uncorrupted form.[11] This is, of course, Isaiah's version of the perennial question of how faith and culture are to relate to each other.

Isaiah 13–23: Not Only Jerusalem

Although in this collection of oracles the perspective is broadened to include all the major cities and powers of the prophet's time, the message is essentially the same. One way or another, the arrogance that accompanies human achievement will be brought down, and cities, the sites of such power, will become desolate. A summary of this is put in God's mouth in 13:11-12: on the day of the Lord,

> I will put an end to the pride of the arrogant,
>   and lay low the insolence of tyrants.
> I will make mortals more rare than fine gold,
>   and humans than the gold of Ophir.

Isaiah then makes the rounds of the relevant cities and civilizations. Thus, for Babylon,[12] the Medes are to be the instrument of the Lord's judgment (13:17), and the city will be inhabited only by various kinds of wild beasts (13:19-22; 14:23). The Lord will afflict Philistia with famine (14:30). The cause of Moab's downfall was pride (16:6) and its future rests with "a remnant, very small and weak" (16:14, NAB). Damascus will become a ruin (17:1) and its allies, including Ephraim (i.e., Israel, the northern kingdom) will become feeble. The cure would be to trust in the Lord, not in "the work of their hands" (17:8), and to cease despoiling Judah (17:14).

All the frenetic activity of Ethiopia (18:1-2) does not impress the Lord, who "will quietly look on" (v. 4, NAB) and await the gifts that they will eventually bring to Mount Zion (18:7). In the case of Egypt, the leaders and wise men lead the country astray (19:11-15), as was the case just prior to the Exodus; this is reminiscent of Israel's own situation as Isaiah diagnosed it in the early chapters. The Egyptians will eventually be won for Israel's God because they will cry out to the Lord (in the way that the Israelites did; Isa. 19:20 and Exod. 2:23-24) and, along with Assyria and Israel, will become the Lord's people (Isa. 19:24-25). In the meantime, Israel is warned not to make alliances with Egypt and Ethiopia against Assyria (chap. 20). The prophet then returns to the subject of the fall of Babylon. Its princes are called from their eating to defend it (21:5), perhaps guilty of the same kind of negligence with which Isaiah charged Israel's leaders in the oracles that make up the first part of the book.

In the following chapters, Jerusalem is once again characterized as a noisy, chaotic, wanton city whose leaders desert it in time of need (22:2-3, 13). It is reliant on its own supply of weapons and emergency activities but does not "have regard to him who planned it long ago" (22:8-11). Two examples of self-serving leadership are given: Shebna, the master of the palace, who was determined to impress people by his spectacular tomb (22:15-19), and Eliakin son of Hilkiah, the opportunism of whose family brought about his downfall (vv. 20-25).[13] Finally, the prophet speaks of the ruin of the great non-Israelite ports of Tyre and Sidon, again because of their pride in human achievement. So Tyre, "the bestower of crowns, whose merchants were princes, whose traders were the honored of the earth" (23:8), suffers an unspecified disaster (v. 5) because "the LORD of hosts has planned it—to defile the pride of all glory, to shame all the honored of the earth" (v. 9). Sidon is "oppressed" and "has been turned into a ruin" (vv. 12-13, NAB). The prophet concludes this whole section by noting that Tyre's restoration will occur after seventy years (v. 17), but what she has then will be sacred to the Lord and "her merchandise will supply abundant food and fine clothing for those who live in the presence of the LORD" (18).

Isaiah's understanding is that, despite the experience of his day, the wealth that is produced by cities is intended for the well-being of the populace (especially those who acknowledge the Lord), not for the glorification of the few who arrogate power to themselves. It sounds familiar. Modern readers can surely name cities in need of Isaiah's message—those in which whole areas have been turned over to businesses catering only to the very wealthy, or where long-time residents of city centers have been displaced because of "gentrification" of their neighborhoods.

Overall, then, Isaiah of Jerusalem has little use for cities and the way they currently operate. At worst, they oppress Israel or lead it astray. They occasionally happen to do the Lord's will for a time but then go too far because they do not understand the situation: one is reminded of the judges Gideon and Jephthah. Even Zion, the city of the Lord's own people, is socially polarized and radically unjust. Its leaders forget that their service is supposed to benefit everyone in the city, and so they use their position to gain wealth for themselves at the expense of the poor and powerless. Isaiah is convinced that, in the end, there will be peace for all, nations and natural world alike, but it will come about as the Lord's doing, not as the *direct* result of any human achievement.[14] The impression given is that Zion's part in this will be determined by the extent to which the people acknowledge God and serve any who are in need of their ministrations, such as the refugees from Moab in 16:3-4.[15]

In all of this, there is no reason to suppose that the prophet thinks human achievements as such are inherently evil. They are, however, harmful to the extent that they lead people to forget the broader context in which they live (i.e., that they are God's creatures) and to oppress others. For Isaiah, ruins inhabited by owls and bats are preferable to such oppression, although his life is so much bound up with Jerusalem that it is impossible to believe that he could hold this view for long.

Isaiah 24–27: Wider Still

Having delivered God's judgment on the various powers of his day (chaps. 13–23), the book of Isaiah goes on to speak of it more broadly in the next four chapters. This section is often termed the "Apocalypse of Isaiah" and is generally regarded as being from a later time than that of the eighth-century Isaiah of Jerusalem. The Lord's verdict is clearly against the (now unnamed) city. There "desolation is left in the city, the gates are battered into ruins" (24:12).

A city without gates is no city at all. The ruin extends much more widely, however: it affects not only Israel but also the entire earth, whose inhabitants have "polluted" it to an extent that "few people are left" (vv. 5-6). Even for those who remain, "all joy has disappeared" (11, NAB). The components of civilized living that Isaiah earlier associated with the corruptions of city life have ceased to exist:

> No longer do they drink wine with singing;
> strong drink is bitter to those who drink it.
> The city of chaos is broken down,
> every house is shut up so that no one can enter
> (Isa. 24:9-10).

Although the survivors "proclaim the majesty of the LORD" (v. 14, NAB), the prophet knows that the earth itself stands under God's judgment: "the windows of heaven are opened[16] and the foundations of the earth tremble" (24:18). Yet "the LORD of hosts will reign on Mount Zion and in Jerusalem" (24:23). The next chapter takes up the theme of the ruined city: "the castle of the insolent is a city no more" (25:2, NAB). Now the poor and needy in distress have a refuge and shelter from the elements: the Lord, who "on this mountain" provides food, life, and consolation "for all peoples" (vv. 6-8). Once more, the Lord is recognized as a God who saves those in need of it (9) and who brings low the pride of (in this case) Moab.

Somewhat paradoxically, although not altogether surprisingly, given the prophet's strong Jerusalem connections and his conviction that Zion is God's city, there remains in Judah a fortified city, but one that is set up by God (26:1; see Rev. 21). Isaiah 26 celebrates it in song. Fundamental to its inhabitants is an attitude of trusting in the Lord (vv. 3-4). The contrast is with trusting in one's own achievements, which is presumably what "the inhabitants of the height" do (5). The Lord brings down "the lofty city," which the needy and the poor then trample (5-6)—a violent pair of images that result from the hurt and resentment caused by earlier oppression. Ironically, this is how God is seen as establishing justice (9-11), peace (12), the right relationship with people (13), the prosperity of "the nation" (15), and salvation (18-19). The picture is wider, of course. God is to punish "the inhabitants of the earth for their iniquity" (21) and deal with Leviathan, the primeval monster that would otherwise remain to threaten creation (27:1).[17] The focus then returns to Jacob/Israel, now once more the "pleasant vineyard" (27:2) and the object of the Lord's attentive concern, destined to "fill the whole world with fruit" (v. 6) provided that "it cling to me for protection" (5). At least for a while, there is no city:

> For the fortified city is solitary,
> A habitation deserted and forsaken, like the wilderness;
> the calves graze there (Isa. 27:10).

The image next metamorphoses into broken branches (of the vine, presumably) that are burned. Yet the final picture of this section is of the ingathering of "the lost in the land of Assyria and the outcasts in the land of Egypt"; they "shall come and worship the LORD on the holy mountain, in Jerusalem" (27:13, NAB). Like the author of Revelation, Isaiah's author must ultimately use city imagery, because genuinely human achievement, albeit transformed by God, is a necessary component of the divine project. Whatever else it may be, people's activity is not theologically insignificant.

Isaiah 28–39: Whom to Trust

Throughout, the prophet has assumed that what people want is peace and prosperity. How, though, is this to be secured? The context of chapters 28–39 is the military threat from Assyria, when the people are turning in desperation to whatever sources they think will enable them to survive. Isaiah is convinced that they are looking in all the wrong places, so these chapters emphasize the need to trust in the Lord rather than in alliances that are liable to fail. A key expression is found in Isaiah 31:3:

> The Egyptians are human, and not God;
> their horses are flesh, and not spirit.

Spurred by the urgency of the situation, Isaiah here presents Israel with a radical choice: to opt for "flesh" rather than "spirit" is to choose death (28:15), even though it may feel like political expediency. On the other hand, choosing "spirit" can bring about political safety. The Lord is concerned about Jerusalem and well able to deal with flesh-and-blood enemies such as Assyria (31:5, 8-9), if Israel will get rid of its dependence on idols and return to the Lord (31:6-7).[18] Isaiah's experience of Jerusalem is of a city where fools and tricksters seem to be in charge. Despite this, he refuses to relinquish the possibility of a society that has a king who is just and princes who function as "a hiding place from the wind, a covert from the tempest" (32:2). There people of noble character will flourish (vv. 1-8). In the meantime, the "complacent ladies" of the "wanton city" (9, 13, NAB) are put on notice (9-14) because of the city's impending fall and desolation and its replacement with wasteland—

> until a spirit from on high is poured out on us,
> and the wilderness becomes a fruitful field,
> and the fruitful field is deemed a forest (Isa. 32:15).

Once again, the future that Isaiah envisages and hopes for is a paradise of justice and peace, calm and security to replace the destroyed city, the citadel of Jerusalem (32:17-18). In place of a nerve-wracking dependence on foreigners (33:18-19), Israel will have Jerusalem as "a quiet habitation, an immovable tent, whose stakes will never be pulled up and none of whose ropes shall be broken" (v. 20). There, in another image derived from Israel's earlier history, the Lord will be judge, lawgiver, king and savior (22), and all members of society will be fully functional (23-24). The section concludes with the same theme taken up in terms of the transformation of the desert, so that the Lord's redeemed can joyfully "return, and come to Zion with singing; everlasting joy shall be upon their heads" (35:10). Isaiah never gives up on his city.

Conclusion

What, then, do we learn from this consideration of Isaiah 1–39? First, what we already knew: that societal malfunctioning, including the violence that comes from injustice and oppression, can exist under a monarch (or a president, or any local official), just as much as in the absence of one. The form it takes may be different but the uncomfortable reality is not. Second, that, in line with some of the traditions of the Pentateuch, Isaiah regards cities and their achievements with a high level of suspicion. In particular, he is horrified at the Jerusalem of his own day, where the differentiation of society has resulted in the establishment of a class of leaders who prosper at the expense of the people as a whole, who oppress the weak, and who are inclined, at least in the prophet's view, to risk serious compromise by forging alliances with surrounding nations. On the other hand, he finds in Israel's history resources that might be used to effect its renewal: traditions (doubtless romanticized) about Israel's formative period in the desert and about God's relationship to the people prior to the establishment of the monarchy. Fundamental to such a renewal would be an attitude of trust in the Lord that persisted through whatever societal developments might occur.

To the extent that Isaiah finds attractive the possibility of going back to rustic simplicity, he could be regarded as naïve: Cain may have built the first city and his ancestors forged the first implements, but human living as a whole would be infinitely the poorer without them. Yet the prophet's view is not so simple. For underlying what appears to be a dream of simple living is a conviction that the whole earth is in the Lord's control and is somehow involved in God's good plans for humanity and the rest of creation. The desert is not simply desert or even the place where Israel first came to know the Lord: it is an area at present unproductive, or even frightening, that God will transform into a surprisingly beautiful element in the total scheme of things. Isaiah says the same and more about the city of Zion, his immediate concern. Even though there is much about Jerusalem that needs to change, the city itself remains a vital component in the prophet's view of how world events are to work out. Viewed as the focus of the Lord's future saving activities, it cannot be abandoned. Therefore it must be reformed by conversion, particularly that of its leaders, however difficult such a process might be in practice. The alternative is that those leaders and the city that expresses their authority will not survive attack by Israel's enemies, whose activities would then be understood as the Lord's way of punishing the people for their unjust behavior. Underlying all this is Isaiah's firm conviction that God's holy mountain, Zion, is to be the focus of God's eschatological activity, an activity that affects all nations and indeed the whole of creation, not Israel alone.[19]

In Isaiah's strong reaction to the possibilities of human corruption, readers from our own century can find a measure of their own dismay as they survey their cities and other aspects of civilization. Yet the prophet offers repeated reminders that his understanding of reality is infinitely wider than even the most appalling urban sprawl. Indeed he invites readers to see the whole of human culture, with all its grandeur, ambiguity, and wretchedness, as situated within the context that was set out in Genesis 1: as components of a divine project that includes the whole universe. Within this, human activity is highly significant and never simply of local concern, and deliberately maltreating any part of it is quite inappropriate. Furthermore, Isaiah believes that God, as Creator, will bring the project to eschatological completion, so that those who know that their lives are lived within that context and who act accordingly need fear no failure. New Testament writers will re-express essentially the same worldview, but with additional imagery made available by the life and work of Jesus of Nazareth.

Before moving to the New Testament, we shall first consider three more Old Testament texts. These are much shorter than the units taken so far and are soundings that attest to the further riches that could be tapped there by those who have followed and accepted the argument of this book so far: that the Bible offers a rich variety of resources to those who wish to stop the spiral of violence and engage in peacemaking.

10

THREE SOUNDINGS

Sounding 1: Abigail as Mediator—1 Samuel 25

As it now appears in 1 Samuel 25, this story is set in the days of Israel's first king, Saul, not long before 1000 B.C.E. It follows two significant events. The first, told in chapter 24, is one of several dramatic scenes of reconciliation between the king and David, the man who would succeed him. The second event that establishes the context for the story of Abigail is found in the opening verse of chapter 25, which reports the death of the prophet Samuel and his burial by "all Israel" at Ramah. Samuel's death left David in a weaker position with regard to Saul. For it was Samuel who had earlier anointed Saul as king (chaps. 9–10) and later told him that he had forfeited the kingship (chap. 15), after which Samuel anointed David (chap. 16), even though Saul was still functioning as king and David was part of the royal retinue. Therefore it is easy enough to see why Samuel's death might be the occasion for David to leave Ramah and go once more to the desert area south of Hebron (25:1), because it was deep into Judahite territory and well away from Saul. It transpires that at least six hundred men are with David there (v. 13).

There are not many ways in which large groups of people can make a living in the desert. One possibility is to appoint themselves as guards for isolated property that might otherwise be subject to the attention of marauders. As is true of protection rackets the world over, the owners of the property may not realize that they are involved in such a scheme until they are presented with the bill. Such is the situation here: David and his men decide that they will "protect" the considerable flocks of a Calebite named Nabal. Biblical tradition links the Calebites with Judah, the tribe to which David belongs.[1] So perhaps the author tells readers of Nabal's tribal affiliation to give some justification for David's initiative with regard to his flocks. Quite understandably, that is not how Nabal sees the situation when informed about it at the end of the shearing season by emissaries of David, who now want compensation for their unsolicited services. Nabal clearly knows who David is, for he refers to him as "the son of Jesse." He also seems to know that David belongs in Saul's (or at least someone's) retinue (25:10). It is less apparent whether Nabal is aware of how much he has benefited from David's help, to which one of his own servants will later testify (vv. 15-16). In any case, the sheep farmer refuses to allow that he has any obligation at all to David and his band. He vigorously insults them all in terms that have at least some plausibility: David as a servant who has defected from his master,[2] and his followers as opportunistic scroungers (vv. 10-11). They have no place on Nabal's payroll or in his life.

On learning of this, David responds decisively in the well-tried manner of young males who have been slighted—with a call to arms. Leaving behind two hundred armed men to protect the group's property, he sets off with four hundred others. Although readers do not learn the details until later (v. 22, with hints in v. 17), David's intention is very simple: to kill all the men of Nabal's household.

David's behavior here is consistent with that which he displays elsewhere, but there is a higher degree of caricature in the portrayal of the other main figures in the story.[3] For "Nabal" means "fool," and he is "surly and mean" (v. 3). Despite his great wealth, he seems to have only one wife,

Abigail, who is "clever and beautiful" (3). The rest of the story is a demonstration of how Abigail uses her intelligence and skills to bring about a creative reconstruction of the apparently intractable situation that her husband and David have produced between them.

Abigail's already-existing moral capital is of primary importance here. Without it, there would be no story except that of a massacre, for she did not witness the scene between her husband and David's messengers (v. 25). She soon learned of it, however, because she is accessible to Nabal's servants in a way that he expressly is not. Whereas they experience their master as "so ill-natured that no one can speak to him" (17), his wife evidently can be expected to understand the potentially disastrous situation into which his foolishness has put the household, and to do something intelligent about it. So she is approached by a servant who has witnessed David's actions in the desert and also her husband's insulting behavior to his messengers. Admittedly, the young man could merely be acting to save his own skin, as it is only from David and the servant himself that readers learn of David's effectiveness as a guard and Nabal's rudeness to him (7, 14-16). Foreseeing a contest between his "surly and mean" master and a furious David accompanied by six hundred young men bent on slaughter, the servant may have thought it prudent to back the side that was obviously going to win. In any case, he tells Abigail what Nabal has done, testifies to the effectiveness of David's efforts on her husband's behalf, and boldly assumes that she will move to avert the crisis (14-17).

The servant has judged correctly. Without a word (and, quite deliberately, without telling her husband what she is about to do), Abigail sets about her task with energy. Having quickly assembled an abundance of provisions, she sends ahead her servants, whose mere presence will convey to David that Nabal's insult was not the last word and, perhaps, stay his hand for a while (vv. 18-19). No company is described as Abigail rides a donkey into the desert, carrying the gifts; even if she is attended by the "five maids" who go with her on a later journey (42), as Nabal's wife she is still very vulnerable to the men she has come to meet. By "[coming] down under cover of the mountain" (20), she perhaps tries to ensure that she sees David before he sees her, so she can be ready to appease him. Then, "David and his men came down toward her; and she met them" (20). In verse 22 the reader learns for the first time the full extent of David's murderous intentions toward Nabal and his household. For Abigail, the stakes are even higher than she yet knows.

In what follows, the author depicts Abigail as taking all possible measures to put right the damage that Nabal did to David's honor and, incidentally, to protect herself and her household from David's wrath. (Unlike the servant, Abigail is inextricably tied to Nabal: *she* cannot change sides.) First, the full description of her actions leaves the reader in no doubt that she is deliberately and systematically trying to rectify the situation. Over a period of weeks, if not months, Nabal had either ignored or been unaware of David's presence with his flocks. If the cause was ignorance rather than ill will, Nabal's "ill-natured" disposition (v. 17, cf. v. 3) may have had something to do with it— why would people take trouble to keep such a one informed? When David sent messengers to him, he refused them any recompense and went out of his way to insult them. Abigail, by contrast, journeys into the desert to find David, bringing the provisions that her husband has refused to give. On seeing David, she hurries to reach him and alights from her beast. Next the writer says that she bows to the ground, falling on her face, at David's feet (vv. 23-24). These last three specifications show the extent to which she uses her body to defuse David's wrath that is directed against her husband and his household: when situations become desperate, people use the resources they have.

From this position, Abigail continues her project of mending relationships with David by addressing him at length. Her speech of 181 words in Hebrew (291 in the NRSV) consists of two unequal parts. In the first, thirty-six words in Hebrew, Abigail speaks of her husband Nabal and the past (vv. 24-25). This is where she currently belongs, as Nabal's wife, and the reader knows that if David does as he has planned, Nabal's house (including Abigail herself) has no future. In the second, much longer part of her speech, Abigail puts before David the Lord's plan to establish David's house, and then has him imagine his intended treatment of Nabal in light of that. If David accepts both Abigail's solidarity with Nabal and the argument for forgiveness that she bases on David's prospects, he may choose to allow her to be part of his future, a possibility she raises in the request with which she concludes her speech. She asks that David remember her when the Lord has made him prosper (v. 31).[4]

Nabal's family and David will never be reconciled unless Abigail takes the initiative and effects it in her own person. There is no other location in which the two sides can come together, for Nabal would never make a move to accommodate David. Even in his own house he refused to entertain the messengers that David sent to him. Nabal's humiliation of David left unfinished business between them. So David would have returned to Nabal—with his four hundred armed men (vv. 13, 21-22). That visit would be followed by Nabal's wider kinship group taking similar vengeance on David's family for the lives of Nabal and the other men of his family. Because taking sanctuary in one of the designated cities of refuge is not possible for those who kill deliberately,[5] the vendetta would continue.

To prevent this, Abigail appeases David, using all the resources that come from her intelligence and her social location as wife of the wealthy Nabal. Her essential task is to make contact with this angry man in a way that will enable him to give her a fair hearing. So, although in the first part of her speech to David she strongly emphasizes her connection with Nabal, she connects herself with David throughout as well. Twelve times he is "my lord" and six times she refers to herself as "your servant."[6] Abigail would, of course, have cut a more dignified figure if she had been able simply to reason logically with the outlaw, but those whose pride has been hurt are not amenable to simple logic from those they might deem at fault. At some cost to her own dignity, therefore, Abigail puts forward her case in a way that she hopes will be rhetorically effective.

In part 1 (vv. 24-25), Abigail presents herself to David as the representative of Nabal's house, asking him to regard her alone as guilty. In this way, she indicates her willingness to accept full blame for Nabal's stupidity, hoping that she will thereby earn a hearing from David about Nabal's situation and David's own future: "Please let your servant speak in your ears, and hear the words of your servant" (24b). Abigail wisely concludes this part of her discourse by mentioning that she "did not see [the] young men . . . , whom [he had] sent" to Nabal (25b). Thus the section starts and finishes with a reference to herself: Abigail asks David to consider her guilty and yet to realize that she is personally innocent. Enclosed between these two statements is her verdict on Nabal (25a)—he is nothing but a fool. The implication is that he is not even worth noticing, let alone endangering one's future for. Abigail is perhaps also speaking to herself. Loyal wives do not say such things, and by this stage, she has essentially detached herself from her husband.

In the second part of Abigail's speech, Nabal is mentioned only once, in verse 26 as a standard of folly that Abigail hopes David's other enemies will attain. She moves closer to her main goal of obtaining forgiveness when she offers to David "this present that your servant has brought to my lord [to] be given to the young men who follow my lord" (27). With this move, she honors David directly (her two addresses of "my lord" are enclosed in one to herself as "your servant") and indirectly (by acknowledging his retinue and his responsibility for them). She then asks him to forgive "the trespass of your servant" (28).

The reasoning that Abigail uses to back her request for forgiveness is significant. In effect, she asks David to refrain from acting on his present anger over a mere fool, because of how he will feel later on, when the Lord will have established for him a "sure house" (since, she says, David is "fighting the battles of the LORD"!). Here Abigail anticipates a theme that is expressed in its classical form in 2 Samuel 7. There, "when the LORD had given [David] rest from all his enemies around him," David offers to build a house for the Lord (i.e., a temple), an offer that is firmly rejected[7] but countered with the promise that, instead, the Lord will build David a house (i.e., a dynasty). When David shall have received this gift from the Lord, says Abigail, he will want to be free of any "grief, or pangs of conscience from having shed blood without cause" from having "saved" his own honor (25:31). In other words, she suggests that David would have been made unfit to carry out the great plans the Lord has for him, had he acted on his desire for vengeance against Nabal.

Of course, Abigail's speech is carefully crafted so as to flatter David and heal his wounded vanity. Only a very selective reading of the Bible's manifold traditions about David could bear out her prediction that evil would not be found in him as long as he lived (v. 28)! Even David's remarkable success in battle (which she lauds in the same verse) counts against him in some parts of the tradition. For example, in 1 Chronicles 28:3, the aging David reports to a solemn assembly that God had told him, "You shall not build a house for my name, for you are a warrior and have shed blood."[8] On the other hand, there is no reason to suppose that the author of 1 Samuel 25 presents Abigail as insincere in regarding David as one who is, for the sake of Israel, especially under the Lord's guidance and protection. The oath with which she opens the second part of her speech certainly recognizes her respect for Israel's God: "As the LORD lives, and as you yourself live. . . ." (26). Indeed, by forestalling David's plans to kill Nabal and his kinsmen, she is herself, by implication, the instrument by which "the LORD has restrained [David] from . . . taking vengeance" on his own behalf (26).

David makes this explicit at the turning point, in verse 32. Here he blesses "the LORD, the God of Israel" for having sent Abigail to him. He continues:

> Blessed be your good sense, and blessed be you, who have kept me today from bloodguilt and from avenging myself by my own hand! For as surely as the LORD lives, who has restrained me from hurting you, unless you had hurried and come to meet me, truly by morning there would not have been left to Nabal so much as one male (1 Sam. 25:33-35).

Having accepted from her the gift she has brought, David concludes, "Go up to your house in peace; see, I have heeded your voice, and I have granted your petition" 25:35). His bestowal of peace on her is important. For when David had first sent his messengers to Abigail's husband to make their request for recompense, he had instructed them to greet him with a threefold wish for peace—on Nabal, on his house, and on all that he had (v. 6). That greeting of peace met with insult. Now, however, through the exertions of Abigail, David is finally able to make peace with the household of Nabal.

The householder himself is, of course, quite unaware of this—or of much else. Perhaps in celebration of the completed shearing (although the text does not say this) or as one final demonstration of his foolishness, Nabal has hosted a feast "like the feast of a king," and is "very drunk" (v. 36). So Abigail demonstrates her wisdom once more, by waiting until morning to explain to him what she has done on his behalf. Naturally enough, he is uncomprehending and appalled. As the narrator says, the heart that only the night before had been "merry within him" now "died within him; he became like a stone" (37). Ten days later, "the LORD struck Nabal, and he died" (38). Although the reader is obviously intended to regard Nabal's death as a suitable ending for one so foolish and, to that extent, at least permitted by the Lord, there is no reason for understanding its terms as implying divine vengeance. Rather it is presented as a fitting outcome of Nabal's foolishness.[9] The Lord allowed that foolishness to run its course, and now it is ended.

One could claim that David had no business to be running a protection racket and that Nabal's angry response to him was justified. There are many indications that the biblical author did not have that view. One could also complain of the terms on which Abigail became one of David's wives (v. 41, is the storyteller assuming that, as a widow, Abigail needed a family? Did she inherit Nabal's wealth?). Yet the story is compelling as an account of how someone was able to bring peace out of what seemed to be an impossible situation by putting herself in a position from which she could convince David that engaging in deliberate violence would permanently damage his integrity.

Admittedly, an extension of the story that somehow reconciled Nabal would have been even more satisfactory, but even as it stands, the situation is remarkable enough.

What difference does it make that the reconciler is a woman? First, like other "wise women" in Israel's tradition, Abigail succeeds in a situation in which a man would probably have failed because his very presence would have been seen as a potential threat to David's honor.[10] Second, it is much more difficult to imagine the biblical authors telling of a man abasing himself to the extent that Abigail did and still surviving with his honor intact, as she did, since David commended her, in addition to granting her petition (25:35). There are very few comparable examples involving men. One might be the servant/son figure of Isaiah 52–53. Here the prophet admits the deep mysteriousness of the one who "has borne our infirmities and carried our diseases," and by whose bruises "we are healed" (Isa. 53:4-5). In this passage, however, the servant is not shown resuming a normal life among peers, which is where the problem of tarnished honor is liable to arise. Abigail has no such problem, because her future is to be with David, as she all but requested of him (1 Sam. 25:31). It does seem, then, that for effective reconciliation in the world of ancient Israel, Abigail's gender, along with her social standing, gives her an advantage.

At the same time, however, Abigail's situation transcends gender because she uses in a creative way the resources that are available to her, including those that she had built up beforehand without any specific idea of how they would benefit her. She is, in a word, virtuous—someone whose habitual ways of behaving have produced strong and positive character traits that become fully evident only in a crisis. In Abigail's case, these traits include the following: qualities of imagination that allow her to interact with people unlike herself (e.g., the servant and David) and to see what situations require; the willingness to take initiatives; habits of diligence and an ability to organize; and the strength of character that enabled her to survive her marriage to Nabal and to persist in doing what she could to rescue the household from her husband's excesses.[11] Certainly, Abigail herself gains from her exertions. That peacemaking is its own reward is one point of the story. At the same time, though, she is shown exerting herself on behalf of the wider community.

Although such behavior is often costly, there is nothing gender-specific about it as an overall project, as people of all times have found. Biblical examples include those prophets who persisted in their efforts despite popular opposition (e.g., Jeremiah and Amos)[12] and Jesus of Nazareth, who could, arguably have avoided execution by ceasing to teach and heal as he did. The various peace movements throughout the centuries provide many other examples. Those in our own day include thousands whose lives were touched by the South African Truth and Reconciliation Commission.[13] There is nothing easy about putting one's life on the line so as to reconcile others. Community support and religious commitment often characterize people who have done this, yet it can also be done by those convinced that the human project is in itself worth giving one's life for and that violence exacerbates problems rather than solving them. The story of Abigail is a resource for any who need reinforcement of their will to reconcile in ways that make for lasting peace.

Sounding 2: David and Shimei—2 Samuel 16:5-14; 19:16-23

David's initial and violent response to Nabal is typical of his character as the Bible portrays it. Perhaps more than anyone else, he is shown to profit handsomely from living by the sword, eventually dying of old age in his bed, perhaps accompanied by a beautiful young woman (1 Kings 1:1-4).

For the most part, therefore, stories about him are any-thing but a helpful resource for constructing nonviolent responses.

However, the complexity of David's character also ensures that he is occasionally shown in a different light. In the story just considered, Abigail persuaded David to stay his anger against someone who had, arguably, mis-treated and dishonored him by his rude response to David's messengers.[14] The events of the next story take place after King Saul's death, when David has succeeded him. Here the king on two occasions responds with mag-nanimity to Shimei, a member of Saul's family who delib-erately insulted the king in front of his whole court and later apologized. Both times David gives reasons for not punishing Shimei and even resists proposals to execute him on the spot. (Decades later, after David's death and at his command, Shimei pays with his life, but that is another story, albeit a problematic one.)[15]

There are three main issues here. Violence is the first of them. Generally, David has no problem with using it, but this occasion is different. He is fleeing from Jerusalem, where his son Absalom has usurped his throne. David's nonviolent response to Shimei may, therefore, result merely from an awareness of his own weakness. Even so, the story itself is instructive. Second, although David was nowhere near Saul and his son Jonathan when they were killed in battle on Mount Gilboa and therefore cannot be implicated in their death (1 Sam. 30–31), he can never be sure that members of Saul's family fully accept him as king. They could easily be harboring resentment of David's success and dynastic ambitions for themselves. Consequently, relating wisely to Saul's various kinsfolk is vital. Third, and this is where the story begins, the traditions in 2 Samuel show David as much more successful in his public life than he is in dealing with his own family. So Absalom, by far the strongest character among David's sons, has been able to gain temporary ascendancy over his father and has moved into Jerusalem with those Israelites who have taken up his invitation to abandon David. David and his household therefore flee Jerusalem, weeping as they go up the Mount of Olives and toward the wilderness (15:30).

As they approach Bahurim, Shimei son of Gera emerges from it. As he approaches, he curses David, throwing stones at him and his entourage (16:5-6). Since "all the soldiers, including the royal guard, were on David's right and on his left" (16:6, NAB), the behavior presents no physical danger but is clearly an affront to the king's honor. In case that were in doubt, in the midst of his curses and in the hearing of all, Shimei shouts at the king that the Lord has given the kingdom to Absalom because David murdered members of Saul's family (a story not recounted until 2 Sam. 21). "See, disaster has overtaken you; for you are a man of blood," he concludes (16:8). That is to say, violence leads to other evils for those who perpetrate it. It is a reasonable position, one put forward repeatedly by generations of Israel's prophets, but is not calculated to please David in his current predicament.

The prompt and predictable response from Abishai, brother of David's army commander, is an offer to decapitate Shimei. Perhaps surprisingly, David turns it down on the grounds that the cursing may be warranted. The king's explanation, addressed to the whole party, suggests that the terms of Shimei's insults correspond to David's own bad conscience. After all, even his own son wants him dead, and Saul's kinsman has much more cause for cursing the king. "Let him alone," David says, "and let him curse, for the LORD has bidden him. It may be that the LORD will look on my distress, and the LORD will repay me with good for this cursing of me today" (16:11-12). So David and his companions go on their way, no doubt uncomfortably, because they are still accompanied by Shimei, who continues to curse and to throw stones and dust at them.

After David's army has defeated the rebel Israelites and Absalom has been killed, the king is met by the people of Judah, who have come to escort him across the Jordan and back into Jerusalem. Among them is Shimei, accompanied by a thousand of his clan, the Benjaminites. He "hurried to come down with the people of Judah to meet King David" (19:16) and fell at David's feet, admitting that he had done wrong and asking him not to "bear it in mind" (19:19). Again Abishai wants David to have him executed, this time for having cursed the Lord's anointed (19:21). The king insists, however, that Abishai's advice is that of an adversary. On that day, nobody is to die, because David is now secure in his kingship. So he assures Shimei that he will not die, backing up the assertion with an oath (19:22, 23).

The first of these two incidents demonstrates David's piety and his sense of realism. His general awareness of living in the Lord's world is heightened at this time when his life has taken such a disastrous turn. He seems alert to the possibility that the Lord will communicate with him through different aspects of his situation, and he does not want to miss a message from God. Even at the practical level, David would have gained nothing by killing Shimei. For apart from the events to which Shimei alludes (a strange story recounted later in 2 Sam. 21, when the men of Gibeon persuade David to kill seven of Saul's sons to avert a famine)[16] the king has treated well the members of Saul's family. In 2 Samuel 9 he was depicted as going out of his way to show kindness to Mephibosheth, the one remaining son of Saul's son Jonathan. Immediately before David's encounter with Shimei, he transfers that kindness to Ziba, servant of Mephibosheth, when the latter appears to have broken with David and to be making a bid for his grandfather's kingdom (16:1-4). Furthermore, the large company of his kinsfolk with which Shimei comes out to greet the returning David (19:16) suggests that the king might have lost out significantly if he had earlier killed the Benjaminite.

On the second occasion (1 Sam. 19), David's motive for sparing Shimei's life seems to be magnanimity (or a continuing desire to keep Saul's descendants in line), rather than piety; his prior oath receives no mention. Rather David cannot think of killing anyone on the day that he returns to Jerusalem to resume his kingship there.

The two encounters with Shimei, separated by the defeat and death of Absalom, have in common Abishai's offer to have Shimei executed. Each time, David uses the same words to restrain him: "What have I to do with you, you sons of Zeruiah?" (16:10; 19:22). Zeruiah's other son was Joab, David's army commander. In an action that he had expected would please David but in fact broke his heart, Joab had killed the hapless Absalom as he hung suspended from a tree in which he had become entangled (18:9-33). Almost immediately after this, David replaced Joab with his own kinsman Amasa (19:13-14). That appointment made good political sense at the time, for Amasa had supported Absalom and therefore had good relations with the Judeans in the city to which David was about to return. It is also possible, however, that at that time in particular David was uneasy about the immediacy with which Zeruiah's sons resorted to violence. For Joab has, in effect, delivered the kingdom to David, but at the price of Absalom's life.[17] So it is not surprising that David finds offensive the second offer of Joab's brother, Abishai, to execute the wayward but now penitent relation of Saul.

In its wider setting of the death of Absalom, David's encounter with Shimei can act as a salutary reminder that

a violent way of living—or indeed any act of violence—
may achieve its immediate ends but is liable to have further consequences that are unforeseen and damaging. At a
general level, the same is true of any action at all: the total
effects are always unknowable in advance and are frequently
harmful to somebody. Yet deliberate acts of violence
inherently put the future in jeopardy because of the hurt and
resentment they build up in their victims. Positively, the
story about David and Shimei indicates that an awareness
of the larger picture (in this case, David's sensitivity to the
Lord and the responsibility that comes with his reinstatement
as king) can lead to other ways of resolving situations—even
though, in this instance, David does not carry through his
resolve right to the end of his life.

Sounding 3: The Good Samarians—2 Chronicles 28:8-15

After the death of King Solomon, David's son, the division of the kingdom into north (Israel) and south (Judah)
was a politically inevitable move that cut across more fundamental religious lines.[18] The problem of having two separate states that worshiped the Lord was especially acute
when, as occasionally happened, Israel and Judah were allied
with larger powers that were fighting against each other.
Such is the case here in 2 Chronicles 28. At the point at
which we take up the story, the northern kingdom, Israel
(with its capital in Samaria), has the upper hand.

> The people of Israel took captive two hundred thousand
> of their [own] kin,[19] women, sons, and daughters; they
> also took much booty from them and brought the booty
> to Samaria. But a prophet of the LORD was there, whose
> name was Oded; he went out to meet the army that
> came to Samaria, and said to them, "Because the LORD,
> the God of your ancestors, was angry with Judah, he
> gave them into your hand, but you have killed them in
> a rage that has reached up to heaven. Now you intend

to subjugate the people of Judah and Jerusalem, male and female, as your slaves. But what have you except sins against the LORD your God? Now hear me, and send back the captives whom you have taken from your kindred, for the fierce wrath of the LORD is upon you." Moreover, certain chiefs of the Ephraimites, Azariah son of Johanan, Berechiah son of Meshillemoth, Jehizkiah son of Shallum, and Amasa son of Hadlai, stood up against those who were coming from the war, and said to them, "You shall not bring the captives in here, for you propose to bring on us guilt against the LORD in addition to our present sins and guilt. For our guilt is already great, and there is fierce wrath against Israel." So the warriors left the captives and the booty before the officials and all the assembly. Then those who were mentioned by name got up and took the captives, and with the booty they clothed all that were naked among them; they clothed them, gave them sandals, provided them with food and drink, and anointed them; and carrying all the feeble among them on donkeys, they brought them to their kindred at Jericho, the city of palm trees. Then they returned to Samaria (2 Chron. 28:8-15).

After an initial nine chapters dealing with genealogical matters from Adam to King Saul, the two books of Chronicles document events from Saul's death and the accession of King David (around 1000 B.C.E.), through the Babylonian exile, and as far as 538 B.C.E., when the Persian ruler Cyrus conquered Babylon and decreed that the exiles could return to Jerusalem and (re)build the temple there. In the span of time that they cover and in many of the traditions that they include, 1 and 2 Chronicles are similar to (and probably dependent on) the part of the Deuteronomistic History found in 2 Samuel and 1–2 Kings (which ends in mid-exile, in 561 B.C.E.), although the story just given has no parallel in the Deuteronomistic History.

The Chronicler also takes from the Deuteronomistic

History an interpretation of history whereby infidelity to the Lord lies behind the disasters that befall the Lord's people.[20] Chronicles differs slightly from the Deuteronomistic History in having a stronger emphasis on the normative foundation that was laid down by David, (e.g., that the Lord was to be worshiped in Jerusalem only), a foundation that was built upon (with varying degrees of fidelity and therefore success) by his descendants who ruled in Jerusalem. The series of post-Davidic dynasties that ruled the northern kingdom usually receives less attention in this account than in Samuel and Kings.

The current passage in 2 Chronicles 28 is in line with this tendency to concentrate on David's dynasty. The chapter opens with a note about the reprehensible behavior of the Judahite king, Ahaz (vv. 1-6).[21] Consequently, the Lord allowed the king of Aram to capture Judeans and take them to Damascus (5). That "Zichri, a mighty warrior of Ephraim" was able to kill Ahaz's son and other notables serves to underscore the king's fall from grace (7). The capture of 200,000 Judeans by the Israelites is the third military defeat that the Judeans suffer at this time. In the writer of Chronicles' understanding, it also results from God's anger with Judah, as is confirmed by the prophet Oded, who interprets the events for the victors (9).

The story that begins in verse 8 is clearly intended to shock. The 200,000 captives are immediately specified as *kin* (literally, "brothers," vv. 8, 11) of the Israelites who have captured them. Among the prisoners are "women, sons, and daughters." These are entire families, not merely the warriors. Those involved in the raid evidently have no sense that these prisoners are related to them. They regard their captives simply as the defeated: sources of booty and enforced labor for the conquerors. And it seems the Israelites have forgotten that a victory attained by the Lord's people is never simply their own achievement. The biblical understanding is that, like any other successful exploit, winning a battle is always a gift from the Lord and part of the wider scheme of things. As is apparent from the examples of Gideon and Jephthah in the book of Judges (see chap. 8 above), this is an exceedingly difficult lesson to learn. Rejoicing in any kind of success is liable to turn into hubris, which activates the resentment of others and therefore invites disaster. Success in warfare is especially problematic: hence the ritual that frequently attends its preparation, execution, and aftermath (see, e.g., Num. 31).

Even before the triumphant Israelite army has entered Samaria, the Lord's prophet, Oded, confronts its members and spells out the situation in detail (2 Chron. 28:9-11). In doing this, he is fulfilling the traditional role of the prophet in Israelite society, on this occasion at some considerable risk to his popularity. However, he does receive support from a group of four Ephraimite chiefs who are named in verse 12. In contrast to their kinsman Zichri, whose significant exploits against Judeans were documented in verse 7, these men of Ephraim did not take part in the war against Judea, although no reason is given for why that should have been so. Perhaps it is relevant that, during the time of the divided monarchy, the Israelite territory of Ephraim lay immediately north of that of Benjamin, which was part of Judah. Jericho, the city to which the captives were eventually returned, lies on the border between the two territories. So some Ephraimites, at least, may well have been better acquainted with (or more closely related to) their Benjaminite neighbors than was the general population of the northern kingdom. Therefore it is possible that Ephraimite leaders had qualms either about the campaign or about the subsequent enslavement of captured Judeans. On the other hand, any misgivings they had were not voiced until Oded had spoken out against the returning army. Perhaps the Ephraimites' silence comes from their awareness that they had no stake in booty from a campaign in which they had not fought. Yet once Oded has spoken, their moral and practical support for his position turns out to be important. For it is when the Ephraimite chiefs have expressed their agreement with each part of Oded's speech that "the warriors left the captives and the booty before the officials and all the assembly" (28:14). The Judeans are no longer prisoners. But now the positive part of their recovery process must begin.

The description of the vigor and thoroughness with which the four chiefs implement their commitment to this part of the project is perhaps the most impressive part of this story. First, they remove the captives' shame by giving them clothing from among the booty. Without this, the Judeans cannot function as humans at all. Then they are provided with sandals, so they can walk with dignity. The chiefs also give them food and drink to appease their hunger and thirst. In a particularly moving gesture, they anoint them with oil. This presumably requires the chiefs (or perhaps those delegated by them) to touch the bodies of the Judeans, an action that could surely not be done without evident and sustained respect. It may also express the notion that the former captives are now their guests. The chiefs then provide transportation for those unfit to walk. In this way, they return them "to their kindred at Jericho, the city of palm trees" (v. 15). The captives are finally back among their own people and in a city that can provide what is necessary to sustain life, including perhaps the beauty that the palms represent. This brief description shows the Israelite chiefs providing the Judeans with something approaching the full range of human needs. At the end of it, the account says simply that the chiefs "returned to Samaria" (15).

To the original readers or hearers, this story would have had an additional shock effect, because its heroes are people from Samaria. Texts such as Ezra 4 suggest that the newly returned exiles were hostile to Samarians, rudely rebuffing them when the latter wished to have some part in building the new temple in Jerusalem. Evidence from the first century of the Common Era shows that the relationship between those who were by then called Jews and Samaritans had not improved: Jesus' parable of the good Samaritan parallels the story from 2 Chronicles 28, in presenting the unlikely figure of the Samaritan as the one who does right when the priest and Levite fail to do so (Luke 10:25-37).[22]

Like the story of Abigail, 2 Chronicles 28 shows people taking responsibility for clearing up the damage left by others and making an apparently impossible situation viable again. In Chronicles the cause of the damage was not the act of a foolish individual but the accepted practice of going to war for one's own people against others who are perceived as enemies. Yet the biblical understanding that underlies this story is that, despite the division of Solomon's kingdom, Judeans and Israelites are only one people. So war between them is equivalent to fratricide—but does not feel like that because of the developments that occur once the separation has taken place. It takes a prophet like Oded to point out the unperceived logic of the Israelites' situation. However, an accurate perception of the state of affairs is only the beginning. Once people have been hurt, restoring the relationship requires more than merely reestablishing the prior situation or its equivalent.

This kind of situation is not uncommon, for the dynamic is the same even when the process does not go as far as the outbreak of war. Any action or state that holds other people captive diminishes their humanity: persistent negative attitudes toward particular nations, groups, institutions, or individuals will have such an effect. In their day-to-day involvement in society, people tend to get swept into projects and may eventually find themselves acting in ways that seem innocuous (because they have been approached gradually) but that a more detached examination would reveal as compromising. For example, it is all too easy to become convinced that deeds done in the name of family or country are justifiable and to forget one's connectedness to others—especially if those others stand between us and something that we could otherwise gain for ourselves (oil and other natural resources, for example). Prophets such as Oded help people to remember the underlying reality of who they are and therefore the extent of their responsibility for others. People like the Ephraimite chiefs and Abigail demonstrate the need for committing humanity's best resources (including those of the imagination) to the difficult but absolutely necessary task of mending broken relationships at all levels. In an ideal situation even Nabal would be included.

With this story from the final chapters of the last book of the Jewish biblical canon, we can make the transition to the New Testament.[23]

11

ATTENDING TO THE MYSTERY:
HUMAN ACTION IN MARK

The Radical Challenge

At the heart of Christianity lies an extraordinary claim: that God, already known from the Old Testament and the events that gave rise to them, is to be definitively understood through the person and witness of Jesus of Nazareth. The gospel according to Mark is one of several narrative versions of that claim. By far the starkest of the four Gospels and perhaps written for a group of Christians who had scant hope of surviving an imminent persecution, it is especially open to the charge that Christianity is a pathological denial of life.[1] Quite the reverse is the case, however. Rather it is a strong affirmation of life in paradoxical terms that can be verified only existentially. In short, this evangelist is presenting in narrative form the basic Christian position: suffering and death (which are unsought but inevitable) do not ultimately prevail over life and human flourishing.

Writing between the years 69 and 75 C.E., Mark was not the first to give written expression to this insight. In the 50s, Paul transmitted to the church in Corinth, "as of first importance," the tradition that he himself had "received" (1 Cor. 15:3), namely, that the death and resurrection of Jesus is central to an understanding of the world, an understanding that strongly shapes Christians' way of living. Far from being utter defeat, Jesus' crucifixion at the hands of the Romans is transformed by God into a great act of divine power, the resurrection, on which the whole of Christianity depends (1 Cor. 15:13-19). Jesus was, Paul says, "declared to be Son of God with power . . . by[2] resurrection from the dead" (Rom. 1:4). Paul's letter to the Philippians attests to his belief that the sufferings of Christians, understood as a "sharing of [Christ's] sufferings," can give them access to "the power of his resurrection" (3:10) and the possibility of their own rising from the dead (3:11).

Second Corinthians 12:9 includes a very succinct formulation of this counterintuitive position: whether in Christ or his followers "power is made perfect in weakness." The appropriate use of that power does not, therefore, involve putting down other people. To the contrary, it entails their empowerment, so that they, too, can serve others. Nor may this "power in weakness" be used to manipulate those whom one would otherwise be unable to coerce, or to encourage people to endure situations that should not be tolerated.[3] It cannot be emphasized too strongly: the weakness of the crucified Jesus was not chosen for its own sake, and suffering is never good. Yet both weakness and suffering are basic and unavoidable aspects of the human situation. No matter how favorable people's circumstances may be, they find that they are frequently thwarted in satisfying their spontaneous desires during their lifetime and are inevitably defeated in death. The fundamental Christian insight responds to that situation in terms that are at least surprising and, for many people, absurd or scandalous—that God's power can be present precisely in this powerlessness and is able to bring new life out of it.

The gospel according to Mark presents what is for Christians the paradigmatic case of that phenomenon. The evangelist depicts Jesus as exerting himself to the utmost, preaching about the nearness of the "kingdom [or reign] of God" (1:15) and performing the healing miracles that God made possible for those who believed. Jesus is ceaselessly active on behalf of people in various kinds of distress: the "sick" who need the "physician" (2:17). He refuses to stop ministering to them, even though the cost of continuing is to exhaust himself and his disciples[4] and to antagonize people who find his priorities offensive.[5] By the end, he has provoked such opposition that a handful of his own people turn him over to the Romans for crucifixion.[6]

For anyone who thinks of Jesus as just another human being (however exceptional), the story ends there or, at best, provides food for thought in the manner of other tragedies, ancient and modern. However, Christians believe that the outcome in this case is quite different. Their belief rests on claims made about Jesus as vindicated by God, a vindication expressed as resurrection. On this view, what looked like a life that had ended in disaster was not so: "his disciples and Peter" were to see the risen Jesus in Galilee (Mark 16:7). This post-Easter experience would somehow enable them and other followers of Jesus to view their own lives differently. Thus Jesus' followers came to see his death and resurrection not as affecting him alone, but as the key moments of a much larger story that included them too. The rapid spread of Christianity around the Mediterranean and beyond attests the apostolic generation's dedication to preaching about the transformation that their experience of Jesus' resurrection had wrought in their lives, a transformation available also to others who accepted their message. Followers of Jesus were convinced that the power of God shown in Jesus' life, death, and resurrection is available in the present to all who "follow" Jesus—who live and die as he did and in his company.

What does Mark think is entailed in living and dying as Jesus did? It is very simple: to belong to a group centered on Jesus, of which the members use their God-given energies for promoting the good of others despite the antagonism and even violence to which this will provoke some outsiders who (often understandably and not necessarily culpably) experience it as a threat to their way of life. For the most part, behavior runs counter to people's natural drives, which prompt them to act on what seems to be their own immediate self-interest. Yet, Mark suggests, our completion as persons requires that we act in ways that appear to (but do not in fact) deny that self-interest. On the other hand, the instincts for self-promotion and for responding in kind to violence are deeply rooted and show no signs of growing any weaker. So failure and fear—one's own and other people's—are inevitable aspects of Christian living. They are, however, more tolerable to those able to accept that Jesus has access to divine power precisely in his weakness.

Clearly, any writing based on such claims will have an uncommon perspective from which to provide resources for strengthening people's ability to forgo the various forms of violence and to embrace the compassionate service of others. This certainly does not entail the abandonment of the Old Testament. Quite to the contrary: its witness remains of great importance to Christians as foundational to their view of the world, as offering a much wider range of divine-human interaction than is included in the New Testament, and as the sacred book that Christians share with their Jewish elder brothers and sisters. Nevertheless the New Testament is not simply a development of the Old, which is why it has something distinctive to offer to the project of making a more peaceful and human world. This chapter will suggest that Mark can make a significant contribution to that project.

Overture

Mark is not, in fact, particularly interested in violence. For him as for most other biblical writers, it is simply a fact of life. His gospel details the execution of John the Baptist and of Jesus (6:17-29 and chaps. 14–15) and predicts that Jesus' followers will experience persecutions (10:29-30; 13:9-13), wars (13:8), and tribulation (13:19). More problematic still is Jesus' own severe treatment of the fig tree and the temple in 11:12-21. Furthermore, unlike the reworking of Mark by Matthew and Luke, Mark's description of Jesus' arrest lacks any rebuke of the sword bearer who mutilates the servant of the high priest (14:47). In this Gospel, violence is a given, and there is no indication that the evangelist expects it to disappear any time soon. Nevertheless Mark's project as a whole does propose to readers a way of behaving and a rationale for it that should empower them to avoid violent responses of their own and to make sense of violence that others inflict on them. How does this work?

The primary element is, of course, Jesus, who serves others and will "give his life [as] a ransom for many" (10:45).[7] The "ransom" metaphor is not to be taken literally. Unlike the early church,[8] Mark does not suggest how the process works or to whom the ransom was paid. Instead his purpose is to convey a sense of an unexpected liberation that comes about through the efforts of another. Parallels are found in Isaiah 53:5, where the Lord's servant bore "the punishment that made us whole," and in Romans 7, Paul's dramatic proclamation of his experience that what humans cannot do for themselves (i.e., live in the way that they know to be right), God can enable them to do through Jesus (Rom. 7:21-25).

Mark takes for granted that people want to live as fully as they can (Mark 8:35-37). His "good news" (1:1) is that others can indeed live more fully because of Jesus' ministry and the ugly death to which it led. The significance of Jesus' human actions far transcends the effects that are immediately apparent. He undergoes execution, but the result is resurrection and new life. The immediate beneficiary of that new life is Jesus himself. Later it invigorates, first, his initially timorous followers and then countless others down the ages. It gives them concrete reasons for hoping that such suffering as they endure is not without significance and that death will not be the end for them. The young man who encounters the women at the tomb on Easter Sunday provides a summary: "Jesus of Nazareth, who was crucified . . . has been raised" (16:6); that is to say, God raised him from the dead. In God's world, human action—of Jesus, of those who killed him, and even of the women with whose silent fear Mark's gospel originally ended (16:8)—does not have the last word.

Mark further suggests that the same general pattern obtains for those who follow Jesus. Just as God brought new life out of Jesus' suffering and death, Christian discipleship that models itself on Jesus entails having faith in (i.e., entrusting oneself to) what God is doing in the person of Jesus. Mark frequently describes Jesus' actions as being effective through people's faith. Examples include the friends of the paralytic who let him down through the roof (2:5); the hemorrhaging woman (5:34); Jairus (5:36); and the epileptic boy's father (9:23-24). The evangelist also includes Jesus' saying about the faith that can move a mountain (11:22-24).

Living a life of faith is not, however, a formula for a peaceful existence. Overall Mark's version of the gospel strongly implies that any action at all is liable to bring trouble for oneself or others. However, when a selfless concern for the needs of others is part of the mix, a more abundant life may ensue, both within present-day communities and in the eschatological consummation that forms Mark's ultimate horizon. The converse is also true: some of the instincts that program people for success and physical survival need to be replaced by other kinds of behavior, because (as we shall see) following them leads to the loss of the very things that they want most.

Because violence is not one of Mark's main concerns, it is not a structural element of the Gospel. Yet, as with the other biblical books that we considered earlier, readers can find in Mark a position that provides a basis for a non-violent ethic. I wish to follow four related themes that enter the story in a sequence roughly corresponding to the flow of Mark's narrative. Each presents human activity as in some way mysterious. Once introduced, all four remain in play. Seen in this way, the text of the Gospel is like a song for four voices that take it up one after the other, with each contributing to the total richness of the effect.

Soprano: John and Jesus—Success as Invitation to Trouble

From the outset, Mark assumes that people will act and can achieve results. His first chapter shows John the Baptist and Jesus doing just this. John's activity is described immediately after Mark's announcement that his topic is "good news," or "gospel" (1:1). Characterized by Mark as preaching "a baptism of repentance for the forgiveness of sins" (1:4), John had initial success. Thus "people from the whole Judean countryside and all the people of Jerusalem" came to him in the desert, confessing their sins as they were baptized by him (v. 5). John made a difference in people's lives. In 11:32, Mark tells his readers that "the crowd" in Jerusalem "all regarded John as truly a prophet," so they had, presumably, accepted his "baptism of repentance for the forgiveness of sins" (1:4) and his statements about Jesus (1:7-8). Yet overall he seems to fail. For the Gospel gives no hint that the crowd's support for John translated into capital for Jesus, and it certainly did not for John himself. The Baptist did not convince "the chief priests, the scribes, and the elders" (11:27-33), and his criticism of the marital arrangements of Herod Antipas led to arrest and execution (6:17-29). Thus, although John was apparently effective in his ministry and continued to fascinate Herod even as his prisoner (6:20), that did not save him from death.

As Mark presents it, the Baptist's lasting achievement was to baptize Jesus. Although the evangelist mentions neither sin nor repentance in connection with Jesus, the baptism provides the circumstances in which the reader is given information about Jesus' identity that expands that which Mark gave in 1:1. Thus the voice from heaven says, "You are my Son, the Beloved; with you I am well pleased" (1:11).

There follows the account of Jesus' desert sojourn. Here his essential goodness is conveyed indirectly. Thus Jesus survives in the presence of wild beasts (1:13). In Israel's tradition, this can be proof of a person's righteousness. In the book of Daniel, for example, the hero accounts for his having survived overnight in a den of lions by telling the offending king, "My God sent his angel and shut the lions' mouths so that they would not hurt me, because I was found blameless before him" (Dan. 6:21-22). Similarly, Jesus' reception of angelic ministrations suggests that he is one of those who "live in the shelter of the Most High" (Ps. 91:1), for whom God "will command his angels . . . to guard you in all your ways" (v. 11). Clearly, the one whose presence John has announced has God on his side. Immediately afterward, however, the evangelist gives the note of the Baptist's arrest (Mark 1:14).

So any success that John has comes from what Jesus will do, not from his own activities, effective as they were at first. As God's "messenger" sent to "prepare the way of the Lord" (1:3, quoting Isa. 40:3), John's fate is mysterious but not, in the end, unfitting. He "prepares" Jesus' way both by getting the people ready to listen to him and by silently providing readers with an anticipation of what is going to happen to Jesus.

Jesus' pattern of activity is not essentially different from that of John. After initial successes, he also soon draws the enmity of others while going about his ministry, in his case preaching the kingdom of God and teaching (1:14, 21). From the outset, "he taught them as one having authority, and not as the scribes" (1:22), and his miracles of healing reinforce that authority (v. 27). The near-inevitable resentment on the part of existing "authorities" (read, "the scribes") renders unsurprising the sequel: the multiple criticisms of Jesus voiced in the five incidents of 2:1–3:6, his relatives' doubts about his sanity (3:20-21), and the scribes' assumption that the source of his power is "the ruler of the demons" (3:22-30). The people who seek his death as early as 3:6 will have their way in chapters 14 and 15. Even so, the angel's announcement of the resurrection in 16:6 will demonstrate that the ultimate success of Jesus' work is even more surprising than was John's.

Alto: The Divine Perspective

At least in story-time, events proceed much more slowly with Jesus than they did with John. For in chapter 4, Mark steps back and considers the situation from a different perspective. Here, beginning with the parable of the sower, the evangelist defines successful human activity as a gift from God. The origin of that activity and its relationship to what people think they are doing are, therefore, beyond people's control and understanding. This is so whether the agent concerned is Jesus or anyone else—Mark 4:3-20 includes both. (Paradoxically, this teaching will make the self and its activities more significant, not less so.)

The immediate referent of the story about the sower in 4:3-9 is Jesus himself, whom the first chapters of the Gospel have described as constantly doing the work of the sower in the parable: preaching the gospel of God in the towns of Galilee (1:14, 38), teaching in synagogues (1:21-22,

39) and beside the sea (2:13; 4:2), and speaking to people "the word" about repentance and the kingdom of God (2:2; 1:15, 38). The purpose of the parable is to encourage his own labors and those of any other sowers/preachers, by showing the vast extent of the final harvest (4:8). Encouragement is necessary because, in the nature of the case, preachers experience no absolute success in their ministry. Even "converts" who seem to have taken the message to heart may fall away at any time. As with the seeds, the observed facts of Jesus' preaching are that most of what is "sown" will "die" at some time prior to the harvest. That, of course, raises the question: why carry on such useless work? The answer comes in the assurance with which the parable concludes (4:8)—the immense productivity of that which does survive should be sufficient to convince even the most disheartened sower that the activity is profitable and ought to be continued. It is easy enough to imagine Jesus telling this parable to make his followers and perhaps himself believe that his Galilean ministry is worthwhile, despite its apparent lack of sustained results among the people.[9] At the harvest the results will be superabundant, he insists. So Jesus and his friends carry on in that hope.

The alleged "explanation" of the parable in 4:14-20 can be read as a reapplication of it for situations in which the need to encourage preachers had been replaced by a concern for quality control among those who listen to the preaching. In this reinterpretation of the story, Mark focuses on the seed and suggests (however improbably, at the level of imagery) that it has some responsibility for its fate. Yet here, too, the massive yield that will come at harvest time is far beyond all reasonable expectation and cannot be accounted for in terms of human achievement.

As Timothy Carmody has noted, there is something mysterious about success in the Mark's Gospel. Writing about the parable of the sower, he observed that, while the cause of failure is usually obvious—because the various kinds of soil do not allow the seeds to grow—"the brief statement of the success suggests that the miracle of growth of the seed is a mystery that surpasses the virtue of the soil." Thus, although clearly the soil is important, the seed's potential cannot be predicted from its environment alone. Carmody continues: "This leaves a gap in the reader's understanding of what it means to respond correctly to the word."[10] The issue here is not simply that people cannot be sure that what they are doing is right. More fundamentally, Mark suggests that human action in its completeness has also a divine component that cannot be assessed directly but is occasionally sensed. There is thus a gap between what people in fact do and what they tend to suppose they are doing.

Further examples in Mark 4 draw attention to the existence of such a gap and away from the important but secondary moral concerns about the dangers posed by Satan, persecution, and the normal run of human desires (4:15-19). People will receive in measures beyond the requirements of normal human transactions, both positively and negatively. Thus:

> "The measure you give will be the measure you get, and still more will be given you. For to those who have, more will be given; and from those who have nothing [literally: 'have not'], even what they have will be taken away" (Mark 4:24-25).

What is this "more"? Mark's Jesus is particularly enigmatic here, but his promise represents the measure of God's generosity to those who are able to accept what they have as God's gift to them and who are generous with it (4:24). Mark understands that God adds to—augments—

what people achieve, provided their work is genuinely human and not merely aimed at promoting themselves. Consequently, the full significance of human action is realized only within the context of the kingdom of God. However, that is in no way under human control. It is indeed a secret (or mystery: *mystērion*, in Greek, 4:11) known only to those with knowledge beyond the ordinary. Therefore, to the uninitiated it remains as mysterious as the way that, without any further help from the farmer who did the planting, farmland of its own accord (the Greek word here is *automatē*) bears the fruit that eventually he can harvest (4:26-29). Similarly, the tiny mustard seed somehow becomes a huge bush that can offer shelter to birds (4:30-32).

The ministry of Jesus and its reception by its hearers are part of this mystery. Like the sower who sows "the word" (4:14), Jesus "was speaking the word to" the people he encountered (2:2). It is not a straightforward communication but, because of its mysterious content, is best told in parables (4:33). As the parable of the sower claims, Jesus' ministry as a whole will be massively fruitful, giving yields far beyond any natural expectation, for any who continually hear and receive God's word (4:20). Writing around the year 70 C.E., Mark is probably thinking here about the community of Christians that has grown from a small group of frightened disciples. How did the growth come about? The evangelist evidently sees the results of the human actions of Jesus and his followers as having a divine component, but does not actually say so in chapter 4.

Mark makes explicit this notion in 10:23-27. Here the image of the camel trying to pass through the needle's eye illustrates Jesus' reiterated statement of how difficult it is for one with possessions to enter the kingdom of God. His disciples' incomprehension gives Jesus the opening he needs to declare that what is beyond human achievement is, nevertheless, possible with God, for whom all things are possible (10:26, 27). Peter then wonders aloud about those who, like himself and his companions, have "left everything" to follow Jesus (10:28). Jesus' response is in line with the massive yield that the seed is to give at the harvest:

> "Truly, I tell you, there is no one who has left house or brothers or sisters or mother or father or children or fields, for my sake and for the sake of the good news, who will not receive a hundredfold now in this age— houses, brothers and sisters, mothers and children, and fields with persecutions—and in the age to come eternal life" (Mark 10:29-30).

This hard saying makes clear that the gospel requires renunciation of family relationships. On the other hand, the "hundredfold" that Jesus promises consists of the very same things; one might indeed ask how anyone would cope with having a hundred houses and mothers, and potentially hundreds of siblings, children, and fields! Thirty years of life as a vowed religious sister has convinced me, however, that precisely these elements are by-products of a deliberate decision to rethink one's basic commitments. Someone who does this becomes part of a larger community of faith, in which many of the "normal" boundaries between people no longer function as such. Even more surprisingly, relationships that had been "given up" have an interesting tendency to return in a richer form. Mark's implication is that for people who have accepted an initial detachment for Jesus' sake (and the possibility of suffering), possessions and "family" connections will certainly not be lacking and do not hinder reception of eternal life "in the age to come" (10:30). That this also is God's doing is hinted at by the unexpressed source of the bounty (one who leaves all will "receive"—*from whom?*) and by the reversal of order predicted in the next verse: "Many who are first shall be last, and the last will be first" (10:31).

If Mark's point is that divine action finally completes human activity and that humans left to themselves are liable to be at risk from their possessions and relationships, how does that help one seeking alternative strategies to violence? Somewhat superficially, it serves as a reminder that people are highly corruptible. What we have around us can indeed choke us (Mark 4), although it need not (Mark 10). But primarily it underscores the mysterious nature of the project in which people are engaged. They—we—are not ultimately in charge of what happens. No humans are. As Mark presents him, not even Jesus was. In Gethsemane he prayed that the God for whom "all things are possible" (14:36, an echo of 10:27) would not make him endure a fate that seemed unavoidable (14:35-36). On Golgotha the next day, having been gradually deserted by all his friends, Jesus' final words are: "My God, my God, why have you forsaken me?" (15:34). His ministry of preaching the word has led to this scene of pathos. There is no humanly detectable link between his cruel death and the enormous yield promised by the parable of the sower in chapter 4. Yet Mark's narrative implies that the move toward the harvest continues with Jesus' resurrection and his invitation to reassemble the group that wants to be with him (16:7), an invitation that, within a few decades, resulted in the establishment of the church of which Mark is a member and for which he writes this document.

In sum, the gospel according to Mark implies that, since it is not even clear what form the harvest will take, there is no requirement for success at all costs. This may come as a surprise to a "can-do" people who try to foresee and plan for every eventuality in their personal lives and to keep control of corporate projects through financial planning, endless committee work, capital campaigns, program development, and the like. Adopting the way of living that Mark proposes may even be experienced as liberation from the burden of assuming that everything depends on us: "Be still and know that I am God!" says the psalmist (46:10), reminding people of where the responsibility really lies. Certainly, attention to God's word, accompanied by vigilance, fidelity, and a measure of asceticism (e.g., hard work and considering others' needs), is required if the seed's potential is to be realized: complacency is inappropriate. Yet the harvest itself is mysterious and is received as gift when the time comes. Any kind of activism, particularly if it involves or risks doing violence to others, would be modified by such a consideration of the context in which it is occurring, a context that extends, Mark suggests, far beyond any human boundaries.

Tenor: How to Get What You Want

Between chapter 4, when they heard the parable of the sower, and the part of chapter 10 where Jesus uses the "camel" and the "hundredfold" images to teach them more about the significance of possessions (cf. 4:7, 18-19), the disciples have been exposed to some important teaching, the elements of which Mark repeats even more emphatically a third time immediately after 10:31. Occurring in chapters 8, 9, and 10 and enclosed in two accounts of Jesus healing someone who is blind (8:22-26 and 10:46-52), this teaching concerns human activity, the topic that featured largely in Mark chapters 1–3, as we saw above. By Mark 8, the Baptist is dead, despite a popular rumor that was earlier associated with Herod (8:7-28; cf. 6:14). What remains is the twofold question of how Jesus is to fulfill his mission (and thus become the great figure that Mark's church believes he is) and how that affects the behavior of those whom he called "to be with him" (3:14).

The answer, given three times, is similarly twofold. The culmination of Jesus' ministry, in essential continuity with the whole of it, will be suffering, death, and resurrection, events that Mark presents him foretelling in chapters 8, 9, and 10. Immediately after each prediction, Jesus indicates the behavior required of people who want to be his disciples. Thus the first prediction, vehemently rejected by Peter, leads into an exposition of what is entailed in being a follower of Jesus (chap. 8), while after each of the other two, Jesus teaches about what constitutes greatness for his disciples (chaps. 9 and 10). Let us look at these three sets of teaching about discipleship.

First, in chapter 8, self-denial (in contrast to self-indulgence) and taking up one's cross (i.e., doing what is right, wherever it leads) characterize one who wishes to follow Jesus (8:34). The rationale is the ultimate reversal: that one's self, one's *psychē*, the only thing that one really wants and has (8:36-37), is saved by losing it for the sake of Jesus and the gospel (8:35), not by the obvious means of pushing oneself forward. What might this mean in practice?

Quite apart from the gospel, human experience testifies to the paradox to which this saying of Jesus refers: that the things people value most do not long survive attempts at holding on to them. Children trying to keep frogs or fireflies in jars soon discover that life cannot be hoarded—the very idea is absurd. Yet even adults sometimes behave as though by employing sufficient effort and resources they can hold on to their youth and treat death as an option that they choose not to take up. The time (life) that is spent in this way is largely wasted, because it is spent on an objective that cannot be attained.

At the interpersonal level too, the paradox of losing life in order to keep it is evident. Thus, having invested themselves in relationships, people fear losing what they have. So instead of allowing the situation to develop and doing what is necessary to adjust to each new reality as it comes along, they try to "freeze" the relationship in its earlier, more satisfactory configuration. After a while, the ones so "loved" begin to chafe under the external control that stunts their lives. If they can, they break free; otherwise they live in a state of resentment. Either way, the relationship has been spoiled, the very thing that the person responsible wanted to avoid. Allowing others freedom certainly makes it possible for them to opt out of the association, but it also enables the partners to continue developing their relationship in the only conditions that will sustain it long term. As with the "harvest" in chapter 4, the ultimate form that each relationship will take is unknown. So, although it can be more or less wisely nurtured, it cannot be programmed in advance. Jesus' teaching in Mark 8 includes all this human wisdom and more: "life" for Christians entails an essential relatedness to him that comes about through patterning one's life on his, including his natural, human death and God-given resurrection.[11] As the evangelist already implied repeatedly in chapter 4[12] and will in chapter 10 assert openly (10:24-28), God is at work when people save their "selves" in this paradoxical way.

The disciples in Mark are unable to see any of this. Thus they do not understand Jesus' second passion prediction, fear to ask him for clarification, and privately dispute about which of them is the greatest (9:31-34). So Jesus gives them another version of the divine reversal: their perfectly legitimate desire to be first is attainable only by being "last of all and servant of all" (v. 35). He then teaches them that God is to be encountered in those who are generally thought of as being of no consequence, the child in this instance (36-37). Although there is ample evidence that children were prized in Roman and Jewish families, the context assumed in this passage is that of patronage in Hellenistic Roman society. Where patronage was concerned, people's value and the treatment they could expect to receive depended on what they could in return be expected to contribute to the patron's own advantage. Therefore beneficence to wealthy adults was recognized as at least potentially a good investment, because such people would feel honor-bound to return the favor and had the resources for doing so. Children, however, were among those not in a position to reciprocate, so benevolence to them and those like them made no economic sense. It is this attitude that Jesus attempts to change. Finally, he follows up by trying to detach the disciples from their proprietary attitude toward him and his mission. One of them, John, has told Jesus, "Teacher, we saw someone casting out demons in your name, and we tried to stop him, because he was not following us" (9:38). Jesus attempts to set John right: acting in Jesus' name is what matters, he says, not "following us" (38-40).

In Jesus' refusal to allow his followers to think that they can increase their status by means of their association with him, Mark draws attention to a common human propensity: to use any circumstance at all to gain the ascendancy over others. It is of vital importance that the disciples learn to resist this. If they do not, they are not following Jesus, however much they may appear to be or think that they are. Rather, they are imposing their own will on others: essentially a violent action that invites (and often receives) response in kind. In that case, their "ministry" would have the effect of increasing the violence inherent in human society, instead of fostering God's reign of peace. It is a lesson that is extremely difficult to learn, because it runs contrary to behavior that has enabled *Homo sapiens* to achieve a degree of dominance on the Earth and its immediate environs.

Although in Mark 9 and 10 Jesus actually *affirms* the basic human dynamic that makes people want to be first in rank, he there rejects the idea that the way to achieve priority is by pressuring for it. Whether in the area of ministry or more broadly, such behavior can sometimes be effective for a while, but only until the next talented and ambitious person comes along. Then those whose strength once allowed them to overcome the competition of their peers must become increasingly vigilant and resourceful in order to keep their position. Energy that is spent defending turf is not available for the enterprise at hand, and the resulting divided attention causes stress elsewhere. Eventually, people trying to hold on to power in such circumstances are a liability to the project to which they are dedicated and an embarrassment to the ones who care about them. Conversely, those who follow Jesus in selflessly spending their lives in service to others are not involved in this kind of rivalry. The authority of a Francis of Assisi or a Mother Teresa is immeasurable and remains intact until they die and, often enough, beyond that. This is in accordance with the gospel tradition as a whole: the meek[13] are to inherit the earth (Matt 5:5), and the ones pronounced blessed in Matthew's parable about the sheep and the goats are people who ministered to those in need (Matt. 25:31-46).[14] In Mark's version of this insight, the one who is the last of all and servant of all ranks highest (9:35; 10:43-44).

It is easy enough to imagine what a challenge this teaching would have presented to men who were not slaves or servants. But what about those who were? Or what impact would it have had on women, to the extent that they were expected to be self-effacing and to give up their own ambitions for the good of the family? It is not impossible that they were being given an inside track, if they really understood what being a Christian entails. The alternative is that the teaching in this section of Mark could have been misused to keep such people "in their place." So far as we can tell, none ever gets to present his or her case. Would that Philemon had enclosed a note for his master along with Paul's letter, or that a letter from one of Paul's women companions had survived!

The disciples' blindness continues in chapter 10. Here, immediately after the third prediction of the passion (10:32-34), James and John unwisely attempt to advance their cause by asking Jesus for the two seats beside him "in [his] glory" (vv. 35-40). When, in reply, Jesus has told them of the link between glory and suffering, and has implicitly identified God as the maker of the seating plan, the other ten voice their concern that James and John may have gained an unfair advantage over them (41). So Jesus explains the radical difference between authority as generally construed and the form it should take among his followers. As in chapter 9, the one wishing to be great must be servant, and "whoever wishes to be first among you must be slave of all" (44). The logic is impeccable for anyone who wants to follow Jesus: "For the Son of Man came not to be served but to serve, and to give his life [as] a ransom for many" (45). By freely giving up his life when the alternative was to abandon his ministry, Jesus somehow made it possible for others to be free from some of the constraints that had bound them. This hard saying in 10:45 is the key to greatness in a world where God controls ultimate outcomes. The disciples must learn that the strength of the strong is for the good of all, not for self-aggrandizement and certainly not for putting others down.

This section of the gospel (8:22–10:52) and Jesus' pre-Jerusalem ministry conclude with his restoring sight to Bartimaeus, thereby demonstrating for a second time his ability to cure the blindness of those who trust that he can indeed heal them (10:46-52; cf. Mark 6:1-6). Mark implies that the metaphorical blindness repeatedly demonstrated by the disciples in chapters 8–10 could be cured in the same way, although the persistence of their self-concern suggests that it would not be easy. Once Jesus enters Jerusalem, most of the teaching about discipleship takes the form of counterexamples from the disciples themselves, with the occasional action by outsiders that is to be emulated. By this stage, readers should be able to draw their own conclusions. The point remains the same, though: looking out for yourself is not the way to get what you really want.[15]

Bass: Death and Resurrection as Paradigm

Having healed Bartimaeus, Jesus enters Jerusalem, where he will soon die (11:1-11). For Christians, Jesus' passion, death, and resurrection are the paradigm that forms the basis of the gospel message, as we have seen. That is: in a sinful world, human action leads to trouble, indeed to a shameful and agonizing death, and yet, Christians claim, God somehow acts "subsequently" (and even now, 10:29-30) to give much more than could ever have been expected. In particular, God gives the assurance of forgiveness and the companionship of others. Jesus' refusal to stop acting on behalf of those who "need a physician" (2:17) raises questions about the source of the power by which he cures (3:22). As Mark tells the story, Jesus' words and actions gradually bring about the hostility that will lead to his execution and to the mysterious, eschatological divine action of resurrection. Unlike Mark's readers, the women who go on Easter Sunday to anoint Jesus in his tomb are still unaware of this pattern. The silence and fear with which they respond to the "young man's" message is understandable but perhaps intended to be one more example of how Jesus was misunderstood by his followers prior to the resurrection.[16] For as long as it lasts, such behavior deprives Jesus' disciples of the presence that might finally bring home to them the full significance of human activity, a message the early church would then preach to the world and of which Mark's Gospel is a prime exemplar.

Coda: Learning from Bad Examples

An important feature of the Gospel of Mark is that, even though Jesus chooses his special group of twelve disciples (3:13) and expends much effort on teaching them, they seem to learn nothing at all about what Jesus is about, at least during the time of his ministry. Not only do they consistently misunderstand him, as we saw when considering the teaching about discipleship in chapters 8–10, but they also completely let him down. Let us now consider this second aspect of their portrayal and why it is an essential part of Mark's version of the "good news."

According to Mark, Jesus appoints the twelve so that they may "be with him" (3:14). For most of Jesus' ministry they succeed in this at least physically, even if they lack a good sense of who Jesus is. (Unlike Mark and his readers, the twelve do not have the advantage of hindsight.) As the going gets rougher, they begin to desert him. For most, this is a betrayal of their intentions. At the Last Supper, for example, Peter boasts of his willingness to die rather than deny Jesus, and the others concur (14:30-31). Yet Peter, James, and John, whom Jesus chose to keep him company in his agony in Gethsemane, repeatedly fall asleep (37, 40, 41). Judas, "one of the twelve" (43) has already taken steps to ensure that Jesus is handed over to his enemies (10-11, 43-46). After having described Jesus' arrest, Mark notes succinctly of the ones who remained with Jesus, "All of them deserted him and fled" (50). The measure of their desperation *not* to be with him when he is arrested is shown in the evangelist's portrayal of the young man who runs off naked rather than remain there (51-52). Shortly afterward, Peter caves in to pressure, twice from a woman in the service of the high priest and once from someone with a tolerably good ear for a regional accent—three times Peter denies knowing Jesus, before realizing the enormity of what he has done (66-72). When someone is needed to help Jesus with his cross, the soldiers draft a passerby, Simon of Cyrene; the disciples are nowhere in evidence (15:21).

Mark specifies that those who stay with Jesus until he dies are "women looking on from a distance," including some from Galilee (15:40). Two of the women take note of where Joseph of Arimathea (*not* one of the twelve) buried Jesus and, with a third, take spices to anoint the body once the Sabbath is over (15:47; 16:1). Whether Mark thought that the women were doing the right thing is doubtful: the triple predictions of death and resurrection in chapters 8–10 would make anointing the body super-fluous. Yet at least these three women were, in some sense, "with Jesus"; by contrast, another trio, Peter, James, and John, repeatedly slept when Jesus appealed for their support in Gethsemane, and the disciples fled (14:33-42, 50). Despite all of this, the angel's message to the women on Easter Sunday morning is to "tell his disciples and Peter" that they will see the risen Jesus in Galilee (16:7).

What is Mark's point in portraying the disciples in this way? Perhaps to convey that people set out with good intentions but are prone to weakness and selfishness that can have disastrous consequences for themselves and others. However, these defects need not cut people off from Jesus and one another. This is good news for any human beings, but is especially so for a persecuted church, some members of which will inevitably not hold fast when they have to endure violent opposition for the sake of Jesus and the gospel. There is the possibility of renewed life "with Jesus" even after such culpable failure.

Conclusion

The resources that Mark offers people who wish to forgo violence are much more radical than specific strategies for solving that particular problem. Instead they are a proposal for changing the orientation of human life. The new orientation involves setting aside the strong instincts and culturally sanctioned behavior that encourage people to be actively concerned only with themselves and their immediate interests. At least some people accepted this change of outlook, and after a few decades it was flourishing in many of the cities of the empire. What, though, does it have to do with our present situation?

The reorientation proposed in Mark's version of the gospel may be an updated version of our evolutionary inheritance, inasmuch as it fits us for survival in a world in which the extent of interdependence has become increasingly evident. The ever-expanding gap between rich and poor, along with everyone's acute, media-induced awareness of it, is a formula for endless fragmentation and strife. National and supranational legal systems may help to some extent, but the prospect that human relations will be regulated solely by litigation is dismal indeed. So the deleterious effects of division among people are likely to keep on growing, unless a sufficient number of them can become actively concerned, not only about themselves and their immediate families or neighborhoods, but also about the wider society and parts of the world that, seemingly although not in reality, have no connection with them.

Such a turnaround, a conversion in the deepest sense, requires resources that most people do not have in large measure. In particular, it requires a high degree of trust that the "others," whether richer or poorer, will not take advantage of us if we attempt to live seriously in the way Mark proposes. They may well take advantage, of course: Mark expressly says that "persecutions" are included among the expectations of those who follow the crucified Jesus (10:30). There is no masochism here, however. As with Jesus, the suffering is neither sought nor wanted, but results from a refusal to stop acting for the well-being of others. The hope is that the pattern of Jesus holds good— that suffering and even death are not the end but lead to fuller life.

Some people do undertake to live in this way, frequently as an expression of their empowerment by Jesus and their commitment to him and his work. They are the reconcilers, willing to put their own lives on the line in the tradition of Moses and Abigail, to bring together and mediate between enemies. Quite frequently, they have been wronged by the system they are taking on. Perhaps they have lost loved ones to military dictatorships, spent years in prison, or endured the humiliation of lifetime membership in a group deemed inferior. The experience that has broken others has somehow enabled them to seize the bigger picture. Such individuals manage to transcend all their pain and anger in order to work for justice, reconciliation, and peace. Some are known by name worldwide: who has not heard of Nelson Mandela and Archbishop Desmond Tutu? Others have a renown that is more local: for example, Mairead Corrigan and Betty Williams, two women from Northern Ireland who were awarded the Nobel Peace Prize in 1976. Still others are known only through the groups that they formed or joined for this purpose. A prominent example is the Sant'Egidio community based in Rome. Its members take on the work of reconciliation as part of their vocation, in much the same way as did those ancient religious orders that ransomed slaves in the period after the Crusades.[17] Other examples include Pax Christi, many members of the Catholic Worker movement, and the women's (and other) peace movements in Ireland, Latin America, and elsewhere.

Like those revered as saints and like Jesus himself, such committed people have an influence that is disproportionate to their numbers, at least in stirring the imagination of others and sometimes in empowering them to see possibilities where none existed before. A prominent example of this in recent years has been the South African Truth and Reconciliation Commission, mentioned in chapter 10.[18] Possible only because of the acknowledged moral capital of Mandela, Tutu, and others, the Commission gave some measure of hope to a country that was previously assumed to be heading only for a bloodbath. However the practicalities of the situation work out in the future, the fact that the process was conceived and brought to completion in South Africa provides vicarious experience and a possible starting point for those concerned to reconcile other seemingly intractable situations. Truth commissions have been established in several South and Central American countries, including El Salvador, Guatemala, and Chile.

As is obvious from Desmond Tutu's book *No Future Without Forgiveness*,[19] engaging in such reconciliation is costly in the extreme. It involves a commitment that few would have the integrity and courage to take on. Mark's Gospel conveys much the same message. Although one of this evangelist's main themes is the near-certainty of failure and the ever-present possibility of forgiveness (because it is taken for granted that people will fail repeatedly), the terms that it sets out for following Jesus are most exacting. Historically, the evangelist probably thought that those for whom he wrote the Gospel would not have to live that way for very long. This is the most obvious interpretation of Mark 9:1, where Jesus solemnly tells the people, "There are some standing here who will not taste death until they see that the kingdom of God has come with power." The short perspective, together with the indications that followers of Jesus would have to face suffering, may explain Mark's concentration on Jesus as the one who suffers and the starkness of his message about discipleship. Matthew's and Luke's versions of the gospel, written slightly later, also include much about Jesus' death but spend much more time than Mark does on the positive aspects of his life and ministry. It seems that they also found Mark too hard to take. Therefore one may reasonably ask whether it makes any sense to pay attention to Mark two millennia later.

Various objections can be lodged against seeing the world in the way that Mark requires. First, living by the gospel may seem pointless or even dishonest to anyone who does not accept God's beneficent presence to the world and ultimate responsibility for it. Following Jesus goes against most of people's natural instincts and, furthermore, entails repeated failure, as the example of the disciples demonstrates. If there is no God to come through with resurrection, this way seems to have little to recommend it. But is it then of no value at all? Given the history of the last century, it may be worth considering Mark's radical claim that concentrating on others and their needs will somehow result in one's own fulfillment as well.[20] Sometimes it just seems to work out that way, as a glance at a wise (because basically selfless) elder may confirm. Besides, even if some see the world as lacking transcendence, does that mean that those experiencing it differently must deny that experience?

Second, many people find Mark's position deeply offensive and open to abuse. For example, it might be used to justify a subhuman servility, discouraging the initiative that underlies the very real achievements of our species. This is not, I think, a fair charge, for the gospel claim is that God does not detract from genuine human achievement (in distinction from self-promotion), but adds to it: to one who has, *more* will be given (4:25). It seems obvious that human needs are endless, service is reciprocal, and everyone's talents are needed.

A further charge is that reading Mark might encourage people to think of suffering as good. Again this is not borne out by the context. Mark talks about taking up one's cross, not going in search of it. It is a matter of encouraging his community to accept what they cannot honestly avoid. The model here is Jesus, who, having done what he thought was right and accepting the consequences, prayed in Gethsemane that God remove the "cup" from him, but nevertheless accepted the possibility (and later the actuality) that this was not going to happen (14:36). Suffering is never good in itself and is not to be sought for its own sake. On the other hand, in one form or another it is a sure component of any human life. Some of it can be avoided or mitigated, but much remains, because it is a biological and psychological condition of our ability to feel and to relate to people and the world around us. Either it constitutes a surd that threatens to deprive everything else of its meaning or it must somehow be incorporated into the meaning that people find or construct in the universe. Mark offers resources for the latter approach.

Much more insidious is the charge that living by the gospel encourages the form of violence typical of the weak: unfair manipulation of those more competent and assertive than oneself. Although this is a real risk, it lacks grounding in the gospel text and is incompatible with the picture of human living that Mark presents in his gospel.

A third kind of problem is the apparent impracticality of living in the way that Mark advocates. Like most strategies for building peace, this one lacks the precision and immediacy of smart missiles, surgical strikes, and the like. There is ample time and opportunity for things to go wrong. Admittedly, history provides occasional examples of the Matthean beatitude that "the meek . . . will inherit the earth" (Matt. 5:5). Yet the contrary position gives much faster returns and allows people to give full scope to what evolution has best fitted us for: acting to change situations in ways that maximize our own immediate advantage. Going against thousands of years of genetic inheritance seems very risky. Surely it would be quite unnerving to live only by the gospel. Do we really not need military resources as a backup? Besides, even the most committed Christians find it almost impossible to live like Jesus all the time, and those setting out to do so will have many a difficult prudential judgment to make. Mark knows this, of course: his plot and the disciples' abysmal record therein attests that he did not claim it would be easy. Yet as Gandhi, Martin Luther King Jr., and hundreds of saints have demonstrated, putting others first may in the long term indicate our best chance for human flourishing—far superior to stockpiling weapons and cluttering up the atmosphere with defense hardware.

The ultimate question, though, is about the context in which human activity takes place: do science and the humanities tell all that there is to know about the universe, or are people to trust the witness of Mark and other intimations that there may be a broader mystery within which the significance of human actions is both less obvious and much greater than we tend to think? If our individual lives are all that there is, the task would be to grasp whatever success one can manage—and hope that someone stronger will not have his or her eye on it, although knowing that sooner or later they will. Alternatively, one can follow Jesus, try to live like him, and trust that within the community that is committed to doing this, one will find the two things that are necessary (with apologies to Luke 10:42). They are: repeated forgiveness and the presence of the God who is the ultimate and mysterious source of human outcomes and who will somehow bring about the growth that leads to the superabundant harvest.[21] It is, of course, a huge gamble. One cannot tell for sure how things will turn out or, indeed, whether they will turn out at all. However, Mark thinks they will, and so do the other writers whose works are in the New Testament, including, famously, the seer of Revelation, to whose writing we now turn.

12

LION AND LAMB:
THE PERILS OF LANGUAGE

At the end of the Christian biblical canon, the book of Revelation returns us to the problematic situation we encountered earlier—a scriptural work that is generally deemed to encourage violence and glorify it, instead of providing a basis for more creative responses to perceived antagonisms. For many Christians the scandal is even greater than it was with such books as Numbers and Joshua, for John the seer is often accused of bypassing all that the community had learned from Jesus, to which Mark and all other New Testament writers testify. The issue here is this: does John in fact foster violence and make it attractive in a way that is a fundamental betrayal of Christian self-understanding? Or are other things going on here from which one might be able to learn alternative strategies?

Certainly, Revelation contains much violent imagery. Some of it does seem to result from the frustrated anger of a community that resents bitterly its inferior status and reacts by projecting onto God the harmful actions that its members wish they could do to those who hold power over them. As noted among the conclusions to the previous chapter, this is one of the real dangers to which Christianity is prone. In light of the wider biblical canon, texts that display this attitude should be taken as a warning against doing likewise, not as a model for emulation.

On the other hand, it is arguable that, despite this undercurrent of resentment, the book of Revelation makes a theme of violence to a much lesser extent than is generally supposed. In reality, much of the "violent" imagery in this book is an inventive use of traditional language in which the seer expresses vividly the realities of the Christian experience, according to which God delivers people who endure suffering while remaining faithful to the crucified Jesus. In other words, a careful reading of Revelation will demonstrate that John's presentation of Jesus (and of the requirements of discipleship) does not differ essentially from that of Mark and the other New Testament writers.

Nor does John radically differ from them in his assessment of created realities and the trajectory on which they are set. (Indeed he is also in line with the Old Testament understanding of this view of God and creation, although reading them through a christological lens, of course.) For example, Paul and his successors are like John the seer in being interested in what the phenomenon of Jesus revealed about the cosmos as a whole.[1] With regard to specifically human affairs, John is certainly not alone in warning his readers about the havoc that possessions and wealth can cause and the opposition that Christians can expect: Mark and other New Testament writers do the same. They also share with John a general expectation that, at Christ's return, those faithful to him will in some way share his glory. Chapter 15 of Paul's first letter to the Corinthians specifies this further when Paul writes that history is the process in which enemies are "put . . . under [Christ's] feet" (v. 25, based on Pss. 110:1 and 8:7) and ends when "death" is finally "swallowed up in victory" (1 Cor. 15:54). The book of Revelation is not entirely different from the other books of the New Testament.

Yet the details and emphases of John's account convey his particular contribution to the tradition. Two respects in which the narrative of Revelation differs from other New Testament writings are especially significant here, not only in themselves but also because of the way in which they are brought together. First, John attempts to say more about how Christians' present experience within the Roman Empire relates to the ongoing eschatological perspective. He therefore treats in much more detail the part that the created world (including in particular its social developments) plays in Christian life, positively and (mostly) negatively. There is a concern both for the local level (e.g., in the messages to the seven churches in chaps. 2 and 3) and for the broader picture (e.g., the perception of the empire as an incorrigibly evil development of an essentially good created order). Second, much more than other New Testament writers, John focuses on the playing out of God's righteous judgment of humans and the mythologically portrayed elements that underlie the negative aspects of human experience. These two concerns—the created world, in all its complexity and ambiguity, and redemption from sin and evil—he brings together to a much greater degree than is the case elsewhere in the New Testament.[2] This perspective will sometimes lead him to appear to be violent when he is not. For although, in true biblical fashion, John is firmly convinced that creation is good and that God's justice will prevail, he takes very seriously the reality of human sinfulness and its manifestations.

There is an important additional factor that may make Revelation sound more violent than it really is. It is that John presumes the reader's familiarity, not only with the Christian doctrinal and liturgical commonplaces of his day, but also with the contents of Old Testament prophetic writing and the conventions of Jewish apocalyptic thought and literature. Modern readers may have some familiarity with the writings of the prophets but are unlikely to know enough about apocalyptic literature to read Revelation well. Apocalyptic writings include Daniel 7–12, Zechariah 1–6, and many nonbiblical examples such as the Qumran War Scroll, parts of the Enoch literature, 4 Ezra, 3 Baruch, and the Apocalypse of Abraham.[3] Those who write apocalyptically use surrealist and, often, military imagery to express both their experience of the reality and strength of evil and their complete confidence that God will rescue them from it. Therefore apocalyptic literature is writing that typically expresses the cry of people whose suffering is so dire that it *should* indicate that their God has given up on them—yet they absolutely refuse to entertain that possibility. Those to whom John originally wrote Revelation may have known how to interpret apocalyptic texts. Most present-day people do not, so the possibility of unqualified readers going astray is even greater than with other parts of the New Testament. Let readers beware.

Part One

In part 1 we shall first outline the general situation of John the seer and the communities for whom he writes, to suggest the likely origins of his hostile attitude to imperial society. As Revelation is the final book in a work that took its origin from God's choice of Abraham and his descendants, some comparisons with the patriarchs will be made here. Then, still in part one, we shall briefly note how John grounds Christian living in his understanding of church, creation, and salvation. The various sections of part 2 consider how the seer uses imagery to portray Jesus and the wide-ranging effects of his life and work.

Enduring Patiently

John introduces himself to his readers as God's servant and as brother of those other "servants" to whom he is writing (1:1, 9).[4] Both aspects of John's self-designation have their basis not in anything that John has achieved but in the activity of "Jesus Christ . . . who loves us and freed us from our sins by his blood,[5] and made us to be a kingdom, priests serving his God and Father" (vv. 5-6). So, like the patriarchs, John and the rest of the Christian community identify themselves as recipients of an act of God in their favor. As in Genesis, the effects of that divine action are understood to be both secure and yet not fully evident at the present time.

In the way this worked out in everyday life, however, there is a major difference between the patriarchal narratives in Genesis 12–50 and John's understanding of late-first-century Christian experience in the cities of the Roman province of Asia, an area corresponding to modern-day western Turkey. Genesis depicts the patriarchs as able to live easily under the terms of the promise that they are carrying. Once Abraham has left Ur in response to God's call (Gen. 12:1-4), he and his descendants wander in a fairly peaceable way through land that would one day be theirs, even though others occupy it at present. There are, it is true, famines and occasional wars (e.g., Gen. 12 and 14), but Abraham and his family are depicted as surviving these with minimal drama. In any case, such crises affected all their contemporaries and were in no way peculiar to the recipients of the promise. The tensions in the stories about the patriarchs are mostly intrafamilial: how will God fulfill the promise of progeny? To which of the sons will the divine blessing be transmitted?[6] At no time are the patriarchs portrayed as being anxious about how long it will be until they receive the land. (Such anxiety would be misplaced, since the text of Genesis includes God's repeated reassurances that the promise still stands.)[7] Nor do they show any interest at all in the status or fate of the land's current occupants.

A primary factor determining the tone of the patriarchal narratives is, of course, that the stories were written centuries after the time in which the events are set, by people who regarded themselves as descendants of those later generations in whom the divine promise of land and progeny had been fulfilled. One can be much more sanguine about a developing situation when its ultimate resolution in one's favor is known from experience.

It is quite otherwise with John the seer and the community to which he belongs. For he is writing not about earlier generations but about his contemporaries and how they should understand their own circumstances as recipients of God's salvation, mediated by Christ. Although John thinks he knows how the story is *supposed* to end, his knowledge rests on a faith commitment, not on fulfillment in the past. Furthermore, the tension is heightened because Christians are confident that the Lord Jesus will indeed deliver them from their present distress.[8] They hope for this ardently, crying, "Come, Lord Jesus!" (22:20; cf. v. 17). They thus experience an uncertainty and an urgency that the patriarchs, as portrayed in Genesis, do not. In addition, John expects his readers to have a strong interest in the fate of their non-Christian contemporaries, both positively and negatively. His understanding is that those among whom Christians live must turn from their present ways to worship the one God,[9] and that those who do not ("everyone whose name has not been written from the foundation of the world in the book of life")[10] are doomed to be cast into "the lake of fire" (20:15, specified in 19:20 as burning "with sulfur"). It is true that John's churches appear not to regard themselves as directly responsible for such conversions as will occur. They happen as a result of sickness (2:21-23), a great earthquake (11:13),[11] and the plagues associated with the first six trumpets. Revelation does not describe missionary activity of the type that Paul exemplifies. Yet the prelude to the earthquake is the prophetic testimony and violent death of the "two witnesses" (11:3-12).[12] So the Christians to whom John writes could not have regarded those among whom they lived with the detached attitudes that the writers of Genesis attribute to the patriarchs. There was simply too much that remained at stake.

There is more. The patriarchs are presented as being able to differ more or less amicably with those who lived around them. At most, some of their neighbors preferred not to remain close to them for too long. Note, for example, the polite way in which Abimelech removes Abraham from his immediate vicinity (Gen. 20:15) and later asks Isaac to leave Gerar (26:16).[13] By contrast, the Christians' new status brought with it obligations that made them conspicuously different from other members of their society, in ways that led to trouble.[14] Even though Revelation was most probably written during the time of Domitian (81-96 C.E.), when Christians were not yet subjected to systematic legalized persecution, they were always liable to harassment locally because of being an easily identifiable group that refused to accept certain tenets and practices prevalent in society at large, particularly with regard to the imperial gods.[15] Moreover, in an action that set a disastrous precedent, Nero had singled them out as a convenient scapegoat on whom he could blame the fire that destroyed much of Rome in 64 C.E.[16]

The text of Revelation itself gives evidence of a further problem that communities had to live with: as long as the secular authorities assumed, at least tacitly, that Christianity was a branch of Judaism, Christians could benefit from such legal protection as the empire traditionally offered to the Jewish people within its boundaries. In some of the communities to which John is writing, however, relationships with the local Jewish communities had turned very bitter, so that Christians could no longer rely on having this protection.[17]

Therefore Christians' interactions with society at large were characterized by uncertainty and the risk of harm from those among whom they lived. The people to whom John wrote are presumed to experience their public lives as under the control of a powerful, immensely wealthy, highly organized society in which they lived as outsiders. At any moment, the authorities could exert their full might against this small group of people that had the temerity to stand out against the empire. In light of this, many Christians would have been strongly tempted to abandon their isolationist stance and make themselves eligible, at least in principle, for what the empire appeared to be offering: "accept[ing] the mark of the beast," as Revelation 19:20 (NAB) puts it (see 13:16-18).

Much more than Paul and those Christians who learned from him, John is convinced that Christians must be countercultural, given the nature of imperial society. He thinks that those Christian communities that do *not* feel their powerlessness are in even more danger than the ones that do. So he is especially hard on the complacency of the churches in Sardis and Laodicea (3:1, 17). Overall he makes no secret of the high cost of remaining faithful to Jesus. Thus in 17:1–19:10 (and especially 18:11-23) he indicates what the empire can make available. Those who refuse to accommodate themselves to it (and worse, try to convert others to their viewpoint) have no chance at all of access to its luxuries and can never regard as their own even the more ordinary manifestations of civilized life (18:11-13, 22-23). Although John hoped that God would terrify some of their contemporaries into conversion, he took it for granted that Roman imperial society was based on realities that were uncompromisingly evil (e.g., Rev. 17:3; 19:20). The seer is vociferous in his disdain for the values of that society, and in this he is very different from the people who assembled and edited the traditions about Abraham and his descendants.

There is thus a high degree of tension in John's work. Motivating the whole book is the beneficent action of God in Christ (i.e., Jesus' death and resurrection) as John received it in the Christian tradition. Yet the seer's sense of what is required by divine justice in the face of human response to that action occasionally leads him to some very problematic expressions of the way in which God deals with evil. It is as though John's experience of God has fundamentally affected the deepest level of his being, but his day-to-day encounter with the resulting opposition has predisposed him to adopt some of the already violent-sounding imagery available to him in the prophetic and apocalyptic writings.[18]

Another contributing factor to John's attitude was the expectation, prevalent among some groups of Jews, that the ultimate, eschatological fulfillment would involve conflict between the forces of good and those of evil. The ancient Jewish texts found beside the Dead Sea at Qumran document such expectation on the part of another strongly countercultural group. In particular, the War Scroll, probably composed in the second half of the first century B.C.E., describes the expected "attack of the sons of light against the company of the sons of darkness," including prescriptions for how "the sons of light" should conduct their part of it.[19] Even though John thought that in Christ's death the essential work had been done, he may well have been led to entertain such ideas of eschatological conflict when he saw how the churches might at any time fall foul of the imperial magistrates, and he could detect no indications that the situation would ever improve.

At the personal level too, John has substantial reasons for understanding the human situation in terms that are largely conflictive. For he is writing from the island of Patmos, to which he has been relegated because, he says, he "proclaimed God's word and gave testimony to Jesus" (Rev. 1:9; NAB).[20] The Greek word used here for "testimony" is *martyria*, cognate with the English *martyr*. John understands his own suffering as linking him with other Christians who have suffered (2:3, 9) or been executed (e.g., Antipas of Pergamum in 2:13 and those represented by the two witnesses of 11:1-13), and with those whose future suffering is, he considers, inevitable (see, e.g., 2:10; 3:10). Indeed, as John describes the situation, the Christian activity of witnessing to Jesus (the Greek verb is *martyrein*)[21] is likely to take the form of a violent death at the hands of opponents.[22] In such circumstances the fundamental virtue is to hold on to one's identity as a Christian, in defiance of all suggestions that such behavior is at best madness and at worst suicidal. John designates that virtue *hypomonē*, or "patient endurance."[23]

Of course, we have only John's version of the story. He may have been thoroughly paranoid and worthy of being written off as an unauthentic witness to the Christian tradition.[24] However, other parts of the New Testament make it highly probable that at least some of those Christians with whom the seer was in contact did evoke the hostility of those around them, in much the same way as Mark's communities and Paul himself appear to have done.[25] So it is possible that John may have read the situation appropriately enough and that some Christians (e.g., those in the cities addressed in chaps. 2 and 3) would have found helpful the practical advice that he gave. Some later believers evidently recognized in Revelation aspects of their understanding of the world, for the book was ultimately accepted into the biblical canon.[26]

The Basis of Endurance: Experiences of Church, Creation, Redemption

As we have just seen, John finds many difficulties associated with being a faithful Christian in Asia Minor in the mid-90s of the first century. Despite this, there are in Revelation many indications that he is motivated to write, not by his hatred of the empire, but by a strong sense of having been appointed by God to give "witness to the word of God and to the testimony of Jesus Christ by reporting what he saw" (1:2, NAB). This activity will give much-needed strength to his fellow Christians.[27] Just as Paul, before him, told the Corinthians of his absolute obligation to proclaim the gospel (1 Cor. 9:16), so John knows that he has particular responsibilities because he has accepted God's offer of salvation. Also like Paul, he writes in his own name and makes explicit some of the consequences of his situation. These latter affect both daily behavior and the basic understanding of church, creation, and redemption from which such behavior springs.

In everyday life Christians are required to "keep the commandments of God and hold the testimony of Jesus," that is, to bear witness to him with the intention of winning converts (Rev. 12:17). In the perspective of faith, such actions turn out to be part of the garment of "fine linen, bright and pure" that enables humanity to relate fully to the Lamb as his bride (19:7-8): John here explains parenthetically, "the fine linen is the righteous deeds of the saints" (v. 8).

Christians can act in this way because of their perception of what it means to be members of "the churches" (2:7, 17, etc.). In the first five chapters of Revelation John spells this out in his own distinctive way. Jesus, their Lord (22:20-21),[28] is present to the community as "one like the Son of Man" (1:13).[29] This picture John presents vividly from two perspectives. First, in 1:9-20, with regard to the totality of the church, Jesus is in the midst of the seven lamp stands, holding seven stars in his right hand. Second, in chapters 2 and 3, John specifies how Jesus is present to each of the seven representative churches of the Roman province of Asia. For example, Jesus confronts the complacent Laodiceans by emphasizing his fidelity and his all-encompassing influence. Jesus is "the Amen, the faithful and true witness, the origin of God's creation" (3:14)[30] and the one able to supply what they really need (and wrongly think that they already possess; vv. 17-18).

In the following two chapters, John considers a wider picture as he tries to convey his understanding of, first, created reality (chap. 4) and, then, redemption (chap. 5). Revelation 4 reminds his audience that, as God's creatures, they are part of a more diverse set of beings whose nature is to praise "the Lord God the Almighty," the Creator of all things (4:8-11). He does not go into details about non-human creation, preferring to treat the topic by means of traditional symbols from the prophetic books of the Old Testament, and to concentrate on human realities.[31] Yet John takes for granted the position of the book of Genesis that creation is good and that people (the twenty-four elders) are a necessary part of the praise that creation offers to God. In chapter 5 he goes further and writes of Christians' status as those saved by the "Lion of the tribe of Judah" (5:5), the Lamb who seemed to have been slain. This redeemer, like the Creator in Revelation 4, elicits the praise of all creation in the heavenly liturgy (4:9-14). So John presents the worship of God as the ultimate activity, with regard to both creation and redemption (again like Paul, this time in Rom. 8).

Part Two
The Lion/Lamb who Conquers

That the Lion of Judah, borrowed and adapted from Genesis 49:8-12, turns out to be a slain lamb provides a key for understanding John's peculiarly mixed viewpoint in Revelation as a whole. As noted above, underlying all John's experience is his fundamental identity as God's servant whom Christ loves and has freed (1:1, 5).[32] The seer has proclaimed this loudly and in the wrong places, which is why he has been exiled to Patmos and the reason he is writing at all. At the same time, however, John sees the Christian community as being, like Jesus, the target of a violence that must either dominate or be overcome in some way.[33] Just as Israel's warrior God of Exodus 15 emerges from the militarization of the Egyptians who had enslaved them (see chap. 5 above, "The Exodus and the Warrior God"), so also the violent treatment to which the Christians of Asia Minor were at least sometimes liable was a major cause of the violent counterimagery by means of which John seeks to strengthen his readers.

The situation is complex. Although in Revelation the violence (or potential for it) remains very prominent at the level of description, *it is not reflected in the way the images function with regard to Christian activity*, including that of Jesus.[34] This is particularly true of the key image of "the Lion of the tribe of Judah, the Root of David" which "has conquered" (Rev. 5:5; the Greek verb is *nikān*, sometimes translated as "to triumph").[35] The reality that this image depicts is not violent at all. In the book of Revelation, the Lion of Judah does not "conquer" in a lion-like way, by tearing its prey to pieces and devouring it, nor even in the military way that the imagery requires and that King David employed so successfully in Israel's past.[36] Indeed there is in this chapter no mention at all of prey, opponent, or enemy. Although John hears the angel refer to the Lion of the tribe of Judah, what he sees when he looks "between the throne and the four living creatures and among the elders" is "a Lamb standing as if it had been slain" (5:6).[37] In context, this is clearly a reference to Jesus, whom Christian tradition regards as a legal descendant of Judah.[38] However, Jesus' victory that led to the salvation of the redeemed and their appointment as "a kingdom of priests serving our God" (see Rev. 5:9-10) resulted not from an act of physical prowess but from his crucifixion. This was ostensibly a humiliating defeat. Yet God responded to it by raising Jesus from the dead. Christians had come to experience the crucifixion (together with the resurrection) as a soteriologically effective achievement that they expressed in various ways, one of the more prominent of them being on the analogy of the ritual sacrifice of a lamb without blemish.[39] In Revelation, the lamb triumphs not by action (and certainly not by violent action) but by enduring the hostile action of others while remaining faithful to God—in other words, by passion (suffering), understood as an accomplishment of the highest sort. As happens with so many of the images applied to Jesus from the Old Testament and its later developments, the means by which Jews expected God to bring about salvation have been made specific by the historical actuality of Jesus of Nazareth.

The victorious lion/lamb figure in chapter 5 is the paradigm for interpreting other parts of Revelation. Thus the reference in 3:21 to the Son of Man's act of conquering and its repercussions must be understood in light of it. In that verse Christ says, "To the one who conquers I will give a place with me on my throne, just as I myself conquered and sat down with my Father on his throne." Like Christ, Christians conquer, but only in the way he did. Therefore each of the seven references to "the one who conquers" in the messages to the churches of Asia Minor in Revelation 2 and 3 is emphatically *not* about forcing one's will on others. Rather it denotes the God-given result of the "patient endurance" (*hypomonē*) that John shares with them in Jesus (1:9). As Wilfrid Harrington notes, "The reality was that 'conquering' meant dying!"[40]

The same is true in other parts of Revelation. The main examples are in 12:10-11 and 21:7. In the former, John writes that Christians ("our brothers") conquered their "accuser" (Satan) "by the blood of the Lamb and by the word of their testimony." As in the case of Christ, this involves their death. Revelation 21:7 specifies that "those who conquer" will drink from the water of life and be in filial relationship to God. In all these instances where Christians are the subject of the verb "to conquer" (*nikān*), the "conquering" involves fidelity and endurance (and sometimes testimony) rather than hostile action. Because of the vivid nature of the language of violence, however, and also because John characteristically approaches the world in terms of a beleaguered "us" and a hostile "them," it is easy to forget this essential transformation of language when reading Revelation.

Part of the problem is that in this work, "conquering" does sometimes involve the imposition of one will on another: this is certainly the case with 11:7 and 13:7, where the beast "will make war on . . . and conquer," first, the two witnesses and then the holy ones. But this is precisely *not* Christian activity. Nor does the rider on the white horse in 6:2 conquer in the Christian sense. It is clear from the parallel with Luke 21:9-11 that what is involved here is war, the essence of which is overcoming enemies by the use of force.[41] Therefore John's notion of conquering has been transformed because all Christian "conquering" must, of its nature, be controlled by what happened in the case of Christ. In other words, the seer would never regard "Christian" violence as a permissible option.

The Transfigured Sword

Other images are similarly transformed. An important example is the sword as instrument of God's judgment.[42]

Thus, "a sharp, two-edged sword" is associated with the Son of Man (1:16; 2:12), who threatens to use it to "make war against" unfaithful Christians in Pergamum (2:16). Yet when it is first mentioned, the sword is said to come "out of his mouth" (1:16, NAB) and is described as "the sword of [his] mouth" in 2:16, a depiction that suggests verbal sparring rather than physical.[43] The same must be the case when the sword reappears in chapter 19. Here it is said to come out of the mouth of one who is called "Faithful and True" and "the Word of God" (19:11, 13), the implication being that God's word will somehow make ineffective anything that is not in accordance with divine fidelity and truth. Thus, like the "Lion of Judah," the activity of waging war in Revelation 19:11 is not physically violent: the phrase must be interpreted metaphorically, not literally.[44]

Israel's prophetic tradition would have provided John with the image of God's word as able to "slay" in a way that is obviously not literal. For example, in Hosea 6:5, God says of Ephraim and Judah: "I have hewn them by the prophets, I have killed them by the words of my mouth."[45]

Therefore it is not surprising to find such usage in the book of Revelation, which from the outset (and several times thereafter) refers to itself as prophecy.[46] Yet in Revelation 19, the mention of the sword is followed by an adaptation of Ezekiel's gory picture of the birds and beasts assembling to eat flesh and drink the blood of those who have come out against the Lord (Ezek. 39:17-20; Rev. 19:17-21).[47] So readers could, perhaps, be forgiven for losing sight of the metaphorical aspect of the sword when it reappears in Revelation 19:21. The vividness of John's language may seduce readers into taking the images more literally than he intends.

But this would be a mistake. For in the wider tradition,

the word of God not only slays but also heals. Psalm 107:20 says with reference to the sick: "He sent out his word and healed them, and delivered them from destruction."[48] John has told his readers that the one against whom the beast and its entourage "gathered to make war" (19:19) is the equestrian Word of God and his "army." The latter wear clean white linen (19:14), similar to that of the bride in 19:8, where it "is the righteous deeds of the saints." This is, therefore, no ordinary battle lineup, however graphically the carrion birds' activity may later be described.

The "Battle" and Its Aftermath

As one would expect from the seer's general understanding of the opposition elicited by Christ and his followers, the heavenly rider has only to appear for his enemies to assemble against him, ready to fight (19:11-16, 19).[49] (In fact, they have been ready for him since 16:14-16.) But no battle is described: what follows in 19:20 is the capture of the beast and the false prophet whose signs had "deceived those who had received the mark of the beast." These two are then "thrown alive into the lake of fire that burns with sulfur" (19:20), the ultimate fate of the damned.[50] However it is achieved,[51] there is certainly a profound fittingness in having one called "Faithful and True" and "the Word of God" cause the downfall of the pair whose *raison d'être* was to deceive others.

What, though, happens to those others? It may be that John himself implicitly leaves open the fate of those "killed by the sword" in 19:21, because, in fact, at least the leaders of this group reappear in the New Jerusalem in 21:24. Let us now consider this in more detail.

In 19:19 the ones "killed by the sword" are designated "the kings of the earth with their armies." The phrase "the kings of the earth" is one of the many ways in which the seer refers to those who oppose God.[52] Derived from the imperial political vocabulary, it has a particularly negative connotation. This is because, as Susan Mathews suggests, it usually designates a subgroup of "the inhabitants of the earth."[53] These are, by definition, "all whose names were not written from the foundation of the world in the book of life" (13:8; see n. 10, above) and therefore destined for "the lake of fire" (20:15). Because those battling "the Word of God" are "the kings of the earth and their armies" (19:19) and they are all "killed by the sword" (19:21), their ultimate consignment to the pool of fire (20:15) would presumably be the end of them. This appears not to be the case, however. For when he writes of "a new heaven and a new earth" in chapter 21, John says of the New Jerusalem that into it "the kings of the earth will bring their glory" (21:24). "The glory and the honor of the nations" will also end up there (v. 26).[54] John is logically inconsistent at this point: the kings of the earth are both dead and yet contribute appropriately to the new city. If one assumes that this is not simply an oversight, what might its significance be? The seer's position probably results from the complexity of his message and the conventions of apocalyptic literature, the vehicle he has chosen to use for presenting it.

At the level of the message, he is convinced of two incompatible things: first, that any who oppose God cannot ultimately survive and, second, that no truly human achievement can be lost in the final restoration. So, because he regards the local non-Christian Jews as culpable in their refusal to accept Jesus, John writes about them in the vituperative language of a family quarrel, claiming that they are no longer Jewish but "a synagogue of Satan" (2:9; 3:9). Using language that turned out to be very dangerous for later communities of Jews, John expresses his (to us, most embarrassing) certainty about their situation vis-à-vis

God. On the other hand, in 18:9-23 the seer poignantly puts before readers the laments with which kings, merchants, and seafarers will respond to the destruction of Rome ("Babylon") and its empire. This section comprises a long list of valuable items in which Rome traded and John's impressions of the lives and talents of the people of the empire. Yet although they are lamented, these are perhaps not irrevocably lost. Rather, after the passing away of "the former heaven and the former earth" (21:1, NAB), they find their place in the New Jerusalem, brought there by "the kings of the earth" (21:24). When this happens, the figure termed "Faithful and True" and "the Word of God" will have made good on his other name, the one "written on his cloak and on his thigh, 'King of kings and Lord of lords'" (19:16, NAB). Furthermore, then the title given to Jesus Christ back in 1:5, "the ruler of the kings of the earth," will be true in actuality and not just in principle; the kings' former subjects will presumably be included too.[55] Such an outcome requires, however, the transformation of "the kings of the earth" who lose the "war" that the rider on the white horse wages against them, in which they are "killed by the sword that came out of [his] mouth" (19:11, 19, 21).

John's chosen medium of apocalyptic permits such logical inconsistency, just as twentieth-century Roadrunner cartoons or nonrepresentational paintings do. It simply does not make sense to ask how, for example, the Roadrunner manages to survive repeated reduction to two dimensions by motor vehicles or high-speed impact against vertical cliffs. In a similar way, inasmuch as the kings of the earth represent intransigent evil in a God-given world, they must "be killed." Their plight, though, is presented as the result of their having been deceived by the "false prophet." So John has them killed by the sword of the mouth of "Faithful and True," the all-powerful

"Word of God" and the only "weapon" available to his churches. He then does not specify that they are among those found eligible for the fiery pool. In this way, he leaves open the way for expressing his conviction that all that is noblest in human accomplishments can become a component of the new Jerusalem in the "New earth," in a way determined by their divine Creator.

Therefore, when in 19:11 the figure on the white horse comes "waging war [Greek: *polemeō*] in righteousness" and "killing," these actions are not simply destructive in the usual manner of wars and killings. Instead, because he is "Faithful and True" and "the Word of God," there is a strong possibility that Jesus is able to rectify the warping that had taken place and thereby make good what had been corrupted by deception. This interpretation is not justifiable on the basis of chapter 19 alone, which presents the sword as merely a weapon of death that slays those who were deceived and turns them into carrion for the birds. It is, however, quite possible and even necessary if one takes into account John's wider viewpoint.

Thematically linked with Revelation 19 is 17:12-14, a passage in which ten kings subservient to the beast are to wage war (again *polemeō*) against the Lamb, who "will conquer them" (17:14). Because this Lamb "is Lord of lords and King of kings" as is the Word of God (in reverse order) in 19:16, the Lamb's victory should not be taken as military here either. Together these two texts show the intrinsic connection between God's Word and the death by which the Lamb redeems. So although John expects God to overcome any who refuse to acknowledge Christ and worship God, and who even "make war" against God's emissary (17:14), the two sides are not using the same techniques. For whereas the Lamb's enemies engage in a genuinely hostile campaign against him, it seems that John expects those enemies to be overcome by the persuasion of

God's words (or, indeed, by God's Word) and not by crusading with regular swords, regardless of how the opposition may choose to take the field. It may be that in John's mind the end result is the same: God's enemies are vanquished (and the birds get to prey on flesh, in gruesome —although natural—fulfillment of Ezek. 39:17, 20). Nevertheless, John does not understand the victory as a military one, because the Word of God in Revelation is not a warrior in the conventional sense. Furthermore, nothing in the context of 17:12-14 requires one to think that "those with him," who are "called and chosen and faithful," do any fighting at all (17:14). There are reminiscences here of Exodus 14, in which the Lord rescued Israel from the army of Pharaoh, but without any formal fighting. The seer of Revelation trusts God to handle human evil, although he risks charges of vindictiveness in his description of the cleaning-up operation by Ezekiel's birds.

A Clear Example of Nonviolent Conquering

For readers who remember John's presuppositions, Revelation 12:7-12 clarifies the situation further. The pericope begins dramatically, with the announcement that "war broke out in heaven." Michael and his angels are forced to do battle (*polemos*) against the dragon and his angels, as a result of which the dragon is "thrown down [*eblēthē*] to the earth," along with his angels (7-8, 9).[56] It appears that those on God's side are initiating a battle, which would clearly be problematic, especially as it takes place "in heaven." In fact, John is making a very strong bid for the reader's attention by opening the passage with the *interpretation*, the "heavenly" meaning, of *earthly events that he only describes later* in verses 10-12. Those events are simply a reformulation of the Christian understanding of Jesus' death and of the ongoing witness given by his followers: "the accuser of our comrades has been thrown down [*eblēthē*]" not by Michael in heaven but "by the blood of the Lamb" and by the word of the testimony given by Christians on earth (12:10, 11).[57] John is here telling his readers that the deceiver is, in principle, conquered by Christ's death and, for that very reason, active on earth. He uses the myth of the dragon's defeat by Michael only to put across the significance of the gospel story and the need for continuing fidelity.[58] The seer is well aware that Christians continue to suffer from the accusations of the accuser/Satan (11) and from the fury of the Devil (9, 12). But they do not fight. Rather they combat evil by their patient endurance. Their victory, which makes possible that of Michael in heaven, is real but in no way military.

So the problem that many readers have with this passage is rhetorical, not moral, and results from misinterpretation. The image of a "war in heaven" (waged by Israel's traditional champion, Michael) and the description of that war's consequences (12:7-9) are so startling that, by putting them first, John virtually ensures that they will eclipse the real events on earth of which they are the interpretation. In other words, Jesus' death and Christians' subsequent witness to it (12:11-12) are earthly events that John understands as radically altering the balance of power "in heaven." This is how "Satan" is defeated. It is standard Christian doctrine and involves suffering, not fighting. However, before John mentions the Lamb in verse 11, he has already engaged his readers' imaginations with images of Michael and his forces in heaven throwing down to earth "the great dragon . . . that ancient serpent, who is called the Devil and Satan" (v. 9). Because the Lamb is undoubtedly real for John, it is easy to understand why many have mistakenly thought that the seer was talking about a heavenly battle that was real also, but he is not. This is one of many ways in which, despite the New

Testament's insistence on the centrality of Jesus' crucifixion, popular imagination has assimilated God's power to human power.

Yet despite these lamentable consequences of the understandable misreading of Revelation 12:7-12, John's panache is to be admired. As is particularly clear from a careful reading of these verses, the point of the entire book is that, in a world that is ultimately under God's control (see Rev. 4 and 5), the slaying of the Lamb and subsequent Christian witness are sufficient to handle all the opposition that the cosmos can come up with. The seer claims that evil, however powerfully alluring and dramatic, is not ultimate. This is a point he made strongly and early on—in Revelation 6, only the slain Lamb was qualified to take the scroll and open its seals. Neither in Revelation 12 nor elsewhere does the Lamb revert to behaving in a way typical of "real" lions. John insists that, as before, the "victory" in heaven came about not because of what Michael did but because of the Lamb's passion on earth and the fidelity of his followers.[59] The description of Michael's war against the dragon serves to indicate the more-than-earthly significance of Christ's death and Christian witness, events that happen on earth. So John can honestly present Christian witness as the way to deal with the "war" that the dragon is still waging against Christians (see 12:12, 17)[60]—always supposing that the readers are not still absorbed in images of Michael apparently ejecting Satan from heaven so that he can cause problems on earth. This supposition is not, however, to be taken for granted, given the priority and the arresting description of the "war in heaven" in 12:7-10: the risk of misinterpreting the passage is high.

The Importance of Canonical Literacy

What is being claimed here is as follows. Admittedly, the tone and much of the language of Revelation 12:7-9;

17:12-24; and 19:11-21 depict the Lamb/Word of God, or Israel's champion, Michael, as returning in kind the hostility of God's enemies that was expressed in military terms. Although this makes for exciting reading, it is not an interpretation of John's text that one should endorse. For the strange figure of the slain Lamb/Word of God that appears at various points in the book suggests otherwise and should be the determining factor here. The reasons for this are twofold. First, in the New Testament generally, the person and work of Christ determine the images that are used of him (not vice versa), and there is nothing in that tradition that posits Jesus as a warrior of any kind—on this, the New Testament is unwavering.[61] As John the seer insists, Christ's "victory" comes from his being crucified (see 5:5-6 and 11:18). Second, within Revelation itself there is a radical reinterpretation of the images of the Lion of Judah and the sword (in its connection with the various "Jesus" figures). Thus what is introduced as the Lion turns out on inspection to be a slain lamb. The "sword" is highly metaphorical—always issuing from the Jesus figure's mouth—and in chapter 19 associated with the idea of God's word as faithful and true. Interpreting the conventions of apocalyptic writing entails an analogous understanding of what sound like descriptions of actual military engagements.

Exactly how John envisages the victory over evil is difficult to say. The one called "Faithful and True" and "the Word of God" is no ordinary warrior. Nor are his opponents soldiers. Moreover, there is no reason for positing the Word's followers as overtly aggressive—even though John's approach suggests that he would very much like to be.

Chapter 11 might be considered problematic in this respect. For about the "two witnesses" John writes:

> And if anyone wants to harm them, fire pours out from
> their mouth and consumes their foes; anyone who
> wants to harm them must be killed in this manner
> (Rev. 11:5).

They certainly sound dangerous. Yet this text also pre-
supposes John's worldview of a community that almost
inevitably draws to itself the hostility of others and therefore has its defenses ready. Although those defenses will
result in the slaying of those who wish to harm the witnesses, one must ask who does the slaying here, and how.
The Greek verb expressing the necessity of that death
("*must be* killed") is the impersonal verb, *dei* ("it is necessary"). In apocalyptic literature in general (including the
book of Revelation), this usually refers to events that will
happen as part of God's design. For example, John designates his book as "the revelation of Jesus Christ, which
God gave him to show his servants what *must* soon take
place" (Rev. 1:1, emphasis added). All the eight occurrences of *dei* in the book of Revelation express some
aspect of this divine imperative.[62] Thus in 11:5 God's
decree somehow underlies whatever it is that happens to
any who wish to harm the two witnesses. The text says,
they "must *be killed.*" This probably functions as a so-
called "divine passive," a frequently used biblical way of
expressing divine activity while avoiding saying directly
that God did something. Here the form reinforces the
implication that God is somehow responsible for the
"killing." But what might this mean?

To the question: How does the "killing" happen?
John's answer is: when "fire pours from [the] mouth [of
the witnesses] and consumes their foes." Obviously, this is
not a literal description, any more than it was in Jeremiah
5:14. There, with particular reference to false prophets in
Israel and Judah, the Lord says to Jeremiah:

Because they have spoken this word,
I am now making my words in your mouth a fire,
and this people wood, and the fire shall devour them.

Similarly, texts such as Sirach 48:1, which speaks of Elijah as one whose words were like a flaming furnace, help to clarify the image: forceful speaker though he undoubtedly was, Elijah did not literally burn people with his words. More specific still is the dream described and interpreted in the noncanonical 4 Ezra 13 (2 Esdras in NRSV and its antecedents). Like Revelation, 4 Ezra is usually dated at the end of the first century C.E. In this work, which originated in a Jewish milieu but was then expanded and transmitted by Christians, one "like the figure of a man come up out of the heart of the sea" (13:3) "sent forth from his mouth as it were a stream of fire, and from his lips a flaming breath, and from his tongue he shot forth a storm of sparks" (v. 10), all of which

> fell on the onrushing multitude which was prepared to fight, and burned them all up, so that suddenly nothing was seen of the innumerable multitude but only the dust of ashes and the smell of smoke (4 Ezra 13:11).[63]

When Ezra requests an interpretation of his dream, he learns that the man from the sea is God's son, who will:

> reproach [the assembled nations] with their evil thoughts and with the torments with which they are to be tortured (which were symbolized by the flames); and he will destroy them without effort by the law (which was symbolized by the fire) (4 Ezra 13:38).

So what "consumes" the enemies of the two witnesses in Revelation 11:5 is the word of God that they speak, the Christian equivalent of an authentic interpretation of

Torah. That is to say, to faithful witnesses in a hostile world, God provides the word that confounds the enemy, who "must be killed" (11:5). Those who wish to harm the witnesses and are, in John's view, evil by definition, will experience God's word as a truth or a logic that they cannot withstand and which, therefore, overcomes them like a fire. As with the images of the Lion and sword, then, the language of 11:5 sounds violent but the reality is not, given John's premises about the conditions in the world where Christians witness to God's word. The latter will indeed confound people whose evil deeds make them resist it. John's implication of their total destruction is hard to take, and perhaps there is no need to take it. Although dualistic thinking remains very common, those present-day readers whose capacity exceeds that of John when it comes to recognizing gray as an alternative to black and white may find themselves expecting that less than the entire person would be affected by the "consuming" and "killing" that the seer attributes here to God's word. In either case, the underlying conviction is that no evil can coexist with God's final, eschatological fulfillment of a world that was created good.

The same is true of the last "battle" described in this book, in Revelation 20:7-10. In the preparation for it, the released Satan deceives "the nations" and gathers them for battle (vv. 7-8). Despite their huge numbers and tactical advantage in surrounding "the camp of the saints and the beloved city" (9), Satan and company have no chance of winning the encounter. The whole incident is over in an instant, when fire comes down from heaven and consumes them (10).[64]

The immediate background to this is the somewhat problematic 2 Kings 1:10, 12, in which the ninth-century B.C.E. prophet Elijah, resisting apprehension by two successive companies of soldiers sent by King Ahaziah, demonstrates that he is "a man of God" by destroying them with fire that he calls down from heaven. On the face of it, this looks simply like a case of God's annihilating the enemy by means of superior firepower, in response to the prophet's fear of the king (see 2 Kings 1:15).[65] Such may be what John had in mind, but the reality is probably more complex, especially in light of Jesus' refusal to do just that in the tradition preserved in Luke 9:54.[66]

One possibility that allows a more nuanced position is the analogy with the fire from the mouths of the two witnesses in Revelation 11. For if, as we saw above, another late-first-century writer could associate fire with the law and the burning up of the guilty when they are confronted with their sins (as in 4 Ezra 13), the fire from heaven *might* be an enhanced example of this that John deemed suitable for the final statement of God in the face of successive and increasingly severe resistance by the forces of evil. In that case, a relevant biblical image may be the metallurgical one of fire as that which eliminates dross.[67] Accepting that possibility does not commit one to regarding those gathered for battle as nothing but dross. For Satan's entourage consists of "the nations" whom Satan has deceived (20:8), and Satan alone is said to join the beast and the false prophet in "the lake of fire and sulfur," precisely on account of that deception (v. 10). So if the divine fire is indeed a metaphor for God's word to humanity (albeit experienced in a painful form), there may still be hope for those affected by it. Thus the "fire [that] came down from heaven" might function at two levels. Superficially, it is seen as an appropriate response to Satan's action, since the latter was couched in military terms (20:8); God's action here would be on the lines of Elijah destroying the soldiers sent to bring him in (2 Kings 1). More profoundly, God's sending "fire" in Revelation can be understood as a different *sort* of action altogether, because the destruction results from an inability to survive in the face of God's Word and not from physical violence.

There is plenty more violence referred to in the book of Revelation. Most of it is in John's head and expresses his and his community's sense of *ressentiment* at their frustratingly powerless situation in civil society and their (understandable but regrettable and surely unchristian) expectation of taking revenge on those who harm them when, eventually, God turns the tables. Thus, for example, "the Son of God" (2:18) will make Jezebel and her minions suffer intensely, and will "strike her children dead" (vv. 22-23). Only in a very restricted way could this be good news—for people (if any there were) whose lives had been ruined by "Jezebel," whoever she was. John's violent language often depends on reused Old Testament imagery. An example of this is Revelation 2:27, which quotes Psalm 2:9, where the victor (defined in Rev. 2:26 as one who "continues to do [God's] works to the end") is expected to rule (literally, "to shepherd") the nations "with an iron rod," a no doubt satisfying exercise of power that is unlikely to do anybody any good.[68] Sometimes a vivid verbal metaphor is used: the locust plague at the fifth trumpet is described in terms of an army like the one in Joel 2:4-5 (9:1-11). Elsewhere real Parthian troops from the imperial bad dreams of the first century are used as the basis of the description of the plague that comes with the sixth trumpet (vv. 13-19). Like Elijah in 2 Kings 1, John is probably genuinely afraid, for his churches if not for himself. Yet although he portrays God as meting out punishments and judgments, there is no instance at all in which direct military action is initiated either by God or by Christians and, as argued above, the divine responses that are described in military terms are, at root, only metaphorically so, their forms being prompted by the opposition that Christians experienced from those among whom they lived.

This lack of divine and Christian military initiative is, perhaps, surprising, given the apparent strength of John's resentment and of his imaginative powers. It may indicate the seer's recognition that making one's point with words is a more effective and appropriate use of energy than is slaying with a sword. As we saw in chapter 2 above, the God of Genesis 1:1–2:4, who creates by mere declaration, is more impressive than the Babylonian Marduk of *Enuma elish*, who creates the world by slicing in two the dead Tiamat! John's lack of military metaphors is also a testimony to the hold that Jesus has over him.

Summary and Conclusion

In the view of John the seer, evil forces are a fact of earthly and cosmic life. However, they were definitively overcome by the death of the Lamb (Rev. 5), an event that enables John's community to continue their conquest of evil by ongoing testimony (12:11). Those wishing to harm the witnesses may experience that testimony as destructive fire (11:5). The image of testimony is further developed in John's portrayal of the Word of God on his white horse, with his similarly mounted followers (19:11-21). The sword from the rider's mouth is effective against "the kings of the earth with their armies" (19:19) by persuasion, not by killing (despite 19:21). This is because in Revelation, definitive destruction involves being thrown into "the lake of fire that burns with sulfur" (19:20; cf. 20:10, 14-15), not being slain by "the sword" that is, once more, specified as coming from the rider's mouth (19:21). For according to 21:24, "the kings of the earth will bring their glory" into the New Jerusalem.

However much God may allow Satan to deceive nations (20:3, 8) and lead them in battle against "the saints and the beloved city" (20:9), that is a lost cause, according to John. The reason is not that Christians do any fighting but that the God whose word was experienced as fire when it was preached by the witnesses speaks again in such a way that any who are left are consumed by it (11:5). Perhaps, since Satan's army existed at this point only because its members had been deceived by Satan and only the latter is described as being "thrown into the lake of fire and sulfur" for practicing the deception (20:7-8, 10), even the consuming fire from heaven could still represent God's words to humanity and thus constitute an opportunity for a conversion that allows people to survive the judgment described in 20:11-15.

Overall, then, the book of Revelation is like the Gospel of Mark (and other New Testament writings) in offering a view of reality that invites readers to interpret their own way of living (including their sufferings) in light of their experience of salvation by the crucified Jesus. John's account is more complex than Mark's, though, for he shows at greater length and in much more detail how God's saving action in Christ includes the whole of created reality. In so doing, he helps his first-century readers to relativize the might of the Roman Empire, however impressive it may be. Knowing that Rome will not last forever, those to whom John writes are less likely to be distracted by what it can offer and to surrender to its claims. Rather they can persist in rendering faithful witness, in imitation of Jesus and his "patient endurance" (1:5, 9). Living in this way runs counter to some of the strongest human instincts, but John is insistent that it is the way to fullness of human living. Mark would have agreed.

In the course of giving this fuller picture, however, John demonizes the empire and its main city, in particular. For him, Rome is Babylon, which in the sixth century B.C.E. did great harm to the Lord's people, forcibly removing them from Jerusalem and making them live in a land that was not their own. They were unable to organize their lives in the ways they wanted and had to submit to an alien rule. John presumes that his readers in the province of Asia experience the Roman Empire as radically problematic and chastises those who do not.[69]

Yet although Rome is thoroughly demonized by John, not all the city's accomplishments are lost. Although his imagery is considerably more graphic, what John writes about Rome/Babylon is in continuity with the misgivings that earlier biblical writers had about cities, from the founding of the first one by Cain (Gen. 5), through various Israelite cities castigated by prophets such as Amos, Micah, and Isaiah, and extending to nearly all the foreign cities of the region, including Babylon itself.[70] Even though these prophets frequently used the city's impending destruction as their means of calling to repentance, hope for renewal always made its way back into the tradition. The book of Revelation has something of the same pattern. John posits Rome as irredeemably demonic and yet ultimately understands God's final restoration in terms of a new city. Admittedly, it is not a new Rome. The New Jerusalem is, however, enriched by the treasures that the kings of the earth have contributed from the empire.

So, while John insists that the Christians of the cities of Asia Minor separate themselves completely from all aspects of civilization, modern city dwellers can be more like John himself: take very seriously his point about the corruptibility of human institutions and still choose engagement with the world, an engagement that has no illusions about the demonic possibilities of civilization and yet refuses to give up on it.

To the extent that his view is under the control of the gospel (at least for those who read Revelation carefully), the seer offers an inclusive view of God's world that artists of all kinds have taken up with enthusiasm. However, when readers pick up on his resentment through careless reading or, in places, with justification, and allow that to control their interpretation of the world he presents, the book can indeed cause damage. That is a risk inherent in his ambitious project. The book of Revelation is a reminder, in the strongest possible terms, that any gift of God can be corrupted. The seer's deepest understanding, though, is that good, not evil, is the enduring reality and that the full scope of human achievements (which he documents for his own day, both directly and indirectly) will eventually contribute to the rich endowment of the New Jerusalem. It is a noble project, despite the risks.

13

CONCLUSIONS:
THE PEACEABLE BIBLE?

As we saw in the Preface and first chapter, the urge to behave violently is, in one form or another, a near-universal component of human nature. In many ways, it is a function of that which enables us to "be competitive" in a world of limited resources. With exceptions that are labeled pathological, people mostly do not wish to inflict harm in the pursuit of their goals: quite apart from anything else, it is liable to provoke retaliation. Yet the line between successful competition and doing violence to other people or to some nonhuman part of the created world is not always evident or acceptable. It is, therefore, often crossed. Sometimes this is done unwittingly, through lack of knowledge, imagination, or foresight. On other occasions the transgression is deliberate, perhaps because of the satisfaction felt while exerting one's will on someone or something else, especially when the other is seen as rival or obstacle.

Therefore violence is mysterious, as is attested by its continued pervasiveness and attraction, even as it is regularly deplored. Uncovering its roots proves to be exceedingly difficult. From time to time, we learn a little more about what some of them may be. In particular, there does appear to be a connection between violence and the sacred, although the nature of that linkage is not yet clear, despite the persistent efforts of René Girard and those influenced by him.[1]

Meanwhile, there continues the search for specific strategies for living nonviolently. It is to this task, rather than as a more ambitious attempt to develop a comprehensive theory of violence, that the previous twelve chapters of this book are offered as a contribution. They have examined some of the ancient (and, for Jews and Christians, sacred) texts that make up the Bible, to see whether their reputation for depicting violence as an attractive option is a fair one. The conclusion is that sometimes it is but mostly it is not, if only because this interpretation of individual texts is not in keeping with the various contexts in which they are now placed: the wider narrative setting of each story, the biblical canon as a whole, and a world created and cared for by the God who repeatedly insists that people be especially concerned about those who are at risk from the power of others. We have also seen that the Bible proposes themes and ways of being, some of them quite radical, that could, with implementation that is small scale or even local, make for fuller human living in a world where violence is a concern. Let us take a last look at these conclusions by grouping them at four levels: textual, personal, cultural, and evangelical/eschatological.

Level One: Violent Imagery as Distraction

Without a doubt, the texts we have considered contain descriptions of violence. Many more are to be found elsewhere in the Bible—in some of the prophetic books and Psalms, for example. Yet, as we have observed, at least part of that reputation rests on the fact that references to violence have a strong tendency to impose themselves on the imagination.[2] They therefore distract a reader's attention from matters that are sometimes more fundamental to the author's purpose. When this happens, other parts of the same text may be interpreted in terms of violence, whereas they would not be if they were in a different context. One consequence of this is to effectively de-canonize the biblical book or story, because people who assume that they will find it offensive do not read it. Another possibility is that the violent "aura" can lead readers to use the text in a way that is inconsistent with the Bible as a whole: to sanction violence.

In the Christian canon, this phenomenon is especially obvious in the case of the book of Revelation. Few seem to read it as a normal (if somewhat more colorful) component of the New Testament. Rather it tends to be regarded either as far too violent for use in polite society or as the only significant book in the biblical canon. Both views are serious misreadings of the text in light of its historical situation and the conventions operative in its production.

Despite its flaws, Revelation is a serious attempt to cope with a very stressful situation by recontextualizing it. That is to say, John sets out to help Christians live with integrity in the uncomprehending and largely unsympathetic environment of the Roman Empire in the last decade of the first century C.E. He does this by showing his readers the broader stage on which they are playing. Although he is frequently negative about aspects of the culture of the day (because it damages those about whom he is primarily concerned), in the end John does not reduce the importance of human achievements. Rather he offers an account of them that takes into consideration their place in the whole of created reality. As it currently exists in the Roman Empire (although not in its basic existence—see Rev. 4), that reality is inherently sinful and therefore violent. It is, however, loved by God and redeemed by the divine power that enabled Jesus to overcome a violent and ignominious death and thus to "conquer" (Rev. 5). John judges that those who follow Jesus are liable to suffer the same fate. This too, he suggests, they can legitimately, although paradoxically, understand as "conquering."

As we saw, a careful reading of the book of Revelation indicates that, for the most part, the violent imagery to be found there does not function violently. The only "weapon" available to John's audience is the word of God. The seer trusts that, in the end, God will deal with evil. He does not know how, of course, but gives an account of it anyway! In doing this he is essentially in line with other writers of both testaments, many of whom risk the occasional extrapolation, based on their understanding of God's character and requirements. Although, as we have seen, John tends to demonize his opponents (or at least the forces behind them), the imagery he employs is much more violent than the use to which he puts it. Using imagination and energy to explore and develop the primary Christian paradigm, the salvific effect of Jesus' death, John is liable to be misunderstood by readers who forget that the basis of his imagery is always the slain Lamb who, by God's power, somehow emerges victorious.

Something rather similar is seen in Exodus 1–15 and especially in the books of Numbers and Joshua. Like Revelation and also the book of Judges, these are often read as encouraging a glorification of violence. In reality, they do nothing of the sort. Israel as it leaves Egypt is in no way military, although its experience of the Lord as "warrior" leads all too soon to seeing Israel's enemies as the Lord's, as the dangerous example of the Amalekites shows (Exod. 17). In Numbers, the census of the tribes in the first two chapters sounds like the muster for military service but never functions that way within the confines of the book. In addition, Israel is shown to be most reluctant to fight. The book of Joshua suggests, overall, that Israel came to hold land by military means. At the same time, there is a remarkable absence of glorying in military prowess. Further, there is a repeated insistence (occasionally direct but mostly in the way the stories are told) that Israel cannot possibly take credit for its new situation. Indeed, even Joshua, that most pious of warriors, cannot.

It transpires, therefore, that the interesting feature of these books is not that they contain violence but, rather, the strength of their claim that Israel is indebted to its God for the benefits that it gains in the course of moving into the Promised Land. Coupled with the accounts of the patriarchs (chap. 4), the narratives suggest a determination on the part of those who wrote and preserved them to keep "open" the world in which they live. Those who crow over their enemies and gloat about their own possessions cut themselves off from the benevolent influence of others. According to Israel's account of it, such conduct also closes one off from the Lord, the God whom they regard as the source of all bounty.

Sometimes it was not possible for Israel to live in peace with those around. In such cases, the texts we have considered tend to blame those who would oppose Abraham's descendants: the Philistines who encounter Isaac in Genesis 26, for example, or the Amalekites in Exodus 17. Occasionally Israel is the aggressor, although those cases are rarely described at length: typical are some of the notes in Joshua about how Israel came to possess parts of the Promised Land (e.g., the list of kings "whom the Israelites defeated" in Josh. 12). Mostly, though, the thrust of the narratives from the call of Abraham to the death of Joshua is that whatever Israel may have at any given time, it is the Lord's gift. The appropriate attitude to reality in those circumstances is quite different from that of a group that sees itself as having earned what it possesses. Israel did not always manage to have the appropriate attitude, of course. (Who among us does?) That was precisely the point of the Deuteronomistic historians, who interpreted the exile as punishment for what they expressed as idolatry (thanking the wrong gods) but which could just as easily be seen as ingratitude to the Lord.

The book of Judges puts in a different form its claims about how the world is constituted, but the message is essentially the same. Here the writer takes full advantage of the appeal exerted by tales of strong military leaders and their exploits, to present a gripping sample of the tribes' increasingly flawed attempts at living in the Promised Land. The result is a very strong counterexample of what happens when human instincts are allowed free rein. Perhaps it would be possible for someone to take a segment of it and presume to emulate Othniel, Jael, or one of the other vivid characters in the book, but that would be to extract them from the context in which the writer placed them, in which the behavior described leads to the disasters that allegedly put an end to rule by judges and favored the establishment of the monarchy, which itself effectively came to a more or less shameful end with the exile in Babylon.

The predominant attitude in these biblical books should, therefore, move readers in the direction of asking questions about the nature of our tenure of the earth and of created reality as a whole. The answers that come up are mostly not of the sort that would encourage self-glorification at the expense of others and the violence to which it leads.

Level Two: The Challenge of Examining the Unexamined

This second level corresponds to the level of the reader and the way in which most stories exert their effects, namely, by drawing people out of themselves, stimulating the imagination, and challenging assumptions about the nature of reality. The world that is presented to the reader of the Bible is so rich and variform that continuing encounters with it keep on yielding new insights. Although some of those who included the different biblical law codes may have intended readers to infer that keeping the rules is all that is required, the accompanying narratives give quite a different picture. In Old Testament times as in our own, it is rarely possible (at least for very long) to keep in the clear simply by holding to the commandments, whether ethical or ritual: life is simply too complex. Rules can be turned into strangleholds for oneself or others, and new situations keep coming up that may change the meaning of a particular rule or rubric, increasing or decreasing its relevance or ease of compliance. There are nearly always other possibilities that might work better, some of them also biblically sanctioned. For example, even something as simple as the initial prohibition on eating meat that is changed after the flood raises questions about how we are to relate to the rest of creation (Gen. 1:20-30; cf. 9:3-4). There is no "pure" position. We cannot fulfill righteousness, because we keep on growing and changing. Loving God and neighbor may sum up the requirements, but deciding exactly what that might mean in the practical order involves us in debate, frequent uncertainty, and the general messiness that is found in the Bible just as much as in ordinary life. We get caught by things that had not even occurred to us: the story of Cain and Abel provides one such example.

A persistent theme of the two testaments is that if humans are to flourish, it is necessary that everyone's needs be considered and everyone's talents be used for a common project. To be human at all is to be made in God's image and likeness or endowed with the divine "breath" or "spirit" (Gen. 1:27; 2:7). So people cannot simply be written off, however ill adjusted we judge them to be in the social world that we have constructed. Those in need—traditionally, the stranger, the widow, and the orphan (specified sixteen times in the book of Deuteronomy), as well as the sick and the imprisoned (Matt. 25:31-46)—

must be cared for, and the "little ones" are of special importance (Matt. 18:6-14). This insight is extraordinarily difficult to live by in a sustained way. Too busy doing what *we* have to do, we rarely notice those whose gifts do not clearly promote our own projects. Therefore, beginning with Cain and Abel, God is shown readjusting the balance so that the one less recognized is acknowledged—but this leads to trouble for both sides, of course.

What would have been a different scenario for these two characters, one that would not have ended in fratricide? One possible answer: for Cain to have taken God's apparent unfairness as an invitation to consider, perhaps for the first time, who Abel was and what it was like for him to be Cain's brother. The world is full of "Abels": those from whom the powerful think they have nothing to learn. As a rule, their contributions are not recognized. No god "intervenes" in their case—otherwise, none would survive to maturity! Eventually, it may happen that the worm turns. Although weak, they are driven to violence, simply to get a hearing. When this happens, those who had scarcely noticed their existence are shocked. The positioning of the Cain and Abel story right at the dawn of humanity's post-Eden life suggests that the author or editor recognized that there is something vital to be learned here. The message the first time around was loud and clear: God approves of Abel, and Abel is Cain's brother, so Cain needs to pay attention to Abel, ineffectual though he may appear to be in his brother's eyes. The existence of the story is a challenge to Cain figures in every age to reflect on the advantages that they have and take for granted. Otherwise many talents of the human race will go unused and the spiral of violence takes another turn. The story in chapter 2 above, in which Cain is brought up short by God's preference for Abel and his offering, provides a salutary reminder. It is a challenge to live more reflectively.

Level Three: The Ambiguity of Culture

At the third level, we encounter social institutions. Several of the texts that we studied drew attention to the link between cities (as symbols of human culture) and the prevalence of violence. The sequence begins once more with Cain, who, after his murder of Abel and subsequent exile, founds the first city. Not an auspicious beginning to a venture, especially given that, like his father, the son after whom the city is named is not part of the family line leading to the patriarchs.[3] Moreover, Cain's descendants are credited with inventing major elements of culture (4:20-22), a further biblical indication that civilization has its problematic aspects. This theme is developed in the condemnation of Babylon (as Babel; Gen. 11:1-9) and, in Genesis as a whole, in an implicit negative evaluation of cities in general.[4] Isaiah's strong criticisms of the Jerusalem of his day are very much in line with all of this, as also is John the seer's depiction of Rome as "Babylon" ripe for destruction.

Yet Genesis does not condemn culture outright, and Isaiah and John are alike in showing a degree of ambivalence about it. For Isaiah, cities are all but doomed, yet he[5] expects the Lord to establish a fortified city in Judah (Isaiah 26), so that those from other nations (notably Assyria and Egypt) can worship the Lord in Jerusalem (chap. 27). John the seer reveals a much more pronounced appreciation for the human achievements that cities make possible. He does this in two places. First, at length in Revelation 18, he gives the powerful and beautiful lament over what was lost when Babylon was overthrown. Then, very succinctly, in Revelation 21:26, he informs readers that "the glory and the honor of the nations" will be brought into the New Jerusalem, the city that comes down from heaven to the "new earth" (21:1-2). John regards human achievement as dangerous, not in itself but in its power to become demonic and thereby destroy human lives. In the end, though, it will take its place in God's scheme of things.

Both John and Isaiah of Jerusalem experience culture as highly problematic. They also believe, however, that it can and will be transformed by God as part of the eschatological reality. Neither prophet will finally give up on human achievements, for all the antihuman possibilities of human constructions. There is surely food for thought here. These ancient writers were as familiar as we are with the fact that civilization can bring problems of violence and injustice. Although, overall, our experience of what human creativity can make possible is very much more positive than theirs was, the ambiguity remains. In our own day, the same civilization leads to longer, healthier lives but also to appalling degrees of violence, of which the brunt is borne by those whose lives are short.

The viewpoint of these two biblical writers can reinforce the notion that human achievements, although not unequivocally good and indeed capable of doing much harm, need to be taken very seriously. Such a position rules out the possibility of a religiously sanctioned "spiritualizing" of reality or an opting out of the human project, inevitably flawed though it may be. Even for the writers of Genesis, cities exist and must be taken into account. One implication of Isaiah 1–39 and, especially, the book of Revelation is that people need to make the best possible use of what is available to them, for this is what God will bring to completion at the end. Implied here is an insight that we saw taken for granted also in other parts of the Old Testament and in the gospel according to Mark: the denial that human achievement is complete in itself. This insight may be especially salutary for our day.[6]

Level Four: Recontextualizing and Risking Everything

Finally, there is a further level at which Mark (and also

the book of Revelation) operates: what can be termed the level of gospel. Here the challenge is more radical. This is because the emphasis is no longer on violence itself but on a fairly specific proposal, grounded in the death and resurrection of Jesus, about how to deal with the failure, suffering, and death that are inevitable parts of human living, both for ourselves and for all those around us. It is not that such negativities are the only or even the main aspects of life. Mark well knows that people want to live and to be effective—to be first—and that sometimes they succeed. On the basis of the community's understanding of what happened to Jesus and its own attempts at living as he did, however, the evangelist insists that the direct, common-sense way of getting what we want by putting others down does not achieve this end and that the service of others is the route to genuine human greatness. Moses, Joshua, Abigail, Isaiah, and other great figures of Judaism would agree. Christians have no monopoly on heroic service.

On the face of it, such an attitude is totally foolish. Who wants to be a servant? It is surely the last resort of people who cannot compete in the marketplace and who therefore wish to change the rules, so as to thwart the efforts of others and increase their own advantage. Indeed the history of Christianity may suggest that the experiment has not been successfully tried very often, although that is a difficult judgment to make, because "success" here is, by definition, not the fame of an individual but the flourishing of a group. If this is the case, Francis of Assisi and other holy people who successfully promoted some aspect of human living from within the church—healthcare and education, for example—are somewhat anomalous. Yet they exist and are recognized by many as figures to be emulated. At the same time, the success of such community-building schemes is typically very fragile. The forces against human cooperation are many and various. Thus, for example,

Luke's late-first-century descriptions of how the earliest Christians in Jerusalem pooled their resources (Acts 2:42-47; 4:32-36) should probably be read in light of Paul's mid-century appeals to the other churches that they send monetary contributions for the relief of the "saints" in Jerusalem, who were evidently in distress.[7] On the other hand, Luke's stories in Acts 2 and 4 remain as testimony to the possibility of trying to live communally and have inspired later attempts.

Could such a system be seriously proposed as a way of living? That may depend on the wider view of those involved. For a relatively small and homogeneous group, and for a short time, it could be viable even as a humanistic project. In the service of good causes, especially in emergencies, many otherwise unremarkable people do put themselves out to extraordinary degrees. When this is attempted on a large scale, however, the problem becomes one of maintaining the motivation beyond the immediate crisis or after setbacks have occurred. Charles Taylor has given a plausible account of how, in the face of repeated encounters with the tough reality of human imperfectibility, "exclusive humanism" (i.e., a thoroughgoing concern for humanity that lacks a transcendent dimension) is liable to run out of steam or even to degenerate into contempt for those whom one is allegedly serving.[8]

As Taylor also notes, a basis in Christianity (or presumably any other position that assumes a wider reality than the merely human) is no guarantee against the occurrence of such degeneration. Yet if, as Mark claims, the significance of human life is not restricted to our present experience, beset as it is by suffering and frustration and bounded by death, one who is able to accept this does have an additional range of motivations for living at the service of others. Central to Christian understanding are the persistent and amazing notions that forgiveness is available for the asking and that failure and even death can be part of the ultimate scenario, which consists of *life* (somehow without limit) in the company of the creator God and the other creatures. John the seer presents much the same picture, except that his portrayal of the New Jerusalem is more explicit about his hope for the survival of all that is best in human culture. In this view, violence is taken account of but does not have the last word.

APPENDIX

VIOLENCE AND DESIRE:
THE WORK OF RENÉ GIRARD

Biblical interpretation as presented in the chapters of this book does not provide a systematic way of understanding the violence that is found in the Bible. However one approaches the material, it remains disparate and intractable. This is frustrating, for we could, perhaps, make a quantum leap in our understanding of violence (and therefore find more effective ways of reducing the harm that we do to each other) if we could discover and agree on an organizing principle for the biblical texts that deal with it. So far, nothing satisfactory has emerged. This at least partly accounts for the enthusiasm with which significant numbers of Christians interested in the topic have considered seriously the ideas of René Girard, a French literary theorist who has lived and worked in the United States since 1947.[1] Because Girard's name is so well known, I think it worth giving some account of why this should be so and also of why, from the perspective of biblical studies, I do *not* think that his work provides a basis for understanding violence.

What Girard offers is a comprehensive hypothesis to account for human violence. He draws evidence for his position from a wide variety of sources: literary texts (including the Bible), animal behavior, ethnography, and psychoanalytic theory. He can, therefore, exchange ideas with people in many disciplines: this is no hole-and-corner enterprise. Furthermore, his system has two other features that ensure it is of interest to many. The first of these is a kind of common-sense appeal. Although Girard's position is vast and highly theoretical, it is nevertheless easy to grasp, at least in part, and is often recognized by ordinary people as giving a unified explanation for familiar experiences that are not otherwise explicable under a single heading. In other words, people readily recognize their own situations in what Girard describes. Second, his work includes features that reflect some of the main tenets of Christianity. This is all the more interesting because Girard apparently came to his conclusions independently of Christian belief: he was, as he says with typical acerbity, "as hostile to the Judaeo-Christian texts as modern orthodoxy could wish."[2] Let us first consider the basic form of this far-reaching position, then look at how it relates to, first, popular experience and, then, Christian teaching, and conclude with an evaluation.

Acquisitive Mimesis: Desire, Violence, and Culture

Girard's primary area of competence is literary theory. He has written about the novel, Dostoevsky, and Shakespeare, for example. From an early stage, however, his interests have ranged much more widely. This is because he wants most of all to know about the structure and dynamics of human desire, which he sees as the engine that drives human individuals and their societies.

Desire, he finds, is essentially mimetic: people desire that which has been given value by being desired by another. This "other" is, therefore, seen as a model. "I want what she wants" means, more fundamentally, "I want to be like her" and is flattering to the one receiving the attention. However, she is not the totally secure individual that I imagine she is. So, the more like her I become, the more fully do I turn into a rival who threatens her possession of the object in question. She responds by putting up resistance to me and becomes an obstacle to my desire. This sequence of events, beginning with my acquisitive "mimetic desire," is what gives rise to violence.

The dynamic just described is potentially without limits. This is because desire does not cease when the object has been obtained. For I am still not satisfied: if the other relinquishes it, she no longer values it (or at least that is what she conveys). Because it was her desire that I was originally mimicking, the object in question is no longer worth anything to me either. Besides, possession does not make me like her. I have the object and she does not (and doesn't care, or insists that such is the case). So I will soon become conscious of a different object that she or someone else values, perhaps one more difficult to obtain than the last, and the process will begin again. Using an insight from the science of animal behavior, Girard understands mimesis as the foundation of all human learning. Not all imitation is acquisitive—parents can be models for their children without the element of rivalry, for example. Yet the prevalence of such behavior among humans as a whole results in an accumulation of damaged individuals, fraught relationships, and an almost unlimited potential for further misunderstandings.

In a society that does not define and impose limits for acceptable conduct, the unchecked operation of this process would very quickly raise personal and societal animosity to an intolerable level. Even where certain types of conduct are prohibited (because they have been found to promote mimetic desire, says Girard), that point will be reached—it simply takes longer. Then Girard's second major proposal becomes relevant: societies (or, at their founding, individuals) are liable to resolve this tension by arbitrarily deciding on a victim, a scapegoat whom they unanimously deem guilty of all that is wrong and expel from their community, usually by killing him or it.

Suddenly, even miraculously (it seems), the society now finds itself in a state of peace. Because people attribute the new situation to the death of the scapegoat, they turn the victim into an object of worship[3]: there has been, therefore, a "double transference" from the people to the victim, first of hatred and then of reconciliation. For Girard, this is how societies came to formulate the notion of the sacred, which "is violence."[4] Three other developments will occur. First, the community will establish prohibitions, the purpose of which is to prevent further mimetic crises; Girard sees the commandments of the Decalogue as functioning in this way (Exod. 20:1-17; Deut. 5:6-21). The sanctions for breaking these rules are severe and are regarded as coming from the divinity. This is because such transgression threatens the whole community: "It becomes an act of hubris capable of provoking violence, for others will be tempted to accuse the wrongdoer or to imitate and surpass the transgression."[5] Second, the community will create sacrificial rituals that reenact and thereby attempt to perpetuate the effects of the apparently supernatural deliverance that the death of the original victim gave them. These rituals include actions that would normally cause acquisitive mimicry and are, therefore, strongly prohibited outside the ritual arena. For example, Girard thinks that animal sacrifice is a commutation of human sacrifice, in which it originated. Third, the people will compose myths that affirm their particular relationship to the god while, at the same time, concealing the brutality of the mechanism by which that relationship came into being: they will now "agree" that the victim's behavior had threatened the whole community—but they attribute the reconciliation to its divine powers.[6]

A key feature of Girard's system is that all societies have been built upon a "founding murder" of this type, in which, typically, one brother kills the other because of the acquisitive mimesis that inevitably results from their presence to one another as "doubles." Culture then emerges in the development of the corresponding rituals, myths, and prohibitions (with their "divine" sanctions). Thus Girard regards all societal institutions as based on violence, a violence that is deliberately concealed but can be brought to light through the study of the rituals and myths.

Girard in the Popular Imagination

Whatever people may think about the origins of religion and culture, they have no difficulty in believing that mimesis and rivalry are often at the root of the violence that increasingly threatens human well-being. They also know from experience that the satisfaction of one desire leads to disillusionment and the emergence of new ones. They have watched an initially contented child deciding that it wants (immediately!) a particular toy only at the instant when another starts to play with it. They have experienced the rapid reconciliation of erstwhile enemies who have joined forces to victimize another. In western societies, they find it difficult not to connect reports of growing violence with the collapse, over the last few decades, of centuries-old prohibitions. They can easily believe that societies are essentially and originally violent. Girard, like Darwin and Freud before him, offers a mechanism that helps people understand why things are the way they are. There "seems to be something in it," something many people find sufficiently plausible to offset the outlandish proposals that the sacred "is" violence and societies are founded on scapegoats and murders.

Girard and Christian Theology

Several features of Girard's system attract the attention of some Christian theologians. First, he regards religion as an important and integral component of human functioning: it is neither in a separate compartment from the rest of life nor an optional extra. He is an articulate opponent of those who would minimize the importance of religion for understanding the basis of human institutions.[7] Girard understands religion as "an immense effort to keep the peace."[8] For him, it is the means by which humans remove from their communities the mistrust and suspicion that their violence would otherwise generate.[9] They do this by transferring responsibility onto God or a god, making the retribution that is visited on those who disregard the prohibitions divine, not merely human. The Old Testament includes such ideas in its descriptions of God as punishing and exacting vengeance, for example. For Girard, Israel's law and sacrificial practices are related to this, because both are regarded as coming from the Lord. Cain's murder of Abel is the Old Testament's version of the founding murder. That the beginnings of civilization are then attributed to Cain and his descendants is part of Girard's case for seeing all social institutions as violent in their essence.

On the other hand, he recognizes that many elements of the Old Testament are also quite different from and indeed subversive of the versions found in other people's myths. In particular, there is a clear and fairly sustained attempt to thwart the scapegoating mechanism by taking the victim's side against oppressors and by insisting that people are responsible for their own violence. Girard borrows from Matthew 24:35 to characterize this (and people's resistance to it) as a persistent tendency "from Abel to Zechariah." It certainly begins with Abel. For the Lord hears the cry of the blood that Cain has shed, and the killer is banished. Cain's place in the relevant tradition is, therefore, very different from that of Romulus, whose murder of Remus simply frees him from their earlier rivalry. Cain will build the first city, but the biblical author uses this fact and the stories of his descendants to draw attention to the unacceptable but inevitable link between civilization (that is, human culture) and violence.[10] The Bible's version of the myth is also different inasmuch as Abel does not become an object of Israel's worship,[11] and the Lord provides Cain with the mark that will protect him from becoming another victim. Girard insists that Israel's God is quite different from other conceptions of the sacred: not derived from human violence but, rather, a God of the victims, although the Bible also contains much evidence of the more usual, vengeful kind of God.[12]

Other Old Testament figures that Girard uses to demonstrate its siding with the victim include Joseph and his brothers in Genesis 37–50, the prophets, the Servant of the Lord in Isaiah 49–53 and, in a problematic book-length study, Job.[13] For Girard, Job is his community's chosen victim, yet he (with a few minor lapses in e.g., Job 9:20-29 and 16:11-14) sabotages their efforts by refusing to admit his guilt.[14] So he cannot be made into an effective scapegoat. Girard claims that by doing this, Job also exposes the violent God of his persecutors, a God whose here-and-now rewarding and punishing is really effected by the community, which is itself under the influence of mimesis. Job himself puts his trust in the God of victims, who does not intervene in human affairs but will ultimately vindicate him. On Girard's reading of the text, however, Job's apprehension and revelation of this God are wrapped around and partially smothered by more conventional ideas of God. These come mostly from the "friends" with whom he is in dialogue, but even the divinity's natural history lesson of chapters 38–41 has the oppressive effect of putting Job in his place and is, therefore, an exercise of "divine" power, however muted. Yet inasmuch as he trusts a God who sides with those who suffer unjustly and is *not* active in the human sanctions that are allegedly divine, Job is for Girard a figure of Jesus, the scapegoat *par excellence* who reveals God's presence with victims in their suffering and also the vindication that the resurrection represents.[15] Thus Girard concludes that, although a God entirely free of violence is definitively revealed only in the person of Jesus to whom the gospels testify, the Old Testament does include something of this.[16] (Whether that should be sufficient for encouraging anyone to read it is a serious question that Girard's analysis raises for a Christian reader; one shudders to think what someone who is Jewish would be thinking at this point!)

Girard also alleges that the Bible is "permeated by a single dynamic movement away from sacrifice" and that "the sacrificial cult [was] explicitly rejected by the Prophets before the Exile."[17] These claims of Girard are entirely false, however, even aside from the difficulty of constructing the time line. Admittedly, in Isaiah 1 the Lord tells Israel's leaders, "I do not delight in the blood of bulls, or of lambs, or of goats," and that they are to "trample my courts no more," because "bringing offerings is futile" (Isa. 1:11-13). Similarly, the oracle in Micah 6:6-8 appears to reject sacrifices in favor of doing right, loving goodness, and walking humbly with one's God. Nevertheless, the context of both chapters indicates that each prophet's primary objection was to the *combination* of sacrifice and rampant social injustice. It is highly improbable that any oracle regarded as seriously advocating that the sacrificial system be abolished would have found its way into Tanak.

The reason that Girard would like the Old Testament to document the decline of temple sacrifice is that, like most Christians, he regards Israel's scriptures as the early stages of a process culminating in a Christianity that is, nevertheless, construed as something completely new and

unlike all that preceded it.[18] This view, which is both true
(because Christian claims about Jesus *did* turn out to be
incompatible with Judaism) and profoundly false (because
a God who replaces one "chosen people" with another is
manifestly untrustworthy) is the third feature that makes
Girard's system of particular interest to Christians and his
understanding of Jesus (and Christianity) unique.

For Girard, Christianity is not a religion like any of the
others[19] except in those aspects of it that he would regard
as not really belonging to it.[20] It is different because, as
Girard reads the Gospels, the crucified Jesus is not just
another victim but the one who, once and for all, unmasks
the sacrificial scapegoating mechanism for the brutality
that it is, and thereby reveals the innocence of the victim—
that is, of all victims. (The Gospels certainly present Jesus
as innocent of the crime for which he was executed.[21]
Where, though, are their alleged deductions or claims
about other victims?) Girard denies that Jesus' death is in
any way a sacrifice, insisting that all sacrificial interpretations of it are profound misunderstandings. According to
Girard, Jesus is the perfectly innocent scapegoat, the victim
of the purely *human* process of mimetic violence, not a
sacrificial victim required by God. (If Paul and the writers
of Ephesians, Hebrews, and the Johannine letters all misunderstood Jesus, the New Testament canon would seem
to be seriously defective, although Girard's point that God
did not *require* Jesus' death is well taken.)[22] Jesus is killed,
says Girard, because he has dared to point out that "religion
is organized around the more or less violent disavowal of
human violence."[23] (Where did Jesus point this out?)
Furthermore, Jesus' exposure of the sacrificial mechanism
as a merely human institution decommissions it as a means
by which people can henceforth deal with the violence
arising from their acquisitive mimesis—at least for those
who understand what Jesus revealed. This is because

bringing about peace by means of the ritual sacrifice of a victim works only to the extent that people believe that it is effective and that the victim was guilty, which they cannot do now that Jesus has revealed the victim's innocence. Consequently, they can deal with their violence only by each one's "seek[ing] to cast upon [their] neighbor the responsibility for persecution and injustice," even though the universal responsibility for it becomes increasingly apparent.[24] (If Jesus did indeed "expose" and decommission the sacrificial mechanism, why has it taken so long for anyone to realize this? And how, in such circumstances, could anyone have then imagined that Jesus' own death was to be understood in sacrificial terms?)

If Christians had really understood what Jesus revealed, they could not possibly have victimized others. Girard, who was born in France in 1923, is thinking particularly of Jews here, but the point is general and certainly valid. That such victimization has occurred he relates to the strong tendency to (mis)interpret Jesus in the old religious terms. It is not to realize that the "rejected stone" is the foundation of something completely different.[25] Christians who victimize Jews are doing exactly that for which Jesus castigated the Pharisees in Matthew 23:30. They say, "If we had been there, we would not have treated Jesus in this way." Trying to exculpate themselves from the violence in which everyone is implicated, they make others (and particularly Jews) into scapegoats.[26] The task of Christianity, as Girard sees it, is to break loose from the destructive cycle of mimetic desire and become a real human *subject*[27] by imitating Jesus, whose own desire was never acquisitively mimetic but, instead, revelatory of God's all-inclusive love.

Evaluation

Like everybody else, academics are susceptible to the appeal of a position that ties together many otherwise disparate elements. Indeed Girard's claim is very much more comprehensive than I have indicated here. His 1978 discussions with two French psychiatrists show that it can also take in such phenomena as personality cults,[28] the cult of the dead, competitiveness, psychosis, hypnosis and possession, sadism, masochism, and attraction to the same or the opposite sex.[29] Girard's book on Job includes an account of the dynamics of totalitarian regimes.[30] There is something for everyone here, and the system has all the attraction ("seduction," many would say) of a "theory of [nearly] everything." So Girard's works have been widely translated and given a significant amount of attention. Experts from many fields have been drawn into the discussion, and the ideas are being further disseminated by younger scholars who have found here a system on which they can build.

Some of what Girard has to say corresponds to intuitions of common sense and the Christianity that he now professes. He is surely right in rejecting the idea that God in any simple way required Jesus' death and in branding as radically unchristian many actions that have been (and still are) carried out in the name of Jesus. Similarly, imitating Jesus is arguably one of the most ancient of Christian practices, although the link between this and mimesis in Girard's system is more coincidental than foundational. I also agree with him that "there exists in Paul a genuine doctrine of the victory represented by Jesus' apparent failure."[31] Again Girard finds a new way of talking about the idea of the Old Testament as both preparatory to the revelation that Jesus will bring and yet incompatible with it in places. The idea that the Bible often foists onto God (or someone else, e.g., Eve) the guilt for human action that would otherwise be unbearable is well worth entertaining, however much this would have surprised the sacred authors.

Yet, even though some of Girard's insights are helpful, others, particularly those derived from his interpretation of biblical texts, are highly problematic, as my earlier comments on his work have indicated. Many of the biblically based arguments that he offers to support his broader theory about the nature and origin of violence are unconvincing, because they do not take into account the context (both immediate and canonical) in which the biblical passages occur. The Old Testament and the New require much more careful and detailed exegesis than Girard has been able to provide.[32] Because he includes so much in his purview and has such a range of biblical texts to choose from, Girard is liable to disregard the context of the passages he selects and their relationship to others that he uses. He also ignores sections or details that run counter to his position. This may sound like harsh criticism: Girard himself is, after all, a literary theorist, not an exegete, even though he has already stimulated the thought of some biblical exegetes.[33] Yet his writing does not always avoid the risk inherent in using such a comprehensive system—that of imposing itself on the other text. The Bible often ends up being used to furnish illustrations of a system that Girard has constructed on a different basis. That, in itself, would not be a problem. What is problematic is that he tends to find in the Bible scapegoats, victims, sacrifices, mimesis, and safeguards against mimesis where none exist. In the passion of Jesus, for example, he constructs a crowd-led "everyone against Jesus" scenario of "mimetic contagion" that, incredibly, includes even the apostles and takes no account of the dynamic that is evident in each Gospel as a whole.[34] The importation of these ideas allows the text to be interpreted in terms of Girard's theory, but at the cost of ignoring elements that require attention. Furthermore, there are too many instances of special pleading in his consideration of the tightly constructed New Testament texts, and especially of the Gospels, which is where his attention is almost entirely focused.[35]

In the present instance, I have preferred to read the biblical text canonically in an attempt at establishing the extent to which it really *is* violent. Certainly, the Bible does sometimes portray a vengeful God and a violent humanity that are quite incompatible with Jesus' teaching and way of living (and with the Old Testament at its best). Girard's ideas can be helpful here. On the other hand, the overall relationship between the testaments is closer and more complex than Girard suggests. Furthermore, it is simply incredible that Jesus himself was radically misunderstood from the time of his first followers until Girard came along.[36] So, even though Girard's description of acquisitive mimesis (and perhaps, although more doubtfully, the "founding murder") has some correspondences in the biblical text, this is not what the Bible is primarily about. The biblical reality (creation as good, for example, or the causes and consequences of Jesus' death and resurrection) is more complex and more nuanced than Girard's position would allow. In other words, while much appreciating his energetic and sustained striving with these matters, I am concerned about the extent to which Girard's comprehensive system distorts the biblical texts that it is allegedly interpreting. This is a high price to pay for any theory.

NOTES

Preface

1. "Bible" is derived from the Greek, *ta biblia*, "the books." Tanak is an acronym derived from the Hebrew words *Tôrāh*, *Nᵉvi'îm* (Prophets), and *Kᵉtûbîm* (Writings). Reordered in places and, for non-Protestants, with an additional half-dozen books from the Greek tradition, it forms the Christians' Old Testament.

Chapter 1

1. Simone Weil, *The Iliad or The Poem of Force*, trans. Mary McCarthy (Wallingford, Pa.: Pendle Hill, 1983), 25; quoted in John S. Dunne, *Peace of the Present: An Unviolent Way of Life* (Notre Dame, Ind.: University of Notre Dame Press, 1991), 33.

2. The biblical canon is the list of the books included in the Bible.

3. Brevard S. Childs, referring to the Old Testament, in *Old Testament Theology in a Canonical Context* (Philadelphia: Fortress Press, 1985), 184.

4. E. O. Wilson, *Consilience: The Unity of Knowledge* (New York: Alfred A. Knopf, 1998), 6.

5. Gregory Baum, "The Social Gospel on Trial: Kroeker, Augustine, and the Love of God," *The Ecumenist* 2 (1995): 68. The Apocalypse is also known as the book of Revelation.

6. Quoted in Peter Gay, *The Enlightenment* (New York: Alfred A. Knopf, 1967), 394.

7. R. Schwager, *Brauchen wir einen Sündenbock?* (Munich: Kösel, 1978), 58-74, cited in Robert North, "Violence and the Bible: The Girard Connection," *Catholic Biblical Quarterly* 47 (1985): 14-15.

8. The situation does, of course, change radically when a significant proportion of the population is outraged by what is being done in its name, either on moral grounds or because the war is being lost.

9. See Ronald G. Musto, *The Catholic Peace Tradition* (Maryknoll, N.Y.: Orbis, 1986), 76-96. He writes: "It is a historical irony that these documented peace movements have been passed over as extremist, disruptive, and misguided, while the disastrous history of the Crusade movement, which consistently attracted fewer, more disreputable, and more destructive forces, has received the awed respect and solemn judgments of historians" (86). On the next page Musto assembles data to

support his claim that, overall, members of peace movements outnumbered those involved in the Crusades.

10. Gilbert K. Chesterton, *Orthodoxy* (New York: John Lane, 1914), 18.

11. Matthew 26:52 is used by, among others, Tertullian, *On Patience* 3 (noted by Louis J. Swift, *The Early Fathers on War and Military Service*, Message of the Fathers of the Church, no. 19 [Wilmington, Del.: Michael Glazier, 1983], 42); Ambrose, *On the Duties of the Clergy* 3.4.27 (ibid., 101); the twelfth-century Peter the Venerable in a letter to Bernard of Clairvaux (see Musto, *Catholic Peace Tradition*, 89); and the seventeenth-century English Quaker, William Dewsbury (Roland H. Bainton, *Christian Attitudes Toward War and Peace: A Historical Survey and Critical Re-evaluation* [New York: Abingdon, 1960], 158).

12. Although Jesus' exchange with his disciples in Luke 22:35-38 has been used to justify the violence of war (see, e.g., Chester Forrester Dunham, *The Attitude of the Northern Clergy Toward the South 1860-65* [Philadelphia: Porcupine Press, 1974], 135), the sword there is symbolic, not actual. See, for example, Joseph A. Fitzmyer, *The Gospel According to Luke X-XIV*, Anchor Bible, vol. 28a (Garden City, N.Y.: Doubleday, 1985), 1431-32. Note how in verses 47-53 Jesus rebukes the one who injured the high priest's servant and then heals the latter.

13. Alasdair McIntyre, *After Virtue*, 2d ed. (Notre Dame, Ind.: University of Notre Dame Press, 1984), 109-10.

14. Bainton, *Christian Attitudes*, 168-69.

15. See, e.g., Dunham, *Attitude*, 110-13. Strongly dissenting views were also heard on pages 33, 128-29.

16. Ibid., 113.

17. Quoted by Bainton, *Christian Attitudes*, 198. Doubtless, in practice "die" was often a euphemism for "kill." A current version has "live" instead of "die"!

18. For a claim that "the warlike element which was accepted as symbol ushers in the reality itself and the 'spiritual weapons of knighthood' became carnal," see Adolf von Harnack, *Militia Christi: The Christian Religion and the Military in the First Three Centuries*, translated and introduced by David McInnes Gracie (Philadelphia: Fortress Press, 1981), 32.

19. The Hexateuch consists of the first six books of the Bible, from Genesis to Joshua.

Chapter 2

1. God's cursing of the snake (Gen. 3:14-15) could be regarded as a violent response but is better understood as a quasi-judicial action that underscores the seriousness of what has been done, because the story presents the snake as deliberately deceiving the woman.

2. Many ancient documents have titles that consist of the first words of their text. Thus Jews call the first book of the Bible Bereshith and Christians call it Genesis, respectively from the Hebrew and Latin words with which it begins: "In the beginning." Likewise *Enuma elish* means, "When on high," the first words of the Akkadian document that tells of how the Babylonian god Marduk came to prominence. For an English translation of *Enuma elish*, see E. A. Speiser, "Akkadian Myths and Epics," in J. B. Pritchard, ed., *Ancient Near Eastern Texts*, rev. ed. (Princeton, N.J.: Princeton University Press, 1955), 60-72.

3. See, for example, J. Gerald Janzen, "On the Moral Nature of God's Power: Yahweh and the Sea in Job and Deutero-Isaiah," *Catholic Biblical Quarterly* 56 (1994): 462-64 and references there. For a sketch of creation stories found among Israel's neighbors, see Richard J. Clifford and John J. Collins, "Introduction: The Theology of Creation Traditions" in *Creation in Biblical Traditions*, The Catholic Biblical Quarterly Monograph Series, no. 24, ed. R. J. Clifford and J. J. Collins (Washington, D.C.: The Catholic Biblical Association of America, 1992), 1-15.

4. Biblical texts such as Psalm 74:13-14 and Isaiah 51:10 include hints that creating the world may have involved God in a fight with monsters. Many scholars also find in Exodus 15 the song that celebrates the Lord's triumph over the Red Sea, many elements of the Lord's successful struggle against the forces of chaos. These passages are not, however, part of the reader's introduction to the Bible in its canonical form.

5. Genesis 1:4, 10, 12, 18, 21, 25, 31. See *La Bible*, translated and introduced by André Chouraqui (Tournai: Desclée & Brouwer, 1985).

6. See David M. Gunn and Danna Nolan Fewell, *Narrative in the Hebrew Bible* (New York: Oxford University Press, 1993), esp., chap. 1.

7. This is particularly evident in the Targums, the Aramaic translations/expansions of the Bible that were not written down until the early centuries of the Common Era but are thought to have originated, at least in part, much earlier. In all the ancient Targum manuscripts associated with Palestine, in Genesis 4:8 Abel claims that his deeds were more correct than Cain's, and Cain either hints at or rails against divine injustice in the universe. See Martin McNamara, *Targum Neofiti 1: Genesis*, The Aramaic Bible 1A (Collegeville, Minn.: Liturgical Press, 1992), 65-67, and Michael Maher, *Targum Pseudo-Jonathan: Genesis*, The Aramaic Bible 1B (Collegeville, Minn.: Liturgical Press, 1992), 32-33. See also L. Alonso-Schökel, *Dov'è tuo fratello?: Pagine di fraternità nel libro della Genesi* (Brescia: Paideia Editrice, 1987), 35-40. For a range of early interpretations of Genesis 4, see James L. Kugel, *The Bible As It Was* (Cambridge, Mass.: Harvard University Press, 1997), chapter 4.

8. English Bibles frequently use uppercase LORD to translate YHWH, the name of Israel's God that Jews do not pronounce because it is so sacred.

9. Various authors have linked Cain's offering with the harvest festival referred to in, for example, Exodus 23:16, 19; 34:22, 26. However, the latter texts specify that the offerings are first fruits.

10. The "desire" and the mastering were used earlier in 3:16 to denote Eve's now disordered desire for Adam and his hold over her.

11. The traditional Hebrew Bible, the Masoretic text, lacks Cain's words to Abel. This probably results from faulty transmission, because the introductory "Cain said to his brother Abel" is present (v. 8). Cain's proposal, "Let us go out to the field" is part of verse 8 in most of the ancient translations of the Bible, including the Greek and the Samaritan Pentateuch.

12. The preacher, Qoheleth, will later dismiss all reality as such nothingness: of the twelve chapters of Ecclesiastes, only chapter 10 lacks a dismissal of something (or everything!) as "vanity," nothingness. Abel's name may be, as Richard S. Hess suggests, "an anticipation of Abel's premature death" ("Abel," in *The Anchor Bible Dictionary*, ed. David Noel Freedman [New York: Doubleday, 1992], 10). Other scholars have claimed that the name comes, rather, from Akkadian and Sumerian words meaning "heir," a position that Hess dubs "speculative."

13. As a shepherd, Abel does have flocks to his credit. It may also be that the author thinks of him as having escaped the curse that went with tilling the ground (3:17-18), although he does, of course, "return to the ground" (3:19).

14. The text gives no indication that Abel feels inferior—but neither does he get to speak! One could write an alternative version in which the displaced older child resents the attention given to the younger sibling, who is perceived as privileged, but there is no evidence of these dynamics in Genesis 4, where nobody except God is shown responding to Abel's presence.

15. Deuteronomy 27:5 specifically forbids the use of iron tools for making the altar on Mount Ebal (see also Josh. 8:31). And although tools were used in the construction of Solomon's temple, 1 Kings 6:7 specifies that no hammer, ax, or tool of iron was used on the temple site itself during the construction, which might be an echo of the earlier prohibition.

16. Cain's separation from his parents is not mentioned, perhaps because that was the fate of all young men: Genesis 2:24 specified that "a man leaves his father and his mother and clings to his wife." That is not, of course, why Cain left his parents.

17. In Genesis 4:12, God condemned Cain to being a wanderer (expressed by a Hebrew participle, *nād*); "the land of Nod" (*nôd*) plays on this verb.

18. Although Adam and Eve are obviously sexual beings from the time of their introduction to each other (2:23-25), the text does not specify that they have intercourse prior to their eviction from the garden; nor does it say that they do not. Yet Adam's "knowing" Eve is the first topic broached thereafter (4:1) and therefore is presented as the first action of humanity's post-Eden life.

19. Note in Matthew 5:23-24 the sensitivity required by Jesus' plea for reconciliation with another who has something against you. Merely knowing that someone bears you a grudge disqualifies you from offering sacrifice—whether the grudge is justified or not.

Chapter 3

1. Robert Murray plausibly suggests that the incident in 6:1-4 is "a truncated fragment of the myth more fully preserved in 1 Enoch." The passage assigns blame to the gods, rather than to human beings, which makes it unsuitable teaching material and may explain why it is not given more fully in Genesis. See *The Cosmic Covenant: Biblical Themes of Justice, Peace and the Integrity of Creation*, Heythrop Monographs, no. 7 (Westminster, Md.: Christian Classics, 1992), 15. In *The Pentateuch: An Introduction to the First Five Books of the Bible*, The Anchor Bible Reference Library (New York: Doubleday, 1992), 74, Joseph Blenkinsopp claims that the offense here is the breaching of the human/divine barrier, a position disputed by Robert A. Di Vito in "The Demarkation of Divine and Human Realms in Genesis 2–11," *Creation in Biblical Traditions*, The Catholic Monograph Series, no 24, ed. Richard J. Clifford and John J. Collins, (Washington, D.C.: The Catholic Biblical Association of America, 1992). For Di Vito the issue is part of the editor's probing of human institutions: "in Gen. 6:1-4, the object of God's limitation on humanity's vitality seems to be an already violence-prone humanity now 'supercharged,' as it were, by semi-divine beings" (50).

2. Baruch follows Lamentations in Bibles derived from the Greek canon. It is not Scripture for Jews and Protestants, but the latter include it among the Apocrypha.

3. See Di Vito, "Demarkation," 49-50. He sees many of the stories in Genesis 2–11 as offering a critique of certain aspects of human civilization and cultural progress (51-56). In other words, the stories are countercultural for the sake of a more authentic human experience.

4. "Lawlessness" (NAB) may be a more accurate translation of *ḥāmās* in Genesis 6, assuming that it includes the idea of violent behavior. The wider use of the word and its interpretation in later Jewish tradition suggests that its basic meaning is a radical disrespect for law that expresses itself in different ways, some of which may seem trivial (e.g., petty pilfering) but all of them very destructive of society. As we shall see, it denotes the unquestionably violent behavior of Simeon and Levi in Genesis 49:5 and Abimelech's multiple fratricide in Judges 9:24.

5. Genesis 7:2-3 specifies that Noah is to take seven pairs of each kind of ritually clean animal and one pair of those regarded as "unclean."

6. In traditional just-war theory there are two sets of criteria that must be satisfied before a war can be considered to be justified. The first set specifies the conditions for rightness in going to war (*jus ad bellum*). In the developed form of the tradition, these include (1) just cause (eventually restricted to defense against aggression), (2) initiation by a competent authority, (3) right intention, (4) that war be the last resort, (5) the probability of success, and (6) proportionality, in other words, that the goods to be attained by warfare sufficiently outweigh the evils expected to be caused. Second, there are criteria for rightness in conduct of war (*jus in bello*), including (1) the immunity of noncombatants from direct attack, and (2) proportionality, in other words, that the means used in fighting produce goods that sufficiently outweigh the harm that they cause. See William J. Collinge, "War," in *Historical Dictionary of Catholicism* (Lanham, Md.: The Scarecrow Press, 1997), 432, and also Libreria Editrice Vaticana, *Catechism of the Catholic Church* (Mahwah, N.J.: Paulist Press, 1994), 2309-17.

7. Genesis 10:12 mentions "Resen between Nineveh and Calah, that is, the great city" (10:12). The names of several foreign cities are listed earlier, in verse 10, but the Hebrew text there does not include the word *city*, although some English translations have inserted it on the basis of the Greek version.

8. In the Sodom and Gomorrah episode, *city* is used in Genesis 13:12 (which tells of Lot's settlement in Sodom) and in 18:24, 26, 28; 19:4, 12, 14, 15, 16, 25, 29, all referring to the cities to be destroyed. In 19:20, 21, 22 it designates the "modest sized" city, Zoar, in which Lot is allowed to take refuge. Presumably it lacked pretensions.

Apart from the notes explaining how Beersheba and Luz got their names (Gen. 26:33; 28:19), the authors of Genesis use *city* only to designate foreign cities: they are Hittite (23:10, 18), Mesopotamian (24:10, 11, 13), Canaanite (33:18; 34:20; 35:5), Edomite (36:32, 35, 39), and Egyptian (41:35, 48; 44:4, 13).

9. The equivalence of Salem and Zion (and hence Jerusalem) is clear in Psalm 76:3. See Michael C. Astour, "Salem," in *The Anchor Bible Dictionary*, ed. David Noel Freedman (New York: Doubleday, 1992).

10. The Greek translation of Genesis uses *gigas*, *giant*, for *gibbôr* in 6:1-4 and 10:8-9. In Greek mythology, the giants were a rebellious race whom the gods destroyed.

11. It may also be significant that the only other place that cognates of *gibbôr* appear in Genesis 1–11 is 7:18-20 and 24, where the verb repeatedly describes the rising of the flood that destroyed nearly everything.

Chapter 4

1. The Lord changes Abram's name to Abraham in Genesis 17:5 and Sarai's to Sarah in 17:15. In the rest of this chapter, we shall use the second form of each name, except in quotations.

2. See R. J. Clifford, "Genesis," in *The New Jerome Biblical Commentary*, ed. Raymond E. Brown, Joseph A. Fitzmyer, and Roland E. Murphy (Englewood Cliffs, N.J.: Prentice Hall, 1990), 2.23.

3. The first time was in Genesis 26:16.

4. On the other hand, one could argue that Isaac's passivity takes over his life. For he is old and blind when fooled into giving Jacob the blessing of the firstborn (Gen. 27). After that, Jacob leaves for Haran, and Esau moves to Edom at some point (32:3). Although Jacob returns and he and Esau eventually bury Isaac (35:29), the text gives no hint that the old man even met (much less enjoyed the company of) his twelve grandsons, named in verses 23-26.

5. Laban's household gods are stolen in the course of the family's leaving Haran, but by Rachel, not Jacob. The narrator is explicit that Jacob did not know that his wife had stolen her father's gods (31:32).

6. In fact, despite the "four hundred men" who accompany Esau (32:6; 33:1), the wronged brother is highly magnanimous and is only with difficulty persuaded to accept Jacob's gift, which the latter designates as his blessing from God (33:11), corresponding to the blessing that Jacob had earlier stolen from Esau (chap. 27).

7. In Genesis 42:1-2 and 43:1-2, Jacob tells his sons to go to Egypt for food. He expresses his unwillingness to let Benjamin go to Egypt in 42:36-38; 43:6, 14; see also 44:25-34.

8. The same verb is used of Saul's restraint in 1 Samuel 10:27, when some men insult him rather than accepting him as ruler.

9. The major difficulty in evaluating this story is that, although Dinah is more intimately involved than anyone else, she never speaks, and the story is told from the points of view of the conflicting men who treat her as an object that has value to them: something they see, desire, seize, rape, negotiate for, fight for, and finally reclaim for themselves. After being "rescued" by her vengeful brothers (v. 26), Dinah drops out of the story completely. Because the author/editor of Genesis is apparently unaware of anything problematic about all this, we must try to assess how he would have expected readers to interpret the story.

Shechem, the young man who, on seeing Dinah, "seized her and lay with her by force" (34:2), is then said to love her (vv. 3, 8, 19), and repeatedly tells her father and brothers that he will give whatever they ask, if he can marry her (vv. 11-12). His father, Hamor, has already voiced such sentiments, apparently in good faith, although he also sees long-term material benefit for his people (vv. 8-9, 23). That the brothers deal "deceitfully" with Shechem and Hamor seems to put them in the wrong (v. 13). Yet the question with which the story ends in verse

31, "Should our sister be treated like a whore?" may indicate that the author (or a later editor) finds Jacob not assertive enough and prepared to pay too high a price for peace with his neighbors. It is hard to be sure, even in light of the incidents that involve deliberate inactivity on the part of Abraham (Gen. 12:10-20; 20:1-18) and Isaac (Gen. 26:6-16) when their wives were at risk from powerful neighbors who had been led to think they might make additions to their harems.

10. In Genesis 49:5 their actions are termed *ḥāmās*, the kind of lawlessness that eats at the fabric of society (see chap. 3, n. 4). Simeon and Levi are somewhat rehabilitated in "Joseph and Aseneth," where Levi engineers a nonviolent outcome to an incident in which Pharaoh's son threatens to kill them if they will not join him in killing their brother, Joseph. See James H. Charlesworth, ed., *The Old Testament Pseudepigrapha* (Garden City, N.Y.: Doubleday, 1985), 2:177-247.

11. John Skinner, *A Critical and Exegetical Commentary on Genesis*, 2d ed., The International Critical Commentary (Edinburgh: T. & T. Clark, 1930), 507.

12. The verse is hard to translate. *One* here is masculine and thus should probably refer to Joseph, as in the New American Bible, where Jacob gives Shechem to Joseph, "as to the one above his brothers." However, the position of *one* in the sentence would link it more naturally with the feminine noun *shechem*. If the latter refers simply to the city of Shechem, *one* is inappropriate anyway. See E. A. Speiser, *Genesis*, Anchor Bible, vol. 1 (Garden City, N.Y.: Doubleday, 1964), 358.

13. See the note that accompanies this verse in the New Revised Standard Version. The city of Shechem lies between the "shoulders" of Mounts Ebal and Gerizim.

14. The Hebrew words for Hamor (in 33:19) and Amorite (in 48:22) are less alike than they sound in English.

15. It would have been quite inappropriate for Jacob to have bought a second burial cave at this stage, when the cave of Machpelah was still available for burials and Joseph only a youth.

16. O. S. Wintermute, who introduces and translates Jubilees in James H. Charlesworth, ed., *The Old Testament Pseudepigrapha* (Garden City, N.Y.: Doubleday, 1985), 2:35-142, cites evidence of a version of this story that is independent of Jubilees (p. 120). For his reasons for dating the composition of Jubilees in the mid-second century B.C.E., see pages 43-44.

17. See the Testament of Judah 3:7, introduced and translated by Howard Clark Kee, in Charlesworth, *Pseudepigrapha*, 1:796. The reference to Shechem comes in Testament of Judah 4:1. In note 3a (p. 396), Kee suggests that this portrayal of Jacob as a giant killer "is an expansion based on a brief hint concerning Jacob's encounters with the Amorites in Genesis 48:22."

18. Millard C. Lind, *Yahweh Is a Warrior: The Theology of Warfare in Ancient Israel* (Scottdale, Pa.: Herald Press, 1980), 35-45. See esp. 39-42.

19. See ibid., 36-37, where the author refers to the patriarchs' attitude as "counter-nationalistic." The attitude also contrasts with the predominant ideology of the kingdoms of the ancient near east (39-40).

20. God's promise is given in Genesis 12:1-3 and frequently thereafter.

21. Admittedly, all three patriarchs sometimes treated women in ways that are now quite unacceptable. In addition to examples noted earlier (see 12:10-20; 20:1-18; 26:1-11), Abraham's treatment of Hagar is anything but honorable: after the newly pregnant Hagar has been contemptuous of her long-infertile mistress (Gen 16: 4), both Abraham and his wife, Sarah, abuse the slave for their own ends. The ancient author undoubtedly thought that Hagar's promised fecundity (16:10-12) compensated for her return and submission to Sarah at God's command; some modern readers may question that.

22. The ultimate primacy of Judah is suggested in Genesis 49:8-12. Judah is generally prominent in Genesis 37–50, the Joseph cycle (e.g., in 37:26-28; chaps. 38 and 44; 46:28). Sometimes his role there is to reduce conflict within the family (43:1-10; 44:14-34, and perhaps 37:26).

23. For a strong qualification of that, see note 21, above.

Chapter 5

1. See, for example, Tremper Longman III and Daniel G. Reid, *God Is a Warrior*, Studies in Old Testament Biblical Theology (Grand Rapids, Mich.: Zondervan, 1995).

2. For example, roughly contemporary Ugaritic texts from Ras Shamra acclaim the Canaanite storm-and-fertility god Baal in similar terms.

3. Babylon Talmud, *Megillah* 10b in Isidore Epstein, ed., *The Babylonian Talmud; Seder Mo'ed in Four Volumes* (London: Soncino, 1938), 4:59. See also *Sanhedrin* 39b in Isidore Epstein, ed., *The Babylonian Talmud; Seder Nezikin in Four Volumes* (London: Soncino, 1935), 251; and Susan Niditch, *War in the Hebrew Bible: A Study in the Ethics of Violence* (New York: Oxford University, 1993), 150. The basis of the midrash is Exodus 14:20, just before Moses parts the sea for the Israelites (and then the Egyptians) to cross over.

4. The Pharaoh is represented by two successive individuals who are otherwise indistinguishable from each other (1:8–2:23; 5:5).

5. See, for example, Gustavo Gutiérrez, *A Theology of Liberation: History, Politics, and Salvation* (Maryknoll, N.Y.: Orbis, 1973), 154-60. For a sound critique of those who misuse the Exodus narrative, see John Howard Yoder, "Exodus and Exile: The Two Faces of Liberation," *Cross Currents* 23 (Fall 1973): 297-309.

6. Michael F. Steltenkamp, *Black Elk: Holy Man of the Oglala* (Norman, Okla.: University of Oklahoma Press, 1993).

7. Ibid., 151.

8. *Akwesasne Notes* (1974), 61-62, quoted in Steltenkamp, *Black Elk*, 190, n. 4. The 1974 volume is entitled *Voices from Wounded Knee: The People Are Standing up* (Rooseveltown, N.Y.: Mohawk Nation). Analogously, present-day people from military families tend to regard the services in the same light, in other words, as promoters of such values as commitment, loyalty, and the defense of freedom rather than as potential enforcers of one state's will on another.

9. Exodus 15:20 relates somehow to 15:1. It consists of a fragment (or possibly a title) in which "the prophet, Miriam, Aaron's sister" leads "all the women" in singing the opening words of the song in verse 1.

10. See especially 15:13-18, which refer to events and traditions still to come in Israel's story, some of them located in Jerusalem, which Israel did not control until around 1000 B.C.E. Thus Joseph Blenkinsopp, *The Pentateuch: An Introduction to the First Five Books of the Bible*, The Anchor Bible Reference Library (New York: Doubleday, 1992), 159-60, thinks that Hebrew phrases in verses 13 and 17 refer to the temple and Sion rather than to Mount Sinai, as earlier scholars held. The phrases are, in his translation, "thy holy habitation" (v. 13b, used of Sion in 2 Sam. 15:25 and Isa. 27:10); "the foundation for your holy dwelling" (v. 17a, which describes the Jerusalem temple in 1 Kings 8:13); and "the sanctuary which your hands have established" (v. 17b, "frequently used in apposition to Zion," e.g., in Ps. 48:9 and 87:5). Blenkinsopp suggests that the third phrase would be "particularly inappropriate if it referred to Sinai." Other scholars, notably F. M. Cross and D. N. Freedman, argue strongly for a pre-1000 date of the poem. See, for example, F. M. Cross, *Canaanite Myth and Hebrew Epic* (Cambridge, Mass.: Harvard, 1973).

11. Like Baal, the Lord here is a storm God, in control of the elements. Blenkinsopp, *Pentateuch*, 159, refers to scholars who found that the phrase "the mountain of your own possession" (Exod. 15:17) was also used to describe Baal's mountain residence in Ugaritic texts.

12. Exodus 15:1 is reminiscent of Virgil's "I sing of warfare and a man at war" (*Aeneid* I.1), which goes on to tell the Romans who they are and where they came from.

13. Blenkinsopp, *Pentateuch*, 158. His first example is Jonah 2 (a problematic text in its own right); then he shows parallels between the language of Exodus 15:1-18 and various verses of Psalm 69, 101, 96, 99, 118, 77, and 89.

14. The infinitive absolute and, here, the perfect. See Paul Joüon and T. Muraoka, *A Grammar of Biblical Hebrew*, Subsidia Biblica, vol. 14, pt. 2 (Rome: Editrice Pontificio Istituto Biblico, 1991), 123e.

15. The Greek translation reads "has indeed been glorified" at this point.

16. Because Hebrew is a Semitic language, most Hebrew words consist of three root consonants that express the general lexical notion of the word. This root is modified with prefixes, suffixes, and (originally, unwritten) vowels to give the range of possible forms expressed by the root. For example, the three consonants of the Hebrew verb "to fill" are *ml'*; the third one, ', is *aleph*, pronounced, if at all, as a glottal stop (for example, as in "bottle" pronounced without voicing the double "t"). This root *ml'* expresses the idea of "fullness" and is found in various verbal forms conveying such ideas as filling, being filled, being full, etc., and in nouns denoting, for example, that which fills something and, thus, abundance, or a full yield. See Joüon and Muraoka, *Grammar*, I:2d.

17. The fulfillment of the other term of the promise, the gift of the land, will be gradually described during the course of Exodus, Numbers, and the first part of the Deuteronomistic History: the books of Deuteronomy, Joshua, Judges, and 1 and 2 Samuel.

18. Walter Brueggemann has argued plausibly that Pharaoh's behavior is that of a vassal who is being disobedient to his overlord, in this case the universal overlord. See his "Pharaoh as Vassal: A Study of a Political Metaphor," *Catholic Biblical Quarterly* 57 (1995): 27-51.

19. The New American Bible follows the Greek Old Testament in having Exodus 8:10 as 8:6 and 8:22 as 8:18.

20. The covenant between God and Israel is not mentioned directly here but is implied in God's reference to "my people" in Exodus 3:7.

21. The biblical presupposition is that recognition and acknowledgment of the Lord (YHWH) is of the essence of rational creatures (see n. 18 above). The problematic idea that the Lord hardens Pharaoh's heart (e.g., 4:21; 7:3; and seventeen more times in chapters 7–14) attempts to convey God's ultimate sovereignty over what happens. At the same time, however, Pharaoh is clearly regarded as responsible for his conduct toward Israel.

22. See Exodus 7:5, 17; 8:10, 22 (vv. 6, 18 in Hebrew); 9:14, 29; 14:4, 18.

23. The New American Bible translates the Hebrew of Exodus 4:23 slightly differently, but the end result is the same: the death of Egypt's firstborn at God's hand. It reads: "Hence I tell you: Let my son go, that he may serve me. If you refuse to let him go, I warn you, I will kill your son, your firstborn."

24. Their firstborn, Gershom (Exod. 2:21-22), although not so designated here.

25. It could be objected that "firstborn" language is not used in Exodus 4:24-26. Some scholars connect the passage with Genesis 32:22-33, in which a "man" (who turns out to be God) wrestles with

Jacob as he, like Moses, is on the point of returning to his own land. The story about Jacob lacks an expressed intent to kill, however, and the incident leaves the patriarch in possession of a blessing, a new name, and a permanent limp.

26. Blenkinsopp, *Pentateuch*, 143-44, argues against this both in general and in connection with Exodus 1–15, but even on his reading of the texts, the Priestly tradition remains late.

27. Admittedly, there is no hard-and-fast distinction between legal and military language: "punishment" can be inflicted by troops. Nevertheless, the use of one set of terms rather than the other can be instructive.

28. The Hebrew word *ḥᵃmûšîm* is a passive participle from a verb that refers to arranging people in companies of fifty. The word occurs also in Joshua 1:14; 4:12. As in Exodus 13, these passages are about crossing a river, this time the Jordan, but they differ from Exodus 13:18 in that each time other words in the context bring out the military aspect of the group involved: they are "warriors" (*gibbôrê haḥayil*) in Joshua 1:14 and explicitly called a host girded for battle (*ḥᵃlûṣê haṣṣābā' lᵉmilḥāmāh*) in 4:13. There is no such context in Exodus 13:18. The word *ḥᵃmûšîm* also occurs in the book of Judges (7:11) with reference to a Midianite encampment; and perhaps (the text is corrupt) in Numbers 32:17, where the idea of military readiness is present in a context of leading the Israelites through potentially dangerous territory. In other words, *ḥᵃmûšîm* was clearly understood as having military connotations; the question is whether they are to be presumed as present in Exodus 13:18.

29. Clearly, Israel obtains weapons at some stage: it is "with the sword" that Joshua defeated Amalek in Exodus 17:13.

30. Here the surrounding references to army and chariots support translating the neutral "people" with *soldiers* or *army*.

31. I thus agree with Millard C. Lind, *Yahweh Is a Warrior: The Theology of Warfare in Ancient Israel* (Scottdale, Pa.: Herald Press, 1980), 54, that Exodus 13–14 contains battle language but doubt his view that the militarization of Egypt necessarily implies that of Israel. Rather, as the story is told, Yahweh is presented as fighting for Israel and routing the Egyptians because Egypt comes as an army against Israel (14:14, 27; see also 14:24-25).

32. The word that the New Revised Standard Version here twice translates as *army* is not *ḥayil* but *maḥaneh*, related to the verb "to encamp." It was earlier used in 14:19, 20 to denote the group of, first, the Israelites and then the Egyptians; the NRSV translation *army* is correct in the second instance but misleading in the first.

33. Elsewhere in the Bible the distinction between using creation and military means is less clear: see, for example, the hailstones that enabled Joshua to defeat the Amorite kings who had attacked Israel's allies, the Gibeonites (Josh. 10:11).

34. *Host* is literally "camp," but the Egyptians are in the middle of the sea at this point. See note 32 above.

35. See 1 Samuel 15:3 and the New Englanders' view of the Native Americans in Roland H. Bainton, *Christian Attitudes Toward War and Peace: A Historical Survey and Critical Re-evaluation* (New York: Abingdon, 1960), 168-69.

36. The author juxtaposes an etiological note about Israel's complaining (the place is named Massa and Meribah, i.e., "Test" and "Quarreling") and the attack on them by the Amalekites, but makes no explicit causal connection between the two.

37. The root of the Hebrew verb translated "deal shrewdly" in Exodus 1:10 is *ḥkm*, used ironically, because Pharaoh's attempt to outsmart Israel will bring about his own undoing.

38. The character of the Pharaoh in these stories is paradoxical. This is because the biblical author is convinced of two things that are formally incompatible: that God is in ultimate control of events (hence the "hardening of heart" motif) and that people are responsible for their actions (so, because Pharaoh acted violently against Israel, the destruction of his army is just).

39. Analogy is always involved when humans speak about God. Since language is part of the created world, it can be used to convey people's insights about God but will never be entirely adequate to the divine reality.

Chapter 6

1. This is a difficult notion for some people to take seriously but depends on the not-uncommon understanding (or belief) that certain everyday realities are an essential part of a group's identity, usually in relation to its god. Some actions are, therefore, required and others are strictly forbidden. Those who transgress, even unwittingly, are regarded as having put themselves outside the boundaries of the community and must undergo some form of purification to be readmitted. Any large-scale violation of the relevant norms would threaten the group's existence, which is why its members are prepared to go to great lengths (even violence) to protect themselves against incurring ritual impurity.

2. The historical reality was undoubtedly more complex and is much disputed. Although the Bible stresses the distinction between Israelites and Canaanites, this was probably less obvious at the time, and many Canaanites "became" Israelites. See, for example, Philip J. Budd, *Numbers*, Word Biblical Commentary, vol. 5 (Waco, Tex.: Word Books, 1984), xxvi-xxvii, xxix-xxxi.

3. See Martin Noth, *Numbers: A Commentary*, The Old Testament Library (Philadelphia: Westminster Press, 1968), 12.

4. The complete phrase is *kol-yōṣê' ṣābā'*. The first word means "all." See Paul Joüon and T. Muraoka, *A Grammar of Biblical Hebrew*,

Subsidia Biblica, vol. 14, part 2 (Rome: Editrice Pontificio Istituto Biblico, 1991), 121, sections i and n.

5. See George Buchanan Gray, *A Critical and Exegetical Commentary on Numbers*, International Critical Commentary (Edinburgh: T. & T. Clark, 1903), 36; and Budd, *Numbers*, 47-48.

6. Exodus 6:26; 7:4; 12:17, 41, 51. It is usually translated as *company* or *hosts*. The Jerusalem Bible, however, has "in battle order," "armies," and "array."

7. See Numbers 2:4, 6, 8, 11, 13, 15, 19, 21, 23, 26, 28, 30.

8. George E. Mendenhall, "The Census Lists of Numbers 1 and 26," *Journal of Biblical Literature* 77 (1958): 54.

9. There are three main strands that were incorporated in the first four books of the Pentateuch, from Genesis to Numbers. These blocks of traditional material have been recognized by most scholars since the time of Julius Wellhausen in the latter part of the nineteenth century. They are the Priestly (P), Elohist (E), and Yahwist (J, since "YHWH" begins with J in German). There is a fourth strand, from the Deuteronomistic tradition (D), but most scholars do not think it occurs in Genesis or Exodus.

10. Budd, *Numbers*, xviii-xix, claims that there is "a very general acceptance of a total priestly contribution" in chapters 1–9, 15, 17–19, 26–31, and 33–36, and that only chapters 11–12 and 21–24 lack Priestly influence.

11. Twice in chapter 1 and again in chapters 2, 7, 10, 13, 26, and 34.

12. Noth, *Numbers*, 20, suggests that "the census carried out from the military point of view, is for [the author] simply one element in the external organization of the people."

13. If *eleph* really did mean "a thousand" in these contexts, the total in Numbers 1:46 (not including Levites) would be 603,550. That would be a lot of people for a small part of the Sinai desert to support, even by the standards of saga! However, despite its translation as *thousand* in modern Bibles, the word originally denoted a unit rather than actual numbers: see, for example Robert G. Boling, *Joshua*, The Anchor Bible, vol. 6 (Garden City, N.Y.: Doubleday, 1982), 176; and Timothy R. Ashley, "Excursus on Large Numbers," in *The Book of Numbers*, The New International Commentary on the Old Testament (Grand Rapids, Mich.: Eerdmans, 1993), 60-66.

14. The word *ṣābā'* (*hosts* or *company*) is used fourteen times in Numbers 31, but never to refer to previously constituted units.

15. See Ashley, *The Book of Numbers*, 273-74.

16. Genesis 36:9-19 shows the Edomites as descending from Jacob's brother Esau.

17. Joshua was not listed as part of the original muster: in Numbers he is first named (as Moses' assistant) in 11:28 (see also Exod. 33:11), although he had functioned as a soldier in Exodus 17.

18. See Susan Niditch, *War in the Hebrew Bible: A Study in the Ethics of Violence* (New York: Oxford University, 1993), chap. 1, "The Ban as God's Portion," and esp. 31-32, 41-42.

19. It is usually within a context of correcting injustice that some of the prophets depict the Lord as rejecting sacrifice: see, for example, Hosea 6:6 and Micah 6:6-8.

20. Reticence about the Lord's wars could, of course, indicate that the Lord was not a successful warrior!

21. For Niditch, *War*, 81-82, the sparing of even some lives removes this incident from the category of the "ban," *herem*, where the enemy is totally destroyed as a sacrifice to God.

22. Niditch, *War*, chapter 3, "The Priestly Ideology in Numbers 31."

23. Noth, *Numbers*, 240.

24. The narrator presents as unreasonable the behavior of some of Israel's adversaries: minimally, the Edomites, the Canaanite king of Arad, and King Og. Those who speak on behalf of their enemies do not always convey the full picture. Even if they are honest, they may lack the imagination to see how (in this case) Israel's presence would have been perceived by others. Fear is one of the strongest motivators for the violence of people who wish to live according to their best lights.

Chapter 7

1. Annie Jaubert, ed., *Homélies sur Josué* VIII.2, Sources Chrétiennes, vol. 71 (Paris: Cerf, 1960).

2. The assumption in Joshua that Israel is a militant society may affect how Numbers is understood by readers who return to it after reading Joshua: they are more likely than before to read chapters 1 and 2 as indicating a real army, not merely a potential one.

3. This understanding, like any other, can be distorted and result in violence. Although the idea is that Israel not become proud of its victory, those whom they displaced are liable to find it offensive that their new masters credit God with subjugating them.

4. Some of the kings listed as having been conquered by "Joshua and the Israelites" in 12:7 are additional to those mentioned in connection with the Gibeonite affair in Joshua 10–11.

5. A similar point was made by Richard McSorley in *New Testament Basis of Peacemaking*, 3d ed. (Scottdale, Pa.: Herald Press, 1985), 61-64.

6. Norman C. Habel, *The Land Is Mine: Six Biblical Land Ideologies*, Overtures to Biblical Theology (Minneapolis: Fortress, 1995).

7. Despite most English translations, *contingent* is preferable to *thousand* here, as *eleph* is a unit rather than a specific number. See Robert G. Boling, *Joshua*, The Anchor Bible, vol. 6 (Garden City, N.Y.: Doubleday, 1982), 176. That armed men are involved here in 4:13 is a

further specification of Joshua 1:14; the language is closer to that of Numbers 32:20-21.

8. For an indication of some of the factors involved, see Boling, *Joshua*, 177-78, where the author quotes at length George Adam Smith's 1894 description of this part of the Jordan.

9. The Lord tells Joshua in 1:7, "Do not turn from [the law] to the right hand or to the left, so that you may be successful wherever you go."

10. In similar circumstances, David and the elders with him instantly prostrate themselves, covered in sackcloth (1 Chron. 21:16b-17). Contrast Numbers 22:23, 31, where Balaam's donkey is needed to alert the non-Israelite Balaam to the existence of the heavenly figure. See Boling, *Joshua*, 197. Joshua's ability to recognize the Lord's messenger is part of God's gift to Israel.

11. See Niditch, *War*, chap. 1, "The Ban As God's Portion," 28-55, and esp. 34-35.

12. The "commander" is, of course, on the side of those who are telling the story!

13. Etiologies are frequent in this part of the Bible. Another example is the story of the siege and fall of Jericho, which explains the existence of another impressive ruin that was familiar to the original hearers of these stories.

14. The Bible describes the ritual slayings of those who had worshiped the golden calf and Baal of Peor (Num. 25) but says nothing of any Israelites killed in battle. Neither are any mentioned in the debacle of Numbers 14:39-45, although Israel's "defeat" must surely imply casualties. At the end of the major campaign against the Midianites, the company commanders inform Moses that not one was missing of all the men whom they had led into battle (31:49). Clearly, we are in the world of stylized sagas, not field reports of battles. Their purpose is to credit Israel's God with perfect victories and conquests, not to record actual body counts.

15. See Boling, *Joshua*, 228, who adds that the September heat in the Valley of Achor led him to conclude that the place "was appropriately named"! The Greek version of Joshua 7:25, followed by the New American Bible, is shorter and reads simply: "And all Israel stoned him to death."

16. For an intriguing suggestion that water pollution had led to the flourishing of the snail vector of the blood fluke that causes schistoso-miasis, see Boling, *Joshua*, 214-15, and references there. It seems that the effects of this parasitic fluke could have included low fertility and high infant mortality, which might account for the ease by which the city was captured, the fact that Israel did not settle there, and the terms of Joshua's curse.

17. The dynamic is the same as with the Egyptians at the exodus (e.g., 7:5; 14:4, 18) and elsewhere in the biblical narrative: in the end, God is to be acknowledged.

18. Nehemiah 8 describes a similar event after the return from exile in Babylon.

19. For another example, see 1 Samuel 15:9-33.

20. Boling, *Joshua*, 269: "The covenant belonged to the people-forming process, and the problem of inferior forms of membership in the community is precisely what the covenant liturgy was originally designed to counteract."

21. The terms of this description are reminiscent of God's promising Abraham offspring ("as numerous . . . as the sand that is on the seashore," Gen. 22:17; see also 32:12) and of the Egyptians massed at the seashore with "horses and chariots" (Exod. 14:9).

22. See 1:1-9; 3:1–4:24; 5:2-12; perhaps 5:13-15; 6:3-16; 7:1-26; 8:30-35.

23. Booty was taken at Ai only "according to the word of the LORD that he had issued to Joshua" (8:27).

24. See, for example, Ambrose of Milan, in *On the Duties of the Clergy* 1.40.195, noted in Louis J. Swift, *The Early Fathers on War and Military Service*, Message of the Fathers of the Church, no. 19 (Wilmington, Del.: Michael Glazier, 1983), 98. Joshua is even more respected among Jews.

25. See, for example, 10:10-14, 30, 32, 40, 42; 11:6-9, 12, 15, 20, 23.

26. See, for example, 10:15, 42; 23:3, 10.

27. Admittedly, it was a very small area by comparison with the pre-exilic situation at its height.

28. Neither, of course, was post-World War I Germany, although that did not prevent it from trying within a decade or two.

29. Ezra 4; Nehemiah 2:19-20; 3:33–4:17.

30. Habel, *The Land Is Mine*, 57. See the whole of chapter 4: "Land as Family Lots: An Ancestral Household Ideology."

31. See, for example, 14:2 and the first verses of chapters 15, 16, 17, and 19. The Hebrew word for "lot" is found also in Joshua 17:14, 17; 18:6, 8, 10, 11; and in seven verses of each of chapters 19 and 21 (19:1, 10, 17, 24, 32, 40, 51; 21:4, 5, 6, 8, 10, 20, 38).

32. Habel, *The Land Is Mine*, 62.

33. The alleged exceptions here are the inhabitants of Samaria and their allies. Among the latter is Tobiah, whose credentials as a well-connected Israelite are quite impressive (Zech. 6:10, 14; Neh. 13:4). Other biblical texts, however, effectively remove him (or someone of the same name) from among the Israelites, specifying that his descendants are among those unable to establish their Jewish descent from the genealogical tables (Ezra 2:60; Neh. 7:62).

34. Beginning with five occurrences in chapter 1 (vv. 1, 2, 7, 13, 15), the book of Joshua refers to Moses as the Lord's servant twelve more times: in 8:31, 33; 9:24; 11:12, 15; 12:6; 13:8; 14:7; 18:7; 22:2, 4, 5.

35. Joshua's treatment of the Amorite kings in 10:16-39 is an exception here.

Chapter 8

1. A parallel here is the presumption of American settlers that they would have to fight to obtain the lands of the indigenous population. As with the biblical accounts, that struggle eventually became the subject of myths ("westerns") that glamorized the tough and often sordid reality.

2. On the other hand, Shechem, site of the assembly in Joshua 24, was later strongly associated with idolatry. Tradition knows it as the city that the tenth-century King Jeroboam built and dwelt in (1 Kings 12:25). Jeroboam was the first king of Israel, the northern region that seceded from Solomon's kingdom after his death. Later tradition remembers Jeroboam primarily for having led Israel into idolatry: to discourage his subjects from continuing to worship in the Jerusalem temple, he made two golden calves and put one at Bethel (in the south of his kingdom) and the other at Dan (in the north). See 1 Kings 12:26-29 and frequent references to his sin in the rest of 1 Kings and in 2 Kings.

3. As noted in the previous chapter, the Greek version of the book of Joshua gives details of the people's idolatry after Joshua's death.

4. Joshua did indeed spare the lives of the Gibeonites, as the treaty required (Josh. 9:15) but, after discovering that Israel had been deceived into making the agreement (9:3-14), he reduced the status of the Gibeonites to the servile, in contravention of the provision of Deuteronomy 29:9-11.

5. Israel "cries out" in Judges 3:9, 15; 4:3; 6:6, 7; 10:10, 12. Note the ironical parallel in 10:14, where the Lord suggests that the unfaithful Israel should try crying out to their chosen gods. The foundational text of all these examples is Exodus 2:23, where the Lord heard the cry of the enslaved Israelites and responded by delivering them from Egypt.

6. Part of the tradition about Caleb is found here too, probably because of the Calebites' later assimilation to the tribe of Judah. See, for example, Robert G. Boling, *Judges*, Anchor Bible, vol. 6A (Garden City, N.Y.: Doubleday, 1975), 356. Judges 1:12-15 lacks Caleb's diplomatic approach to Joshua found in Joshua 14:6-15.

7. See Boling, *Judges*, 169-70.

8. El-berith, god of the covenant, is a Shechemite deity that Israel had also taken to worshiping, according to Judges 8:33.

9. *Thousand* or (more likely) *companies*" (See chap. 6, n. 13; chap. 7, n. 6.)

10. The inhabitants of Gibeah had subjected to mass rape a woman who had been handed over to them by her Levite husband for such treatment. See Judges 19 and 20:21, 25, 31, 35, 44.

11. Instances of civil strife in Judges include also the strong-arm tactics by which Danites passing through Ephraimite territory relieve

Micah of his Yahwist shrine (of questionable origin and legitimacy) and of the wandering young Levite whom Micah had adopted as his private priest.

12. As already noted, Gideon's son Abimelech becomes king by killing all but one of his seventy-one half-brothers and dies ignominiously after a three-year rule (9:1-6, 53-54).

13. Commentators note Micah's generous treatment of this Levite, who eventually deserts him and turns out to be a descendant of Moses' firstborn, Gershom (18:30), whose absence from the biblical tradition (except here and in 1 Chron. 23 and 26) is surely significant.

14. By this stage in Judges, the idea of living on the land assigned by the Lord has almost completely broken down. For example, Micah lives in the mountain region of Ephraim but is not said to belong to that tribe (Judg. 17:1); his Levite priest comes to him from Bethlehem of Judah, but his family's land was in the north (18:7; Josh. 21:6) and he later goes away with the Danites (Judg. 18:20). The latter have given up trying to take possession of their appointed land and migrated to Judah (1:34; 18:1, 12); the Levite in chapter 19 is described as a resident alien who lived in Ephraim (19:1); the old man in Gibeah who gives him hospitality is from Ephraim but living in Benjaminite territory (19:16). In an account of how the Lord gave Israel land to live in, this moving around is a problem. The book of Ruth provides a certain corrective, at least in the Greek canon, where it follows Judges. For when the Israelite Naomi and her family live in Moab, her husband and sons die and leave no descendants, whereas Naomi's return to the Promised Land with her daughter-in-law Ruth soon results in abundant food and the birth of a child from whose line King David will come.

15. Micah, who earlier took in the Levite, is hospitable to the Danite emissaries too (18:2). Between his behavior and that of the men of Gibeah in chapter 19 there is a further decline.

16. See Boling, *Judges*, 53 and 61.

17. In Lillian R. Klein, *The Triumph of Irony in the Book of Judges* (Sheffield: Almond Press, 1988), 24, Klein claims that together Simeon and Judah conquer only people, not a city. But they do in fact destroy the city of Zephath (1:17).

18. Ibid., 23. In what follows, Simeon is mentioned only in the destruction of Zephath and its inhabitants (1:17) and not thereafter in Judges.

19. Ibid., 33.

20. Ibid., 36.

21. Ibid., 40. That Moab "was subdued" under Israel's power may imply God's activity (Judg. 3:30).

22. When Deborah gives Barak the Lord's message that he is to lead men of Naphtali and Zebulun against Sisera, Barak refuses to go unless she goes with him (4:4-9). Thus Sisera's assassination by Jael is presented

as retribution for the general's lack of confidence and courage: Deborah had predicted, "the Lord will sell Sisera into the hand of a woman" (v. 9).

23. The "thirty-two thousand" of most English translations should probably be "thirty-two companies."

24. "'Sound and light' show" is from Klein, *Triumph*, 55.

25. Gideon does not, however, trouble to qualify the Israelites' flattering claim that he had "delivered [them] out of the hand of Midian" (8:22), despite the repetition in 6:14, 36 and 7:9, 14 that the Lord would deliver Midian into Gideon's hands.

26. Note that Abimelech is nowhere said "to judge" Israel.

27. As previously noted (n. 2), Shechem was regarded as an evil place by Judeans of later times, because of its association with King Jeroboam I. After seceding from Judah, he made two golden calves and put one in Dan, in the north of his territory, and the other in Bethel, in the south, so that people would not go to Jerusalem to worship (1 Kings 12:26-29). Thus "Shechem" is almost synonymous with "idolatry," in many parts of the tradition.

28. Although the text says that God "sent an evil spirit between" Abimelech and the lords of Shechem (9:23), it was surely only a matter of time before the latter regretted having made Abimelech their king, given his character as revealed in the slaughter of his brothers. Sometimes evil does destroy itself, and the biblical writer has no problem with attributing that to God.

29. Note also that Israel's "crying out" in 10:10 is not followed by the accession of Jephthah but by God's angry response and then Israel's abject reply and repentance, to which God responds (10:11-16). The Lord is getting weary! Gideon's case was rather similar: God responded to Israel's cry by sending an unnamed prophet (6:6-8), and Gideon is called immediately after that. The sequence in these two cases is different from that of the earlier judges, where the judge's appointment comes right after the cry.

30. In Klein, *Triumph*, 89, the author, building on the work of earlier scholars, finds that Jephthah "has his facts all wrong" about the Transjordan campaigns, the name of the local god concerned, and the equivalence that Jephthah allegedly assumes between the Lord and that god. Yet Boling produces good reasons for finding Jephthah's account "technically meticulous" rather than mistaken (*Judges*, 201-5).

31. The adjective translated *only* in 11:34 is *yeḥîdāh*, the feminine form of *yāḥîd*, used of Isaac in Genesis 22:2, 12, and 16, when his father is told to offer his only son as a sacrifice.

32. There are some resemblances between this incident and the one in Judges 1:11-12, where Othniel offers his daughter, Achsah, as wife to whoever conquers Kiriath Sepher. Yet Othniel's promise is not termed a vow, does not involve God, and has clear terms, however much they may offend those who think of a daughter as more than a potentially valuable asset.

33. There is a slight possibility that Jephthah's quarrel with the Ammonites may be similarly personal. His daughter tells him, "The LORD has given you vengeance against your enemies" (11:36); *you* is singular. See C. F. Burney, *The Book of Judges with Introduction and Notes on the Hebrew Text of the Books of Kings* (New York: KTAV, 1970), 300. As Burney notes, however, that the Ammonites were Jephthah's personal enemies is hard to reconcile with his outsider status (11:1-11). So the singular *you* may reflect merely the child's perspective on her father's affairs.

34. Throughout, Manoah's wife behaves with good sense. By contrast, her husband does not accept her report of her encounter with the angel and is clearly relegated to outsider status when the angel makes it clear that his wife already knows all that is necessary (13:8, 13). Indeed Manoah does not recognize the angel of the Lord until verse 21 (see v. 16, even though his wife told him her surmise in v. 6). He also needs her to point out to him that their imminent death ("for we have seen God," v. 22) would not be compatible with either God's acceptance of their offerings or the promise of a son (v. 23).

35. See, for example, Boling, *Judges*, 80-83. Othniel is said to be son of Caleb's *younger* brother (1:13), which would be regarded as a disadvantage only by those who have forgotten about the Lord's propensity for disregarding (or even reversing) the prevalent understanding of primogeniture. If his designation as son of Kenaz (1:12) makes him a Kenizzite, he is not an Israelite but descended from Esau (see Gen. 36:11). Later, however, when King David's success had increased the fortunes of his tribe, the Kenizzites were assimilated into the tribe of Judah, and this is the situation that seems to be presupposed by Judges 1:10-15. See J. Kenneth Kuntz, "Kenaz," in *The Anchor Bible Dictionary*.

36. Ehud's left-handedness may not even be a problem in the light of 20:16, which speaks of seven hundred top rank sling throwers of Benjamin who were similarly endowed.

37. The first is a Philistine who, under great pressure because of Samson's boasting, chooses family loyalty over her newlywed husband. The second is a prostitute, and the third, Delilah, takes money from Philistines for betraying him.

38. Moses also was given water from a rock, but Samson is here much more like the people of Israel, whose grumbling against Moses led to that incident (Exod. 17:1-7).

39. The Hebrew word translated as *concubine* is *pîlegesh*. It often denotes a secondary wife. Clear examples include the woman who bore Abimelech to Gideon (Judg. 8:31) and some of the women who bore sons to Abraham and some of his descendants (Gen. 22:4; 25:6; 35:12; 36:12). In the instance in Judges 19, however, there is no evidence that the Levite involved had any other wife.

40. As, for example, New Revised Standard Version, following the Greek text. The Hebrew verb *zānāh* could be translated "became a prostitute" but the preposition that follows the verb is unusual, as Boling, *Judges*, 274, points out. The Greek *orgizein* could represent a different Hebrew verb (also *zānāh*) that means "to be angry," and if prostitution were the issue, it is strange that she would then return home. For the suggestion that the woman's desertion itself constituted infidelity to her partner, see Gale A. Yee, "Ideological Criticism: Judges 17–21 and the Dismembered Body," in *Judges and Method: New Approaches in Biblical Studies*, ed. Gale A. Yee (Minneapolis: Augsburg Fortress, 1995), 162-63.

41. He claims that the men of Gibeah were out to kill him (their intent was homosexual rape, 19:22) and omits mentioning that they were able to abuse his concubine only because he sent her out to them. He may have surmised, perhaps fairly, that they would otherwise have killed him.

42. See Boling, *Judges*, 53 and 61.

43. In Judges 1, Judah does attack first, albeit along with Simeon, while 20:20 merely states, "The Israelites drew up the battle line against them at Gibeah."

44. Readers might, however, think of the close association between Jabesh-gilead and the Benjaminite king Saul. See 1 Samuel 11 and 31:11-13.

45. With careful handling such as the Lord provides, even the timorous Gideon can be recruited to lead Israel in battle.

Chapter 9

1. David, presented in Ruth 4:21-22 as Ruth's great-grandchild, will become Israel's second king.

2. Readers are probably to infer that Elimelech, Naomi's husband, did wrong in taking his family away from Bethlehem ("the house of bread") during the famine, and that this is why they do not prosper in Moab.

3. The link between human well-being and living in the right place (in this case, Bethlehem in Judah) is a positive example of a theme repeatedly found in its negative form in the book of Judges. As we saw in the previous chapter (ch. 8, n. 14), large numbers of people had moved away from their ancestral allotments.

4. Uzziah (Azariah) ruled Judah from around 783-742 B.C.E., with his son acting as regent during the king's last years, because Uzziah had contracted leprosy. J. Kenneth Kuntz notes that Uzziah was one of Judah's most successful kings: he "mended the defenses of Jerusalem, reorganized and reequipped the Judean army, won and capably maintained control over numerous caravan routes to the south, [and] extended Judah's frontiers at the expense of neighboring Philistines and

Edomites" ("Uzziah," *Anchor Bible Dictionary*). Politically, he was able to do all this because neither Egypt nor Assyria had interests in the region. That would change after 743, when the Assyrian Tiglath-pileser III defeated an anti-Assyrian coalition that included Tyre and Damascus.

5. See also Isaiah 65:25, which relates to this passage.

6. See Genesis 4 and chapter 2 above.

7. See Isaiah 7:3-25; 37:2-7, 21-35; 38:1-8 for Isaiah's interactions with two of Judah's Davidic kings, Ahaz and Hezekiah.

8. That the Lord can command a foreign army to chastise Israel is an expression of the people's conviction that injustice deserves retribution—from God, if necessary.

9. In Hebrew, the verb translated in 10:21 as *return* can also mean "repent."

10. Jesse was King David's father: see 1 Samuel 16:1-13.

11. Isaiah 40–55 expresses this as the Lord rebuilding Jerusalem in precious stones (see, e.g., 54:11-12). Isaiah 56–66 is much more explicit about the hoped-for restoration (60:1-22; 61:4-7; 61:10–62:12; 65:17-25; 66:7-14, 18-23) and about how the moral dimension affects Zion's restoration and subsequent prosperity (see, e.g., 61:8; 63:7–65:16; 66:1-6). The book of Revelation also develops this general theme (see chap. 12 below).

12. The intended reference here is probably the Assyria of Sargon II, because the Assyrian kings also held the title of King of Babylon.

13. For a less jaundiced account of the activities of this pair, see Isaiah 36:1-22.

14. Other sections of Isaiah develop this theme poetically. See, for example, 55:12-13.

15. Isaiah is much more explicit about this later in the book: see references given in note 11 above.

16. This imagery is reminiscent of the beginning of the flood in Gen. 7:11, although the word for "heaven" is different in the two texts.

17. The peaceable creation story with which the Bible opens does not mention Leviathan as a component of the primeval chaos, but this monster (as destroyed or tamed by the Lord) remains part of Israel's wider tradition. See, for example, Ps. 74:13-14 and 104:26.

18. Isaiah 46:1-4 draws a graphic comparison of Babylon's gods, who need to be carried by the people, and Israel's God, who has carried "the house of Jacob" since its birth and will continue to carry it for as long as is necessary.

19. Isaiah will later set this out in much greater detail. See, for example, 66:18-24, the final words of the canonical book.

Chapter 10

1. See, for example, Numbers 13:6, where Judah's representative among the spies that Joshua sends to spy out the land is "Caleb son of

Jephunneh," and Joshua 14–15 locates Caleb's land within that apportioned to Judah.

2. For David's separation from Saul's retinue, see 1 Samuel 24:22.

3. Beginning with the story of his encounter with Goliath, David's prowess as a soldier was legendary (1 Sam. 17). It is apparent, for example, in the women's song of 18:7 and in David's lack of hesitation in killing Philistines to meet the price of a hundred of their foreskins that Saul set for his daughter Michal (vv. 20-29).

4. Although Abigail will end up as part of the royal household (vv. 39-42), this cannot be her motivation here, because she is still married to Nabal.

5. See, for example, Exodus 21:13; Numbers 35:6-28; Deuteronomy 4:41-43; 19:1-13; Joshua 20; and 1 Chronicles 6. For David and/or Nabal, the nearest city would be Kiriath-arba, or Hebron (Josh. 20:7).

6. Speaking to David, Abigail refers to herself as "your servant" twice in 25:24 and once in verses 25, 27, 28, and 31, the last of these being the final word of her speech. She calls him "my lord" twice in verses 25, 26, 28, and 31, and once in verses 24, 27, 29, and 30.

7. No reason is given for this in 1 Samuel 7, but see the next note and the text to which it relates.

8. 1 Kings 5:3 (5:17 in the Hebrew) has a less pointed version of the same idea.

9. As we might say, after ten days, Nabal's "stroke" killed him.

10. Examples of wise women include those of Tekoa, whom David's army commander, Joab, sent to David, to convince the king that he should put aside his concerns about Absalom and resume his rule (2 Sam. 14:1-24). Joab knew that she would be able to make David listen, whereas he himself could not. Later another woman successfully negotiated with Joab to prevent the destruction of her city (2 Sam. 20:14-22).

11. Readers may here be reminded of Isaac's wife Rebekah, who took initiatives that first tricked her husband into favoring her younger son, Jacob, and then saved his life by getting him out of the way (Gen. 27–28).

12. See, for example, Jeremiah 20–21 and Amos 7:10-14.

13. The Truth and Reconciliation Commission was set up in South Africa in December 1995, after decades of racial strife. Its formal proceedings concluded with a report made to President Mandela in October 1998. The purpose of the Commission was to bring about reconciliation in a society where a white minority had violated the rights of their fellow citizens systematically and with impunity. Under the leadership of Archbishop Desmond Tutu, the seventeen-person commission established three committees: on Amnesty, on Human Rights Violations, and on Reparation and Rehabilitation. Under this system,

amnesty was offered to anyone who, in a public hearing, made to the Commission a full disclosure of politically motivated violations of human rights (e.g., abduction, torture, killing) committed between 1960, the year of a landmark massacre in Sharpeville, and 1994, when Nelson Mandela was inaugurated as the South African Head of State. There were also public hearings for those victimized by apartheid and provision for reparations. For a first-hand account of the process, see Desmond Tutu, *No Future Without Forgiveness* (New York: Doubleday, 1999). See also Priscilla B. Hayner, *Unspeakable Truths* (New York: Routledge, 2001).

14. Nabal's version of this would be that he had refused to submit to David's extortion. Clearly, the biblical author of 1 Samuel is on the side of the poor, yet resourceful, David.

15. In his final decree before dying, David instructs his son Solomon to ensure that the now-aged Shimei die violently for his action of so many years before (1 Kings 2:8-9). In the end, therefore, Shimei is executed for an offense that David admits he had sworn to forgive (v. 8, 46). The decree is part of a series of arrangements that the dying king makes, as his last efforts to avoid guilt from his own acts or those of his subordinates. The story in verses 36-46 tells how Solomon picks up on the subtlety of his father's request (as David had intended that he should) and Shimei accepts from him what looks like a reasonable chance of survival for an old man: house arrest in Jerusalem. Shimei dies only when he violates that agreement. Perhaps David's (and the Deuteronomist's) high regard for the Lord's anointed takes precedence even over an oath (see his references to Saul in 1 Sam. 24:6, 10; 26:9, 11, 16, 23 and 2 Sam. 1:14, 16).

16. The Gibeonites claimed that Saul had "consumed . . . and planned to destroy" them (2 Sam. 21:5), although the Bible contains no independent account of such action of Saul's, apart from verse 2.

17. The ruthlessness of Zeruiah's sons should indeed have worried David. As David's military commander, Joab was close to the king himself. Consequently, he was best placed to orchestrate the king's overthrow, if he chose to do so. For example, he might one day have judged that he could undermine David's authority by revealing how David had dealt with Uriah (see 2 Sam. 11–12).

18. In 2 Samuel 2:4, the people of Judah anoint David as their king. Seven and a half years later, after his success in subduing potential rivals from Saul's house, "all the tribes of Israel" make a covenant with David and then anoint him king over Israel (5:1-3); verses 4-5 give the time frame of David's reign. Thus first David and then Solomon rule "all Israel." After Solomon's death, however, his son Rehoboam is unable to keep the allegiance of the northern tribes, who then secede under the leadership of Jeroboam (1 Kings 12). "There was no one who followed the house of David, except the tribe of Judah alone" (1 Kings 12:20).

19. Literally, "their brothers" (2 Chron. 28:1, 11). This meant that captors and captives were related, as descendants of Jacob.

20. There are great problems with such a simplistic view of history and of the relationship between human deeds and divine activity. For example, the Chronicler did not have to incorporate into his scheme the Shoah and its atrocities, where Jewish people were targeted simply for being descendants of Jews, whether or not they themselves were observant.

21. Ahaz of Jerusalem is charged with worshiping gods other than the Lord (including the Canaanite Baals, see 2 Chron. 28:2), with having "made his sons pass through fire" (28:3; this could designate child sacrifice, but more likely an ordeal or branding), and with sacrificing in places other than the temple in Jerusalem (v. 4). Therefore, his crimes are cultic in nature.

22. Note too that 2 Chronicles 28 and the parable in Luke 10 also share references to Jericho, and to the care, sustenance, and anointing given to the victim by the Samarians/Samaritan.

23. Although Christian Bibles (following the Greek tradition) place the two books of Chronicles after 2 Kings, the Hebrew Bible (in a tradition at least as old as the Babylonian Talmud) locates them at the very end. Consequently, the Jewish Scriptures in their present form conclude with the edict of Cyrus of Persia, commanding the Lord's people to go up to Jerusalem and build a temple there. (An alternative tradition, found in the ancient Hebrew codices from Aleppo and Leningrad, follows 2 Chronicles with Ezra and Nehemiah, thus representing the historical order of the events described in these books.)

Chapter 11

1. Nietzsche provided the classic formulation of the position that sees Christianity as the enemy of all that is noble in humanity.

2. Some scholars give a temporal sense to the Greek preposition *ex* and translate it "since." In either case, God's power is understood as being made manifest in Jesus' resurrection.

3. Although Christians have frequently been guilty of both these abuses, they remain abuses.

4. Mark expresses the cost of Jesus' ministry in various ways. It is implicit in the fast-paced sequence of preaching, choosing disciples, and healing with which the evangelist introduces Jesus' activities (1:14-45). The pressure under which the disciples live is indicated by 6:31-33, where Jesus tries unsuccessfully to secure a little peace for them. In telling of Jesus' healing a woman with a hemorrhage, Mark notes that Jesus "was aware that power had gone forth from him" (5:30).

5. See, for example, John P. Meier, *A Marginal Jew: Rethinking the Historical Jesus*, The Anchor Bible Reference Library (New York: Doubleday, 1991), 1:177.

6. Although it would be convenient to be able simply to blame "the Romans" for Jesus' execution (because there would be no chance that the present inhabitants of Rome would think that it had anything to do with them), there seems to be no doubt that Jesus deeply and repeatedly offended some of his fellow Jews, who found the implications of some of his words and actions incompatible with living as a member of the covenant people. The Roman authorities were, no doubt, willing enough to remove from their midst such a potential source of civil strife. This is, of course, a far cry from implicating in Jesus' death any more than a few of his contemporaries: anti-Judaism is profoundly unchristian.

7. The New Revised Standard Version omits "as" here. So does the Greek, but its inclusion seems warranted by the sense and for clarity's sake.

8. For examples, see Gustav Aulén, *Christus Victor: An Historical Study of the Three Main Types of the Idea of Atonement* (New York: Macmillan, 1967), 47-50.

9. The parable could also have encouraged John the Baptist in prison (1:14).

10. Timothy Carmody, "To The One Who Has, More Will Be Given: Discipleship Training in Mark's Parable Discourse and the Sea Journeys." Paper presented at the national meeting of the Catholic Biblical Association in August 1999.

11. "Imitating" Jesus is a notion that is foundational to Christian self-understanding: note, for example, how the dying Stephen in Acts 7:58-59 follows Jesus by praying for his executioners (cf. Luke 23:34, in many manuscripts) and hands over his "spirit" to Jesus, as the latter did to his Father in his dying prayer in Luke 23:46. Most Christians who consciously imitate Jesus adopt certain attitudes and practices and reject others as incompatible with their commitment. This involves making prudential judgments and is very context-dependent. For some, it does indeed involve having no family and restricting associates to those with similar ideals. Yet the imitation is never slavish, even in Francis of Assisi, who took this devotion as far as anyone.

12. The yield in 4:8 vastly exceeds mere biological possibilities; greater measure than one's own will be given (4:24); more will be given to one who has (25); the seed grows *automatē* (26-30); the product of the tiny mustard seed can eventually shelter the birds (31-32).

13. The Greek word here, *praüs*, translates the Hebrew *'anāwîm* in texts such as Psalm 37:11 (which Matt. 5:5 is quoting) and Isaiah 61:1. The *'anāwîm* are the poor who are the object of God's special concern. The singular form, *'ānāw*, is used of Moses in Numbers 12:3 to express his humility and piety. Provided that the nuance of devotion to God is retained, the word could be translated *gentle* in current English.

14. It is possible that the "least" who receive the ministrations are Christian leaders who are suffering for carrying out their mission. In

that case, the text would parallel Matthew 10:40-42, where welcoming a disciple is equivalent to welcoming Jesus (and God). The parable in Matthew 25 is usually interpreted more broadly to include charity done to anyone in need.

15. That is not to say that one may not look out for oneself at all. Mark probably knows his community well enough to know that there is little risk of that happening. Nevertheless, there are people for whom Mark's words could be dangerous, because their self-esteem is so low. The solution (rarely easy in practice) is that other members of the community must look out for such people.

16. That the women "fled from the tomb" may also be significant, because Mark earlier wrote that the disciples and the unidentified young man "fled" at Jesus' arrest (16:8; 14:50, 52). The Greek verb (*pheugein*) is the same in each case, although the context in which it is used in 16:8 perhaps softens the effect there.

17. The Sant'Egidio community was founded in Rome after the student uprisings of 1968 and currently has more than forty thousand members in more than sixty countries. See http://www.santegidio.it/en and further documentation there, or Robert Imbelli, "The Community of Sant'Egidio," *Commonweal* 121 no. 20 (November 18, 1994): 20-23.

18. See chapter 10, note 13.

19. Desmond Tutu, *No Future Without Forgiveness* (New York: Doubleday, 1999).

20. In this connection, note that the righteous, the "sheep" in the parable of the sheep and goats in Matthew 25:31-46, are most surprised that it turned out to be "the king" whom they had served as they ministered to the needy (vv. 37-39).

21. Mark's emphasis is on God's general offer of forgiveness (1:4; 2:5; 3:28) and on the way that the disciples are forgiven for their repeated misunderstanding and eventual desertion of Jesus. In 11:25 he insists on the need to forgive others before praying, but does not otherwise offer his readers help with how to go about this. The parable of the unforgiving servant in Matthew 18:23-35 will supplement Mark in this matter by suggesting that people's awareness of having received much forgiveness from God should empower them to forgive others. This does not, of course, make it easy, especially for victims of torture, rape, or systematic abuse of whatever kind. Yet it can be done. Over thirty years ago, I heard Metropolitan Anthony Bloom speak of a pact that he and his mother made as the Nazi threat to them grew greater. They swore that, whatever happened, neither of them would hate Nazis.

Chapter 12

1. See Romans 8 and the christological hymns of Philippians 2, Colossians 1, and Ephesians 1.

2. *Sin* here means a deliberate wrongdoing considered as an offense against God and therefore harmful to created beings.

3. For the texts, see James H. Charlesworth, ed., *The Old Testament Pseudepigrapha*, vol. 1 (Garden City, N.Y.: Doubleday, 1985).

4. See Revelation 7:3 and 19:5 to support the understanding of "his servant" (1:1) as meaning God's servant rather than Christ's, although the latter is not impossible in view of such texts as 5:13 and the New Testament tradition found in, for example, Mark 9 and 10.

5. That is, by his death, which includes also his resurrection. In Revelation 5:9 Jesus' action is termed "ransoming," as in Mark 10:45. Basic to Christian self-understanding is the improbable, unexpected experience of having been freed by God from various kinds of bondage through Jesus' death and resurrection. There are many attempts at explaining how this works, none of them entirely adequate, but the experience itself remains as the bedrock of Christianity.

6. Examples of such tension include Abraham's attempts to produce an heir by means of Hagar, the position of the older brothers, Ishmael and Esau, and the fragmented nature of Jacob's family throughout most of the Joseph cycle in Genesis 37–50.

7. See Genesis 15:1-21 (Abraham); 26:1-6 (Isaac); 28:13-19; 35:9-13; 46:1-4 (all Jacob).

8. See Revelation 1:3, 7; 2:16; 3:11; 22:6-7, 12.

9. See, for example, Revelation 2:21; 9:20, 21; 16:9, 11.

10. See Revelation 13:8; 17:8; 20:15. The literary purpose of the "book of life" is to express John's understanding that God knows who will be saved and who (if anyone) will not. This relieves the seer of the need to specify any further the limits of salvation—which, of course, he was not in a position to do.

11. The people who remain alive after the earthquake "were terrified and gave glory to the God of heaven" (Rev. 11:13).

12. John also gives prophetic testimony (Rev. 1:2-3). The two witnesses in Revelation 11 may represent the whole church, as it actively witnesses during the time of suffering (the three and a half years variously depicted in 11:2 and 3), or they may just be the martyrs in the narrower sense.

13. In the first case, Abimelech says to Abraham, "My land is before you; settle where it pleases you" (Gen. 20:15). To Isaac, he is blunter: "Go away from us; you have become too powerful for us" (26:16).

14. Jews contemporary with John had similar obligations, of course, but that is not the concern of Revelation.

15. See Revelation 2:13; 3:4; 13:16-17.

16. Even Tacitus, who had no respect for Christians, implies that Christians were innocent of the charge: see John Jackson, ed., *Tacitus*, vol. 4, Loeb Classical Library (Cambridge, Mass.: Harvard University Press, 1937), 4.282.

17. See, for example, Revelation 2:9; 3:9.

18. See, for example, Isaiah 47:8; 63:1; Ezekiel 14:21; 21:14; 38:17-20; Joel 1–2.

19. An English translation of the Qumran War Scroll, with a brief introduction, may be found in Geza Vermes, *The Complete Dead Sea Scrolls in English* (New York: Penguin Press, 1997), 161-86. The quotation here is from page 163. For a convenient summary of the scroll, see Joseph A. Fitzmyer, *Responses to 101 Questions on the Dead Sea Scrolls* (New York: Paulist Press, 1992), 30-32.

20. Although there is no contemporary evidence that Patmos was used as a penal settlement, Roman provincial governors did sometimes use deportation to an island as a form of punishment, especially for those of higher social standing. See Frederick J. Murphy, *Fallen Is Babylon: The Revelation to John*, The New Testament in Context (Harrisburg, Pa.: Trinity Press International, 1998), 15, 86.

21. See, for example, Revelation 12:17; 19:10.

22. Apart from John's own witnessing and that of Christ, most of the uses of *martyria* and its cognates in Revelation involve the violent death of one or more Christians. See 2:13; 6:9; 11:3, 7; 12:11, 17; 17:6; 19:10; 20:4. Of these, only 19:10 and (although only formally) 12:17 lack such a reference.

23. In Revelation, patient endurance (*hypomonē*) is referred to in 1:9; 2:2, 3, 19; 3:10; 13:10; 14:12. Mark 13:13 uses the cognate verb in Jesus' promise that one who endures to the end will be saved: even though enduring death, such a person will not ultimately lose his or her "self" (*psychē*, Mark 8:35-37).

24. It is not impossible that John had, independently of his Christianity, a bad case of *ressentiment* from other social causes. Little is known of his social status, although there is evidence from Julius Paulus, an authority in Roman law from around 200 C.E., that, for some crimes at least, *deportatio in insulam* was a punishment reserved for *honestiores*, or in other words, not for the lowest ranks of Roman society. John may have found Christianity attractive at least partly because it freed him from an uncomfortable state in which he could not advance further in the empire. On such cognitive dissonance, see Wayne A. Meeks, *The First Urban Christians: The Social World of the Apostle Paul* (New Haven, Conn.: Yale University, 1983), 173-74 and references there.

25. See Paul's references to his imprisonment and the other punitive measures he experienced. They include Philippians 1:13; Philemon 1, 9, 23; 2 Corinthians 4:9; 11:23-26. According to Luke in the book of Acts, Paul repeatedly evoked animosity from both Jews and Gentiles: see, for example, Acts 14:1-7, 19-20; 16:16-24; 19:23-40; 21:27-36.

26. Various parts of the church showed a reluctance to accept Revelation as canonical, sometimes because the apostolic authorship

was disputed and at other times because of the millenarian teaching that it contained. See John Sweet, *Revelation*, TPI New Testament Commentaries (Philadelphia: Trinity Press International, 1990), 47.

27. John's encouragement of those to whom he writes can be seen in such texts as Revelation 2:7, 11, 17, 26-28; 3:5, 12, 20-21; 22:11b-12.

28. See also Revelation 11:8; 14:13; 17:14; 19:16.

29. The phrase "one like the Son of Man" (Rev. 1:13) is deliberately reminiscent of "one like a human being" in Daniel 7:13; John's subsequent description of this figure reuses imagery that originally described "the Ancient One" in the same chapter of Daniel (v. 14). John is referring to Jesus in language that in its original form and context applied to "the people of the holy ones of the Most High" (i.e., Israel, Dan. 7:27) and to God.

30. For the New Testament background to these terms as applied to Jesus, see such texts as 2 Corinthians 1:19-20 and Colossians 1:15-20.

31. The twenty-four elders are the first to be referred to once John has finished trying to describe the divine throne. They probably represent a combination of the twelve tribes of Israel and the twelve apostles: John here reminds his community of its Jewish roots. The four living creatures, which also praise God, symbolize in an economical way what he wants to say about the created world at this point, although there will be more later: see the description of the new Jerusalem in 21:11–22:5.

32. The freedom is from the bondage of sin. Some Greek manuscripts of Revelation have the baptismal image, "washed," *lousanti*, instead of the more usual "freed," *lusanti*.

33. The situation presumed by Mark, some thirty years earlier and in a different region, has become more polarized.

34. The only possible exception here is the rider on the white horse in 19:11-12: "in righteousness he judges and makes war." Yet his weapon is a sword "from his mouth," which suggests that his warring is with words, and not physical (v. 15).

35. See Genesis 49:9-12 for the background to the "Lion of Judah," where Jacob, near death, blesses his twelve sons. The relevant part of Judah's blessing is: "Judah, like a lion's whelp, you have grown up on prey, my son. He crouches like a lion recumbent, the king of beasts— who would dare rouse him? The scepter shall never depart from Judah, or the mace from between his legs, while tribute is brought to him, and he receives the people's homage" (Gen. 49:9-10).

36. See Psalms of Solomon 17:21-25 for evidence that at least one Jewish group (probably during the first century B.C.E.) expected the Davidic messiah to use such military methods in the future. In verse 25 the sight of this descendant of David suffices to make the nations flee. For an account of the wide range of Jewish expectations about the messiah current in the first century C.E., see Jacob Neusner, William S. Green, and Ernest Frerichs, eds., *Judaisms and their Messiahs at the*

Turn of the Christian Era (Cambridge: Cambridge University Press, 1987) and John J. Collins, *The Scepter and the Star: The Messiahs of the Dead Sea Scrolls and Other Ancient Literature,* Anchor Bible Reference Library (New York: Doubleday, 1995).

37. Frequently in this work, what John hears conveys the inner reality of what he sees, with the understanding of that inner reality always determined by the concrete Christian experience. See, for example, Sweet, *Revelation,* 125-32. (In Rev. 5:6, "standing" indicates that the Lamb has been raised from the dead; see also 7:9 and 15:2, where it applies to the redeemed.)

38. See Paul's succinct statement in Romans 1:3 and also the genealogies in Matthew 1:1-17 and Luke 3:23-38.

39. See, for example, Exodus 12:5; Ezekiel 46:13; Hebrews 9:14; 1 Corinthians 5:7; 1 Peter 1:19; and probably John 1:29, 36. Isaiah 53:7 is also relevant to the whole picture of "lamb" christology. On this, see Sweet, *Revelation,* 124-25.

40. Wilfrid J. Harrington, *Revelation,* Sacra Pagina, vol. 16 (Collegeville, Minn.: Liturgical Press, 1993), 226.

41. See G. B. Caird, *The Revelation of St. John the Divine,* Harper's New Testament Commentaries (New York: Harper & Row, 1966), 80. Allen Kerkeslager plausibly argues that this first of the four riders represents "the complementary elements of false messiahs and false prophecy" ("Apollo, Greco-Roman Prophecy, and the Rider on the White Horse in Rev 6:2," *Journal of Biblical Literature* 112 [1993]: 116).

42. The Greek word for "sword" used here is *rhomphaia.* It is also used in Revelation 6:8, one of the four traditional means by which the four horsemen (or at least some of them; the text is unclear) bring death. The background here appears to be the expected consequences of breaking God's covenant. See, for example, Jeremiah 24:10; 29:17; and 32:24, which specify sword, famine, and pestilence, as in Revelation 6:4. Ezekiel 14:21 inserts "wild animals" as its third item; it comes last in John's list. The same instrument, the sword, is denoted by a different Greek word, *machaira,* in Revelation 6:4.

43. The clearest New Testament parallel is in Ephesians 6:17. There, in a Christian expansion of Isaiah 59:17, "the sword [*machaira*] of the Spirit" is simply equated with "the word of God." In Isaiah 49:2-3 the servant of the Lord says that God made his mouth "like a sharp sword" (*machaira*). Wisdom 18:14-16 contains the idea of God's word as being like a powerful sword (*xiphos*).

44. This is not the case with the other two uses of *machaira* in 13:10, 14. The first refers to a real possibility of Christians being killed and the second to the apparently mortal wound from which the Beast recovered, perhaps a reference to Nero's suicide, for which he used a sword; there were persistent rumors that he was not really dead.

45. See also Isaiah 11:4.

46. See Revelation 1:3; 10:11; 22:7, 10, 18, 19.

47. See Daniel Berrigan, *The Nightmare of God* (Portland, Ore.: Sunburst Press, 1983), 123-29.

48. Similarly, Wisdom 16:12 reads: "For neither herb nor poultice cured them, but it was your word, O Lord, that heals all people." This is probably a reference to the Law.

49. In Wisdom 2:12-24 a similar sentiment is graphically expressed in personal terms rather than as a military metaphor.

50. See Revelation 20:10, 14-15. John's overall point is that evil will not overcome that which is on the side of life and creativity. Is such a viewpoint liable to include malicious glee? Certainly. Should it do so? Probably not, since the destruction of anything represents an absolute resistance to the creator's will that God does not prevent (as John understands it). Here John is making an act of faith in God's power to deal with those whom he sees as implacably hostile to the Christian community of his day.

51. John may wish to imply that there was a battle that he chooses not to describe, or he may envisage a situation like that described in Psalms of Solomon 17:24-25, where the Davidic messiah has only to warn the "unlawful nations" to cause them to "flee from his presence" (R. B. Wright in Charlesworth, ed., *The Old Testament Pseudepigrapha*, 2:667).

52. "The kings of the earth" are referred to as such in 1:5 (on this, see below, in text); 6:15; 17:2, 18; 18:3, 9; 19:19; 21:24; see also 16:14 and 17:20, 12. Other ways in which John refers to his opponents are "the inhabitants of the earth" (3:10; 6:10; 8:13; 11:10; 13:8, 14; 17:8); "the nations" (2:26; 5:9; 7:9; 10:11; 11:2, 9, 18; 12:5; 13:7; 14:6, 8; 15:3, 4; 16:19; 17:15; 18:3, 23; 19:15; 20:3, 8; see also 21:24, 26; 22:2); "the rest of humankind" (9:20); "a synagogue of Satan" who "say that they are Jews and are not" (2:9; 3:9); "those who claim to be apostles but are not" (2:2); the Nicolaitans (2:6, 15); the Balaamites (2:14); and the Jezebelites (2:20).

53. Susan Mathews, unpublished paper presented at the national Catholic Biblical Association Meeting, Washington, D.C., August 1992, p. 4, n. 1.

54. The Jerusalem Bible and the New American Bible translate the Greek as "treasure and wealth," rather than "glory and honor."

55. For Paul's version of the expectation that all will eventually be subject to Jesus (under God), see 1 Corinthians 15:24-28.

56. The tradition of a primordial battle between good and bad angels is not in the Bible but occurs in such texts as the late-first-century 2 Enoch 29:4-5: see Charlesworth, ed., *The Old Testament Pseudepigrapha*, 1:148.

57. George Beasley-Murray pointed to John 12:31 as the best commentary on this passage. There Jesus says with reference to his imminent passion/glorification: "Now is the prince of this world being driven out [*eblēthēsetai exō*]." Beasley-Murray, *The Book of Revelation*, New Century Bible (London: Oliphants, 1974), 203.

58. See Caird, *Revelation of St. John*, 153.

59. This goes counter to the expectation deducible from the Qumran document 11Q13. See Vermes, *Complete Dead Sea Scrolls*, 500-2. There the leader of the "Sons of Heaven," called Melchizedek (but "identical with the archangel Michael," p. 500), prevails in heaven and seems to be the cause of the Messiah's saving actions on earth.

60. In Revelation 12:17, Christians are "the rest of [the] children" of the woman who, in 12:1-6, gave birth to the child who would rule.

61. There is no question that Jesus profoundly offended some people; that is why he was executed. Yet the Gospel writers are adamant that, although they understand Jesus to be God's anointed one, he was not a militant Messiah—whatever the Romans chose to think.

62. Those at 1:1; 4:1; and 22:6 all contain the words *ha dei genesthai*, "the things that must happen," as in Daniel 2:28, 29 (NAB), and refer to the general working out of events in a divinely directed world. In Revelation 10:11, John is told that he must prophesy again, clearly a divine command; 13:10 is closest to the example in 11:5, for it is about the suffering of the faithful; and 17:10 and 20:3 refer to the (presumably divine) restriction of those who oppose God.

63. Charlesworth, ed., *The Old Testament Pseudepigrapha*, 1:551-52.

64. See Leviticus 10:2; 2 Kings 1:10, 12, 14; Ezekiel 38:22; and, in the New Testament, Luke 9:54-55.

65. Perhaps the prophet's earlier activity of calling down fire on the sacrifice on Carmel (1 Kings 18:36-38) underlay this story intended to enhance Elijah's prestige, although it should not in fact do so.

66. In Luke 9:54, a Samaritan village refuses to welcome Jesus and his disciples as they travel to Jerusalem. James and John enthusiastically offer to command fire from heaven, to consume the village, but Jesus "turned and rebuked them," after which the entourage continues on its way.

67. Examples of this idea include Psalm 66:10; Job 23:10; Proverbs 17:3; Judith 8:27; Wisdom 3:6; Sirach 2:5; 1 Corinthians 3:12-13; 1 Peter 1:7. See also Isaiah 33:14, where sinners ask anxiously, "Who among us can live with the devouring fire? Who among us can live with the everlasting flames?" The reply is "Those who walk righteously and speak uprightly, who despise the gain of oppression."

68. Scholars connect the image in Psalm 2:9 with its ancient near-eastern milieu. For example, Egyptian kings are said to have broken pottery jars inscribed with enemies' names at their coronation and jubilee ceremonies. Mesopotamian rulers are said to have shattered their enemies as pottery is shattered. The image is of "universal, judiciary, absolute power," according to Hans-Joachim Kraus, *Psalms 1–59: A Commentary*, trans. Hilton C. Oswald (Minneapolis: Augsburg, 1988), 133. The closest biblical parallel is in Jeremiah 19, where God tells the prophet to break a pottery jug to symbolize the coming destruction of Jerusalem and its inhabitants.

69. See, for example, Revelation 3:14-19, the message to Laodicea.

70. See, for example, Amos 2:6–3:2 (regarding Samaria), Isaiah 1 (regarding Jerusalem), Micah 1–3, (regarding "Samaria and Jerusalem," 1:1).

Chapter 13

1. See the Appendix. The English title of one of Girard's books is *Violence and the Sacred*.

2. Another feature of narratives dealing with violence is the tendency for the violence to escalate as the narrative progresses. This is certainly a feature of parts of the biblical canon, the movement from Exodus to Judges being an especially obvious example. Although the last stage is a strong warning about the dire effects of violent living, there are points at which divine or human violence seems to beget more of the same, and to make it seem less problematic. In this respect, the Bible stands guilty as charged.

3. See Genesis 4:17; 5:3-32; 11:10-26.

4. See chapter 3 above; notes 7 and 8.

5. Or, more accurately, those who assembled chapters 1–39. Most scholars regard Isaiah 24–27 ("the Apocalypse of Isaiah") as a later disciple's addition to the work of Isaiah of Jerusalem.

6. For an illuminating presentation of the roots and limitations of "exclusive humanism," which claims that human good is all that there is, see Charles Taylor, "A Catholic Modernity," *A Catholic Modernity?* ed. James L. Heft (New York: Oxford University Press, 1999), 13-37.

7. See 1 Corinthians 16:1-3; 2 Corinthians 8–9; Romans 15:25-32. Acts 11:27-30 suggests that a famine during the time of the emperor Claudius (C.E. 41-54) underlies the Jerusalem community's later indigence, to which Paul may have been responding.

8. Taylor in Heft, ed., *A Catholic Modernity*, 30-35.

Appendix

1. For an introduction to Girard and his thought, see the following articles: Robert North, "Violence and the Bible: the Girard Connection," *The Catholic Biblical Quarterly* 47 (1985): 1-27, and James G. Williams, "The Innocent Victim: René Girard on Violence, Sacrifice, and the Sacred," *The Religious Studies Review* 14 (1988): 320-26. For a more popular introduction to mimetic theory, see James Alison, *Raising Abel: The Recovery of the Eschatological Imagination* (New York: Crossroad, 1996), 18-25. Girard's most recent book available in English is *I See Satan Fall Like Lightning* (Maryknoll, N.Y.: Orbis Books, 2001).

2. That is, he was not then committed to the Catholicism in which he was reared, although later he accepted it again. See Girard, *Things Hidden Since the Foundation of the World* (Stanford: Stanford

University Press, 1987), 76. French original: *Des choses cachées depuis
la fondation du monde* (Paris: Editions Grasset & Fasquelle, 1978). The
book is characterized as "research undertaken in collaboration with
Jean-Michel Oughourlian and Guy Lefort," two psychiatrists.
Quotations in what follows are from the English translation.

3. The victim is analogous to the scapegoat of Leviticus 16:20-22
only in its expulsion from the community as the bearer of the community's sins: the goat used on the Day of Atonement was not killed (and
so is not, strictly speaking, sacrificial), nor was it ever an object of worship.

4. Girard, *Things Hidden*, 32.

5. Ibid., 41.

6. Ibid., 115.

7. See, for example, ibid., 68.

8. Ibid., 32.

9. Ibid., 42.

10. Ibid., 153.

11. Nor did Remus, of course—Girard is slippery in places.

12. Girard, *Things Hidden*, 166, distinguishes between "the religion that comes from man" and "the religion that comes from God."
Christianity, with its basis in the religion of Israel, is his only example
of the latter.

13. For Joseph, see ibid., 149-53; for the prophets, ibid., 154; for
the Servant of the Lord in Isaiah 49–53, ibid., 155-56. For Job, see
Girard, *Job, the Victim of his People* (Stanford: University of Stanford
Press, 1987). French original: *La route antique des hommes pervers*
(Paris: Editions Grasset & Fasquelle, 1985).

14. Job 1 has a different account of this: God allows Job to be tested,
and scapegoats do not feature at all.

15. See Girard, *Job*, especially chapters 16–21.

16. Girard, *Things Hidden*, 157 and 158.

17. Ibid., 239 and 154.

18. Ibid., 175-78.

19. Ibid., 177-78

20. Girard's view is that initially these were essentially alien elements, temporary accommodations to early Gentile converts who had
not benefited from Old Testament teaching about victims and sacrifice
(ibid., 252), but he also thinks that the culture subsequently founded by
Christianity is illegitimate because it is a sacrificial reading of the
Gospels (ibid., 219).

21. For example, Luke and John include in their passion narrative
a threefold declaration of Jesus' innocence from Pilate himself (Luke
23:4, 14-15, 22; John 18:38; 19:4, 6).

22. The following New Testament texts are among those that explicitly interpret Jesus' death as a sacrifice: Romans 3:25; 1 Corinthians 5:7;

Ephesians 5:2; Hebrews 2:17; 7:27; 9:26; 10:12; 13:12; 1 John 2:2; 4:10. The implication is there also in texts such as Mark 10:45; 14:24; and parallels.

23. Girard, *Things Hidden*, 166.

24. Ibid., 170.

25. Ibid., 178.

26. Ibid., 174-75.

27. Ibid., 199.

28. In Girard's terms, "ambivalence," as this is understood in psychoanalysis. "Excessive responsibility for currents of public opinion and sentiment" is attributed to "figures who have been artificially isolated or placed in the spotlight" (*Things Hidden*, 37). If the second transference, the positive one, does not occur, they will be energetically hated.

29. For the cult of the dead, see *Things Hidden*, 80-83. For the rest of the list, see ibid., book 3, chapters 2–4, "Interdividual Psychology."

30. Girard, *Job*, 114-23.

31. Ibid., 192.

32. "The Gospels tell us that to escape violence it is necessary to love one's brother completely—to abandon the violent mimesis involved in the relationship of doubles. There is no trace of it in the Father, and all that the Father asks is that we refrain from it likewise" (*Things Hidden*, 215). On what basis should readers of the Gospels interpret them in terms of "mimesis" and "doubles"? Girard's occasionally cavalier attitude to the biblical text (as exemplified by his "reasons" for preferring the text of the Jerusalem Bible in *Job*, 71-72) has quite understandably infuriated some biblical scholars, for whose academic discipline he has no good word.

33. Early examples include Robert G. Hamerton-Kelly, *Sacred Violence: Paul's Hermeneutic of the Cross* (Minneapolis: Fortress Press, 1992); Alison, *Raising Abel* (see n. 1); and Gil Bailie, *Violence Unveiled: Humanity at the Crossroads* (New York: Crossroad, 1997). More recently, see Willard M. Swartley, ed., *Violence Renounced: René Girard, Biblical Studies, and Peacemaking*, Studies in Peace and Scripture 4 (Telford, Pa.: Pandora Press, 2000).

34. Girard, *Things Hidden*, 167, 193, 247. Here are some further examples. First, at the expulsion from Eden, "God takes the violence upon himself and founds humanity by driving Adam and Eve far away from him" (ibid., 142). Second, Girard sees Cain's mark (Gen. 4) as "the establishment of a differential system, which serves, as always, to discourage mimetic rivalry and generalized conflict" (ibid., 146). I doubt that it is so complicated in the first case and so simple in the second. And how can Noah's lone survival really "amount to the same thing as a single victim" (ibid., 143)? What is the evidence that the two meals that his sons offered to Jacob are "a sacrificial institution" (ibid.,

143)? And what particular justification is there for designating the dead who left their tombs and were seen in Jerusalem after Jesus' death (Matt. 27:52-53) as "victims buried by mankind" (ibid., 235)?

35. See, for example, *Things*, 188, where Mark and Luke posit a vengeful master of the vineyard because "minor defects have managed to creep into the text" as perhaps "simply a rhetorical effect," so that Matthew's version which Girard prefers, alone testifies to the original intention. Later Girard asserts that the humanity Christ wills to save is "unable to see that all the old sacrificial solutions are now bankrupt and completely empty" (ibid., 241). On the next page, he describes Christ as exposed to "the violence of a community unanimously bent on retaining sacrifice" (ibid., 242). I find nothing in the Gospel text to support such conjectures as these.

36. Compare ibid., 227.

WORKS CITED

Alison, James. *Raising Abel: The Recovery of the Eschatological Imagination*. New York: Crossroad, 1996.

Ashley, Timothy R. *The Book of Numbers*. The New International Commentary on the Old Testament. Grand Rapids, Mich.: Eerdmans, 1993.

Aulén, Gustav. *Christus Victor: An Historical Study of the Three Main Types of the Idea of Atonement*. New York: Macmillan, 1967.

Bailie, Gil. *Violence Unveiled: Humanity at the Crossroads*. New York: Crossroad, 1997.

Bainton, Roland H. *Christian Attitudes Toward War and Peace: A Historical Survey and Critical Re-evaluation*. New York: Abingdon, 1960.

Baum, Gregory. "The Social Gospel on Trial: Kroeker, Augustine, and the Love of God." *The Ecumenist* 2 (1995): 65-69.

Beasley-Murray, George. *The Book of Revelation*. New Century Bible. London: Oliphants, 1974.

Berrigan, Daniel. *The Nightmare of God*. Portland, Ore.: Sunburst Press, 1983.

Blenkinsopp, Joseph. *The Pentateuch: An Introduction to the First Five Books of the Bible*. The Anchor Bible Reference Library. New York: Doubleday, 1992.

Boling, Robert G. *Joshua*. The Anchor Bible 6. Garden City, N.Y.: Doubleday, 1982.

Brueggemann, Walter. "Pharaoh as Vassal: A Study of a Political Metaphor." *Catholic Biblical Quarterly* 57 (1995): 27-51.

Budd, Philip J. *Numbers*. Word Biblical Commentary 5. Waco, Tex.: Word Books, 1984.

Burney, C. F. *The Book of Judges with Introduction and Notes on the Hebrew Text of the Books of Kings*. New York: KTAV, 1970.

Caird, G. B. *A Commentary on the Revelation of St. John the Divine*. Harper's New Testament Commentaries. New York: Harper & Row, 1966.

Catechism of the Catholic Church. Mahwah, N.J.: Paulist Press, 1994.

Charlesworth, James H., ed. *The Old Testament Pseudepigrapha*. 2 vols. Garden City, N.Y.: Doubleday, 1985.

Chesterton, Gilbert K. *Orthodoxy*. New York: John Lane, 1914.

Childs, Brevard S. *Old Testament Theology in a Canonical Context.* Philadelphia: Fortress Press, 1985.

Chouraqui, André, trans. *La Bible.* Tournai: Desclée & Brouwer, 1985.

Clifford, Richard J. "Genesis." In *The New Jerome Biblical Commentary*, edited by Raymond E. Brown, Joseph A. Fitzmyer, and Roland E. Murphy, 2.23. Englewood Cliffs, N.J.: Prentice Hall, 1990.

———, and John J. Collins. "Introduction: The Theology of Creation Traditions." In *Creation in Biblical Traditions*, edited by Richard J. Clifford and John J. Collins, 1-15. The Catholic Biblical Quarterly Monograph Series 24. Washington, D.C.: The Catholic Biblical Association of America, 1992.

Collinge, William J. *Historical Dictionary of Catholicism.* Lanham, Md.: The Scarecrow Press, 1997.

Collins, John J. *The Scepter and the Star: The Messiahs of the Dead Sea Scrolls and Other Ancient Literature.* Anchor Bible Reference Library. New York: Doubleday, 1995.

Cross, F. M. *Canaanite Myth and Hebrew Epic.* Cambridge, Mass.: Harvard University Press, 1973.

Dunham, Chester Forrester. *The Attitude of the Northern Clergy Toward the South, 1860-65.* Philadelphia: Porcupine Press, 1974.

Dunne, John S. *Peace of the Present: An Unviolent Way of Life.* Notre Dame, Ind.: University of Notre Dame Press, 1991.

Epstein, Isidore, ed. *The Babylonian Talmud; Seder Mo'ed in Four Volumes.* London: Soncino, 1938.

Fitzmyer, Joseph A. *The Gospel According to Luke: Introduction, Translation, and Notes.* 2 vols. Anchor Bible. Garden City, N.Y.: Doubleday, 1985.

———. *Responses to 101 Questions on the Dead Sea Scrolls.* New York: Paulist Press, 1992.

Gay, Peter. *The Enlightenment.* New York: Alfred A. Knopf, 1967.

Girard, René. *I See Satan Fall Like Lightning.* Maryknoll, N.Y.: Orbis Books, 2001.

———. *Job, the Victim of his People.* Stanford: University of Stanford Press, 1987.

———. *Things Hidden Since the Foundation of the World.* Stanford: Stanford University Press, 1987.

Gray, George Buchanan. *A Critical and Exegetical Commentary on Numbers.* International Critical Commentary. Edinburgh: T. & T. Clark, 1903.

Gunn, David M., and Danna Nolan Fewell. *Narrative in the Hebrew Bible.* New York: Oxford University Press, 1993.

Gutiérrez, Gustavo. *A Theology of Liberation: History, Politics, and Salvation.* Translated and edited by Sister Caridad Inda and John Eagleson. Maryknoll, N.Y.: Orbis Books, 1973.

Habel, Norman C. *The Land Is Mine: Six Biblical Land Ideologies.* Overtures to Biblical Theology. Minneapolis: Fortress, 1995.

Hamerton-Kelly, Robert G. *Sacred Violence: Paul's Hermeneutic of the Cross.* Minneapolis: Fortress Press, 1992.

Harnack, Adolf von. *Militia Christi: The Christian Religion and the Military in the First Three Centuries.* Translated and introduced by David McInnes Gracie. Philadelphia: Fortress Press, 1981.

Harrington, Wilfrid J. *Revelation.* Sacra Pagina 16. Collegeville, Minn.: Liturgical Press, 1993.

Hayner, Priscilla B. *Unspeakable Truths: Facing the Challenge of the Truth Commissions.* New York: Routledge, 2001.

Imbelli, Robert. "The Community of Sant'Egidio." *Commonweal* 121 no. 20 (November 18, 1994).

Janzen, J. Gerald. "On the Moral Nature of God's Power: Yahweh and the Sea in Job and Deutero-Isaiah." *Catholic Biblical Quarterly* 56 (1994): 458-78.

Joüon, Paul and T. Muraoka. *A Grammar of Biblical Hebrew.* Subsidia Biblica. Vol. 14, pt. 2. Rome: Editrice Pontificio Istituto Biblico, 1991.

Kerkeslager, Allen. "Apollo, Greco-Roman Prophecy, and the Rider on the White Horse in Rev 6:2." *Journal of Biblical Literature* 112 (1993): 116-21.

Klein, Lillian R. *The Triumph of Irony in the Book of Judges.* Sheffield, England: Almond Press, 1988.

Kraus, Hans-Joachim. *Psalms 1–59: A Commentary.* Translated by Hilton C. Oswald. Minneapolis: Augsburg, 1988.

Kugel, James L. *The Bible As It Was.* Cambridge, Mass.: Harvard University Press, 1997.

Lind, Millard C. *Yahweh Is a Warrior: The Theology of Warfare in Ancient Israel.* Scottdale, Pa.: Herald Press, 1980.

Longman, Tremper, III, and Daniel G. Reid. *God Is a Warrior.* Studies in Old Testament Biblical Theology. Grand Rapids, Mich.: Zondervan, 1995.

Maher, Michael, trans. *Targum Pseudo-Jonathan: Genesis.* The Aramaic Bible 1B. Collegeville, Minn.: Liturgical Press, 1992.

Meeks, Wayne A. *The First Urban Christians: The Social World of the Apostle Paul.* New Haven, Conn.: Yale University Press, 1983.

Meier, John P. *A Marginal Jew: Rethinking the Historical Jesus.* The Anchor Bible Reference Library. New York: Doubleday, 1991.

Mendenhall, George E. "The Census Lists of Numbers 1 and 26." *Journal of Biblical Literature* 77 (1958): 52-66.

McIntyre, Alasdair. *After Virtue: A Study in Moral Theory.* 2d ed. Notre Dame, Ind.: University of Notre Dame Press, 1984.

McNamara, Martin, trans. *Targum Neofiti 1: Genesis.* The Aramaic Bible 1A. Collegeville, Minn.: Liturgical Press, 1992.

McSorley, Richard. *New Testament Basis of Peacemaking*. 3d ed. Scottdale, Pa.: Herald Press, 1985.

Murphy, Frederick J. *Fallen Is Babylon: The Revelation to John*. The New Testament in Context. Harrisburg, Pa.: Trinity Press International, 1998.

Murray, Robert. *The Cosmic Covenant: Biblical Themes of Justice, Peace and the Integrity of Creation*. Heythrop Monographs 7. Westminster, Md.: Christian Classics, 1992.

Musto, Ronald G. *The Catholic Peace Tradition*. Maryknoll, N.Y.: Orbis Books, 1986.

Neusner, Jacob, William S. Green, and Ernest Frerichs, eds. *Judaisms and their Messiahs at the Turn of the Christian Era*. Cambridge: Cambridge University Press, 1987.

Niditch, Susan. *War in the Hebrew Bible: A Study in the Ethics of Violence*. New York: Oxford University, 1993.

North, Robert. "Violence and the Bible: The Girard Connection." *Catholic Biblical Quarterly* 47 (1985): 1-27.

Noth, Martin. *Numbers: A Commentary*. The Old Testament Library. Philadelphia: Westminster Press, 1968.

Skinner, John. *A Critical and Exegetical Commentary on Genesis*. 2d ed. The International Critical Commentary. Edinburgh: T. & T. Clark, 1930.

Speiser, E. A. "Akkadian Myths and Epics." In *Ancient Near Eastern Texts Relating to the Old Testament*. 2d ed., edited by J. B. Pritchard, 60-72. Princeton, N.J.: Princeton University Press, 1955.

Steltenkamp, Michael F. *Black Elk: Holy Man of the Oglala*. Norman, Okla.: University of Oklahoma Press, 1993.

Swartley, Willard M., ed. *Violence Renounced: René Girard, Biblical Studies, and Peacemaking*. Studies in Peace and Scripture 4. Telford, Pa.: Pandora Press, 2000.

Sweet, John. *Revelation*. TPI New Testament Commentaries. Philadelphia: Trinity Press International, 1990.

Swift, Louis J. *The Early Fathers on War and Military Service*. Message of the Fathers of the Church 19. Wilmington, Del.: Michael Glazier, 1983.

Taylor, Charles. "A Catholic Modernity." In *A Catholic Modernity?*, edited by James L. Heft, 13-37. New York: Oxford University Press, 1999.

Tutu, Desmond. *No Future Without Forgiveness*. New York: Doubleday, 1999.

Vermes, Geza. *The Complete Dead Sea Scrolls in English*. New York: Penguin Press, 1997.

Williams, James G. "The Innocent Victim: René Girard on Violence, Sacrifice, and the Sacred." *The Religious Studies Review* 14 (1988): 320-26.

Wilson, E. O. *Consilience: The Unity of Knowledge.* New York: Alfred A. Knopf, 1998.

Yee, Gale A. "Ideological Criticism: Judges 17–21 and the Dismembered Body." In *Judges and Method: New Approaches in Biblical Studies,* edited by Gale A. Yee, 146-70. Minneapolis: Augsburg Fortress, 1995.

Yoder, John Howard. "Exodus and Exile: The Two Faces of Liberation." *Cross Currents* 23 (Fall 1973): 297-309.

ACKNOWLEDGMENTS

It is time to acknowledge with much gratitude the many people who have enabled me to bring this project to completion.

For all but the final stages, I was a faculty member at Mount Saint Mary's College, Emmitsburg, Maryland. I am grateful to the college for encouraging scholarship and, in particular, for allotting me summer grants in 1992 and 1993 and a semester's sabbatical in the spring of 1998.

It would be impossible to express how much I have valued the companionship, help, and encouragement of my departmental colleagues. Bill Collinge set the whole thing going with his invitation to contribute to his "Peace and War" seminar in 1991. Bill Portier read draft after draft and kept me on task, both as department chair until January 1999 and thereafter as mentor and friend. Bill and his wife, Bonnie, also allowed me to spend whole weeks and more in their house on the Outer Banks in North Carolina, where many of the chapters were written and edited. Their daughter, Anathea Portier-Young, gave me much valuable criticism, and for this and her friendship I am most grateful. Jim Donohue and David McCarthy also helped me to keep moving forward, by their energy and companionship and their willingness to read drafts on request. Being a member of the theology department of Mount Saint Mary's was a privilege. It was also a spur to production: I had to have something to contribute to Provost Carol Hinds's bookshelf!

Those are the people who have endured the decade-long gestation, as have the members of my religious community, in the United States and England. More recently, others kindly lent me their time and expertise, as they responded to drafts and offered suggestions for improvement. They include John P. Meier, Gerard S. Sloyan, Marilyn Schaub, George Lawler, Elizabeth Nagel, Margaret Mary Loughran, Ben C. Ollenburger, Robert D. Miller II, Amy-Jill Levine, Alice Laffey, Walter Brueggemann, Ladislas M. Orsy, Mary Kate Birge, Pamela Hussey, and Nunzio D'Alessio.

I have also benefited from the kindness and expertise of the library staff at Mount Saint Mary's, especially the reference librarians Joy Allison, Kathleen Sterner, Laurel Thrasher, and Bruce Yelovich.

Finally, I should like to thank my Ushaw colleagues Michael Sharratt and Jeremy Corley for valuable help in the final stages, and Sarah Kehrberg, of Herald Press, for her skillful handling of the manuscript and the author.

Ushaw College, Durham
December 2003

SCRIPTURE INDEX

SUBJECT INDEX

ABOUT THE AUTHOR

Patricia M. McDonald is a lecturer in New Testament at Ushaw College, Durham, England. She taught in the theology department at Mount Saint Mary's College, Emmitsburg, Maryland, for twelve years. A native of Scarborough, Yorkshire, she belongs to the Society of the Holy Child Jesus.